The Legacy of John Paul II

The Legacy of John Paul II

Edited by

Michael A. Hayes
Gerald O'Collins, S.J.

burns & oates

Burns & Oates
A Continuum Imprint

The Tower Building	80 Maiden Lane
11 York Road	Suite 704
London	New York
SE1 7NX	NY 10038

www.continuumbooks.com

First published 2008

British Library Cataloguing-in-Publication Data
A catalogue record for this book is available from the British Library.

ISBN 9780860124405

Typeset by Newgen Imaging Systems Pvt Ltd, Chennai, India
Printed and bound by CPI Antony Rowe, Chippenham, Wiltshire

Contents

Participants in the Conference

Dr Simonetta Calderini. After taking a degree in Oriental languages and civilizations from the Oriental Institute, Naples (Italy), she received her Ph.D. in Islamic Studies from the School of Oriental and African Studies, University of London. A senior lecturer in Islamic Studies at Roehampton University, she has co-authored *Women and the Fatimids in the World of Islam*, *The Intifada* and *Mauritania*. Her articles in academic journals and works in collaboration cover such topics as Islam and human rights, gender studies, and cosmology and authority in Medieval Ismailism. Having received an AHRC grant (*A rating), she is currently on leave to research 'arguments for and against women imams in classical and modern Islamic sources'.

Dr Philip Endean, S.J., is a tutor in theology at Campion Hall, Oxford and since 2001 has edited a journal of Christian spirituality, *The Way*. His *Karl Rahner and Ignatian Spirituality* (Oxford University Press, 2001) is a based on his doctoral thesis supervised by Archbishop Rowan Williams. He is co-translator of *St Ignatius of Loyola, Personal Writings* (Penguin, 1996).

Dr Michael Hayes, after serving as head of the School of Theology, Philosophy and History at St Mary's University College, Twickenham, is currently a Vice-Principal. He is editor of *The Pastoral Review*. His doctoral thesis (University of Surrey, 2005) investigated the interface between psychotherapy and spiritual direction. A priest of the Archdiocese of Southwark, he is also a qualified psychotherapist. His publications include nine edited books: for instance, *New Religious Movements in the Catholic Church* (Burns & Oates, 2005) and *Contemporary Catholic Theology: A Reader* (Continuum, 2000).

Rt Revd Christopher John Hill studied at King's College, London, and was ordained a priest in 1970. Throughout his ministry he has been involved in ecumenical affairs. From 1974 to 1981 he was Co-Secretary of the Anglican-Roman Catholic International Commission (ARCIC), and from 1982 to 1989 the Archbishop of Canterbury's Secretary for Ecumenical Affairs. After being Bishop Suffragan of Stafford (Lichfield diocese) from 1996, he was appointed Bishop of Guildford in 2004.

Professor David Albert Jones is Professor of Bioethics at St Mary's University College, and runs an MA programme in bioethics and a foundation degree in Healthcare chaplaincy. On behalf of the Roman Catholic Bishops Conference of England and Wales, he has given evidence on various bioethical issues: to the Department of Health, to the House of Commons Science and Technology Committee, to the National Institute for Health and Clinical Excellence, to the Nuffield Council on Ethics, and to the House of Lords Select Committee on Stem Cell Research. After helping to prepare Cherishing Life, a statement on life issues for the Bishops Conference, he is a member of the working party preparing guidance for Catholics on the Mental Capacity Act. His *The Soul of the Embryo* (2004) was short listed for the Michael Ramsey Prize. In 2007 he published *Approaching the End: A Theological Exploration of Death and Dying*.

Professor Brendan Leahy. A priest of the Archdiocese of Dublin, he qualified in philosophy and law before studying theology to the doctorate level at the Gregorian University (Rome). Formerly registrar of Mater Dei Institute (Dublin), confessional lecturer at the Irish School of Ecumenics, and visiting lecturer at Edgehill Methodist College (Belfast), he is currently Professor of Systematic Theology at St Patrick's College, Maynooth. As secretary to the Bishops' Conference Advisory Committee on Ecumenism and a member of the Irish Inter-Church Meeting, he has a lively interest in ecumenism and interreligious dialogue. His publications include: *The Marian Profile in the Ecclesiology of Hans Urs von Balthasar* (London: New City, 2000) and, as co-author, *Christianity: Its Origins and Contemporary Expressions* (Dublin: Veritas, 2003). He has also co-edited *Vatican II: Facing the 21st Century: Historical and Theological Perspectives* (Dublin: Veritas, 2006) and compiled *No Peace without Justice, No Justice without Forgiveness:Messages for*

Peace from Pope John Paul II (Dublin: Veritas, 2005). He is a corresponding fellow of the Pontifical Theological Academy.

Dr John McDade, S.J., is a lecturer in systematic theology and the Principal of Heythrop College, University of London. After receiving his doctorate at the University of Edinburgh, he has taught at Heythrop College since 1985 and has served as the President of the Catholic Theological Association of Great Britain (1999–2005). A widely known and valued speaker, he has contributed numerous articles to popular and professional journals.

Archbishop Kevin J. P. McDonald. Born in Stoke-on-Trent, he attended St Joseph's, the Christian Brothers' Grammar School (1958–65) and then read Latin at Birmingham University (1965–68). As a student for the Archdiocese of Birmingham he trained at the English College in Rome (1968–75), being ordained priest (1974) and securing his licentiate in moral theology (1975). After teaching moral theology at Oscott College (1976–85), he worked as an official at the Pontifical Council for Christian Unity in Rome, where he had special responsibility for Anglican–Catholic relations. During this time he completed a doctorate at the Angelicum (Communion and Friendship: A Framework for Ecumenical Dialogue and Ethics), with Fr Bruce Williams, o.p., as his supervisor. On his return to England he became parish priest of English Martyrs, Spinkhill (1993–98), an area of Birmingham with a large Muslim population. It was there that he developed his interest in interreligious dialogue. After serving as rector of Oscott College (1998–2001), he was ordained Bishop of Northampton in 2001 and was named Archbishop of Southwark in November 2003. On 29 June 2004, Archbishop McDonald received his pallium from Pope John Paul II in St Peter's Square, Rome. In the Bishops' Conference of England and Wales, he is chairman of the Department of Unity and Dialogue, as well as chairman of the Committee for Other Faiths and the Committee for Catholic–Jewish relations.

Professor Gerald O'Collins, S.J., Born in Melbourne, Australia, he received his BA and MA from Melbourne University, his S.T.L. from Heythrop College (now University of London) and his Ph.D. from Cambridge University (1968). From 1973 to 2006 he taught theology at the Gregorian University (Rome), where he was also dean of the theology faculty (1985–91). In 2007 he became a research professor in theology at St Mary's University College, Twickenham. He has lectured for many universities, colleges and seminaries around the world, and has received five honorary doctorates and other awards. He has published hundreds of articles in professional and popular journals, and – either alone or with others – 50 books. His most recent works include: *Catholicism, Jesus Our Redeemer, Salvation for All* (all three with Oxford University Press), *Easter Faith, The Lord's Prayer, Jesus: A Portrait* (all three with Darton, Longman & Todd), *Incarnation* (Continuum), and *Living Vatican II: The 21st Council for the 21st Century* (Paulist Press). In 2007 he co-edited with Daniel Kendall and Jeffrey LaBelle *Pope John Paul II: A Reader* (Paulist Press).

Sr Margaret Shepherd, nds. The current provincial of the UK/Ireland province of the Sisters of Our Lady of Sion and a former director of the Council of Christians and Jews, she has a Master of Theology in Biblical Studies from King's College, a Diploma in Jewish Studies from Leo Baeck College, a BA in humanities from the Open University, and a Diploma in Education from Maria Assumpta College. She is a member of the Committee for Catholic–Jewish Relations of the Roman Catholic Bishops Conference of England and Wales, and a member of the executive board of the International Council of Christians and Jews (ICCJ). Her publications include contributions to such works in collaboration as *Public Life and the Place of the Church* (2006), *He Kissed Him and They Wept: Towards a Theology of Jewish-Catholic Partnership* (2002), and *The Holocaust and the Christian World* (2000).

Mr Edward Stourton. A presenter of the 'Today' programme on Radio Four, he is also a member of the presenting team for 'the Sunday Programme' on the same network. He has presented numerous current affairs and religious programmes for radio and television. Educated at Ampleforth and Trinity College, Cambridge, he began his journalistic career with Independent Television News in 1979. He has worked as a Washington correspondent (for Channel Four News), a Paris correspondent (for BBC News) and Diplomatic Editor (for ITN). He was a presenter of 'The One O'Clock News' on BBC One for 7 years before taking up his present job. His documentary work includes Absolute Truth, a four-part series on the Catholic Church for BBC 2, which was accompanied by a book of the same name. His most recent publication is *John Paul II: Man of History*. He is currently working on a new book called It's a PC World: The Story of Political Correctness, due to be published by Hodder & Stoughton in November 2008.

Professor Christian W. Troll, S.J., was born in Berlin (1937), studied philosophy and theology at the universities of Bonn and Tübingen (1857–61) and Arabic and Islam at St Joseph's University in Beirut (1961–63). In 1976 he obtained his Ph.D. at the School of Oriental and African Studies (London), with a dissertation on the nineteenth-century Indian Muslim, Sayyid Ahmad Khan. After being a Professor of Islamic Studies at the Vidyajyoti Institute of Religious Studies (Delhi) (1976–88), he became a senior lecturer at the Centre for the Study of Islam and Christian-Muslim Relations (Birmingham) (1988–93). From 1993 until 1999, he was Professor of Islamic Institutions at the Pontifical Oriental Institute (Rome) and a regular guest professor for the Faculty of Theology at Ankara University. Since 1990 he has been a member of the Commission for Religious Relations with Muslims (Pontifical Council for Interreligious Dialogue, Rome) and since 1999 a member of the Subcommission for Interreligious Dialogue of the German Bishops Conference. Currently he is Hon. Professor for the Study of Islam and Christian-Muslim Relations at the Philosophisch-Theologische Hochschule St. Georgen (Frankfurt). His published books include *Sayyid Ahmad Khan: A Reinterpretation of Muslim Theology* (1978); Muslims Ask, Christians Answer (2005; also published in German and Turkish); Unterscheiden um zu klären. Orientierung im christlich-islamischen Dialog (2008). He edited *Islam in India: Studies and Commentaries*, 4 vols. (1982–89), and co-edited *Faith, Power and Violence: Muslims and Christians in a Plural Society, Past and Present* (1998).

Professor Jared Wicks, S.J. He received his doctorate from the University of Münster (for a dissertation on Martin Luther's early instruction on Christian life), gaining much from professors of the Catholic and Evangelicals theology faculties. They included Joseph Ratzinger, now Pope Benedict XVI, and Walter Kasper, now a cardinal and head of the Pontifical Council for Promoting Christian Unity. After teaching at the Jesuit School of Theology in Chicago, Fr Wicks moved to the Gregorian University (Rome) in 1979 and also served there as dean of the theology faculty (1991–97). Since 2004 he has been writer-in-residence at John

Carroll University (near Cleveland, Ohio). On commissions of Lutheran–Catholic ecumenical dialogue, he took part in discussions about justification and the Church (1986–93) and then about the apostolic character of the Church, which led to the study-document The Apostolicity of the Church (2007). He helped draft the landmark Lutheran–Catholic agreement, the Joint Declaration on the Doctrine of Justification, formally signed in 1999. Following the lead of some Gregorian University doctoral students who worked on theological currents at Vatican II, Fr Wicks now researches and writes on the theologians who contributed as expert consultants at the Council.

Preface

During a programme for Polish television aired on 16 October 2005, the anniversary of the election of Pope John Paul II in 1978, Pope Benedict XVI said: 'I consider it my essential and personal mission not so much to produce many new documents but to see to it that [John Paul II's] documents are assimilated, because they are a very rich treasure, the authentic interpretation of Vatican II.' We too have found a rich legacy in those documents, which repeatedly expressed and reflected not only the pastoral activity of the late Pope within the Catholic Church but also his outreach to innumerable other groups and individuals.

Three years after the death of John Paul II in 2005, it seemed worthwhile to gather experts in various fields with a view to exploring collaboratively some major aspects of his legacy. The conference, which was held at St. Mary's University College, Twickenham (UK) 25–26 March 2008, brought together a group of scholars, pastors and writers from Germany, Ireland, the United Kingdom, and the United States. To promote discussion, advance scholarship and establish stronger connections between the different contributions, we encouraged those presenting papers to circulate them in advance to all those attending the conference.

This volume in no way aims at being comprehensive. It does not, for instance, take up the late Pope's teaching on sacraments, science and religion, and social issues – in particular, his three encyclicals, *Laborem exercens* (Performing Work) of 1984, *Sollicitudo rei socialis* (Concern for Social Matters) of 1987, and *Centesimus annus* (The Hundredth Year [since Leo XIII's groundbreaking encyclical *Rerum novarum* (Of New Things)]) of 1991. Nor do we examine, for example, the apostolic exhortations that he issued in the aftermath of the special synods for the bishops of five continents: the Assembly for Africa (1994), America (1997), Asia (1998), Oceania (1998) and Europe (1991 and 1999). Rather than attempt anything like total coverage, we decided to limit our evaluation to aspects of his theological legacy and set ourselves to probe the lasting value of his life and teaching in certain areas.

In Chapter 1, Professor Gerald O'Collins, S.J., presents three areas in which the official teaching of Pope John Paul II proved innovative and has contributed to the healthy development of Catholic doctrine. First, while maintaining the Vatican II teaching on divine self-revelation, he went beyond the Council by helping to illustrate how God's self-disclosure enters human experience. Second, no previous Pope had ever developed so much teaching on the redemptive and revelatory value of suffering and martyrdom. Third, when considering the cultures and religions of the world, he highlighted the presence and activity of the Holy Spirit. To be sure, John Paul II broke new ground in other areas of his teaching, as will be explained in several other chapters in this book (especially in chapters by professor David Albert Jones, Sister Margaret Shepherd, professors Christian Troll and Jared Wicks). This chapter limits itself to exploring three major areas in which the late Pope left valuable teaching that continues to invite further assimilation.

In Chapter 2, 'John Paul II: the Man and His Ideas', Edward Stourton traces the relationship between the late Pope's unusually intense experiences as a young man and the theology and ecclesiology that informed his thinking as an archbishop and later as Pope. It focuses particularly on the period of the Nazi occupation of Poland – which was marked by especially brutal repression, even by the standards of the time – and uses his early writings to examine the way he responded to an immoral and capricious authority. The chapter also suggests that John Paul II's understanding of the relationship between the Church and the world was profoundly influenced by the way he experienced the Catholic Church during this period, which coincided with the formation of his vocation.

In Chapter 3, 'John Paul II and Hans Urs von Balthasar', Professor Brendan Leahy traces the extent to which the paths of two great figures of the twentieth century (one a bishop and then Pope and the other a major theologian) crossed. How far did Balthasar influence John Paul II? This chapter argues that, in terms of material content, there are some grounds for saying that Balthasar exercised an influence on the Pope's theology.

Nevertheless, the theology of John Paul II was shaped primarily through encounter with other teachers and by different experiences.

Above all, the late Pope was very faithful to the agenda set by Vatican II, an agenda that had shaped his theological outlook. Balthasar was above all very faithful to his Ignatian formation and to his encounter with Adrienne von Speyr's mission that proved the prism through which he reread the vast cultural, philosophical and theological insight he had gained through his studies.

Both the Pope and the theologian came to prominence in the last 25 years of the twentieth century. They admired each other's fidelity to the mission assigned to them by God. Some distinct aspects of the Swiss theologian's cross the horizon of the intuitive, charismatic Pope's writings and actions. Nevertheless, the panoply of influences that shaped Karol Wojtyla, both before and after being elected Pope, establish that, despite a certain convergence of thought and interests, Balthasar was but one, limited influence upon John Paul II. That takes nothing away, however, from the great esteem in which the late Pope held the Swiss theologian and the degree to which he proposed Hans Urs von Balthasar as a model theologian at the service of the Church.

In Chapter 4, 'John Paul II and his Ecclesiology', Dr. John McDade, S.J., complements the previous chapter by exploring the Marian centre and the Petrine authority that characterize the Church.

In Chapter 5, 'John Paul II and Moral Theology', Professor David Albert Jones argues that, in the development of Roman Catholic moral theology at the end of the second millennium, John Paul II left an important legacy. To establish this claim, Professor Jones must first explore briefly the history of moral theology and its current state. Against this background, one aspect of the late Pope's moral theology is cited to demonstrate his distinctive contribution: his use of the Scriptures. In his fundamental moral theology and on specific moral issues, John Paul II used the Scriptures, not just as 'proof texts' for conclusions provided by the tradition or established by natural reason, but to 'do the work'. Engaged in a sustained exegesis of scriptural passages, he was attentive to what they teach on moral issues. An Anglican moral theologian, Oliver O'Donovan, has appreciated the way the Pope used the biblical passages – 'not quoted as a proof but teased out as a way of framing a question in scriptural terms'. O'Donovan draws attention to 'the unforgettable treatment of the rich young ruler at the beginning of *Veritatis splendor*, or of Cain and Abel in *Evangelium vitae*'. In order to appreciate John Paul II as a theologian (without either excessive deference or excessive defensiveness), it may be helpful to 'forget' that he was Pope. Now that he is dead, we can appreciate better the extent of his legacy precisely as theologian.

In Chapter 6, 'The Legacy of John Paul II: Ecumenical Dialogue', Archbishop Kevin J. P. McDonald recalls an integral part of the late Pope's pontificate: ecumenism. Building on the theological foundations laid by the Vatican II and the practical steps taken by Pope Paul VI, John Paul II joined leaders of the Oriental Orthodox Churches in signing common Christological statements; he also set up the Catholic–Orthodox dialogue with the Byzantine Orthodox Churches. He made significant progress in the dialogue with the Churches and Ecclesial Communities of the West (see the chapter by Jared Wicks S. J.). On his travels, Pope John Paul II consistently met and prayed with the leaders of other Churches and Ecclesial Communities, and reiterated his commitment to Christian unity. On their visits to Rome, he welcomed many other Christian leaders and made such visits highly significant and deeply appreciated. Apropos of the difficulties on the road to Christian unity, he was realistic and clear that it must be based on unity of faith.

The revival of Eastern-rite Catholic Churches after the fall of Communism occasioned fresh problems with the Orthodox. Despite promising developments in the dialogue with Anglicans, the ordination of women created a fresh obstacle. Yet Pope John Paul II always remained positive and hopeful about ecumenism and handed on a rich legacy to his successor.

In Chapter 7, 'John Paul II and Lutherans: Actions and Reactions', Professor Jared Wicks, S.J., shows how the late Pope became a major ecumenical figure, by underscoring, for example, Catholic-Lutheran agreement on fundamental truths about God and Christ. He included central truths about justification as shared by Catholics and Lutherans, while continuing to make observations about differences remaining in ecclesiology. John Paul II's forthright assertions of doctrine and discipline led to some Lutherans putting him in bad light. Other Lutherans, however, saw deeper, as when one theologian singled out for praise his theological anthropology. His personal contacts with Lutherans were marked by a religious tone and his encouragement of ecumenical processes was already underway. In 1989 he accepted that the Catholic Church should look towards a possibly binding reception of the results of Lutheran–Catholic dialogue; this led to the Joint Declaration on the Doctrine of Justification of 1999.

In St. Peter's Basilica, Lutheran episcopal primates three times joined him at the high altar in presiding at Vespers to commemorate St. Bridget of Sweden. But he regularly said that common participation by Lutherans and Catholics in Holy Communion must wait until there is a full consensus in faith.

In *Ut unum sint* (1995), John Paul II confirmed what Vatican II had taught about the ecclesial character of churches, like the Lutheran Church.

They are in real but imperfect communion with the Catholic Church, in spite of such communities lacking some ecclesial elements and there still being areas of doctrinal difference to be clarified. In the same encyclical the Pope formulated essential Catholic terms for a broad ecumenical discussion of the disputed Petrine ministry of universal oversight and service of unity.

In *Ut unum sint*, John Paul II set forth the Catholic vision of the ecumenical goal of unity, which, however, some Lutherans have challenged, especially after *Dominus Iesus* (2000). They hold that doctrinal differences may continue to exist in ecclesial communion, even without or before working out reconciled diversities – as was done in the Lutheran–Catholic Joint Declaration on Justification.

In Chapter 8, Professor Christian W. Troll, S.J., focuses on John Paul II's theological outlook on Islam as a distinct religious vision and as a body of normative practices and beliefs. He perceived the reality of the worldwide Muslim community – in its wide and constantly changing spectrum of sects, movements, tendencies and ideological trends. Hence this paper leaves to one side John Paul II's (1) innovative initiatives in the field of Christian–Muslim relations, and (2) his perception of dialogue and its relation to mission and proclamation. The chapter analyses some highly significant statements about Islamic faith to be found in the late Pope's Crossing the *Threshold of Hope* (1994). It then draws on papal addresses to highlight those elements of Muslim faith and practice to which John Paul II attributed special theological significance: faith, spiritual and ethical core values, and the ideal of sanctity. The Pope conjured up a specifically Islamic collective religious identity, called to form with Christian and other collective religious identities a global religious identity, made up of different religious identities that support each other and thus contribute to the common good of all people. The chapter concludes with brief comments on two recent Muslim esssays concerned with the very theme of this chapter.

In Chapter 9, 'John Paul II and Catholic–Jewish Dialogue', Sister Margaret Shepherd, n.d.s., shows how the late Pope fostered and developed a new relationship between Catholics and Jews. His personal history had formed him for this role, since right from childhood he had close Jewish friends.

During the Second World War he witnessed the fate of Jews at the hands of the Nazis. As Pope, he repeatedly recalled the *Shoah* and condemned Anti-Semitism in the strongest terms. He focused on the unique bond between the Church and the Jewish people. Two key moments demonstrated the power of gesture to convey John Paul II's convictions: his 1986 visit to the Synagogue of Rome, and his visit in 2000 to Israel and the Palestinian Territories. In his speech in the Rome Synagogue he dwelt on the essential relationship between Jews and Catholics and pointed to the truth that God's covenant with the Jewish people is irrevocable. In the Holy Land in 2000 two iconic moments were his visit to *Yad Vashem* and the Western Wall, where he placed a prayer expressing the significant shift that had taken place since Vatican II's 1965 document, *Nostra aetate* – a shift that was further developed in the 2001 document of the Pontifical Biblical Commission, The Jewish People and their Sacred Scriptures in the Christian Bible.

In Chapter 10, Professor Troll adds a chapter that raises a key question and answers in the negative: 'Mohammed – Prophet for Christians also?' It is significant that John Paul II never applied this title to Mohammed.

As the summaries offered above indicate, this volume contains nine presentations and an additional chapter (by Christian Troll). Each presentation was followed by a response that initiated the discussion of that particular paper. To avoid making this book too long, we have included only three responses. Given the high importance of his field, we have also included as an additional chapter a second paper by Christian Troll S. J.

We are most grateful to all those who participated in the conference. Our special thanks go to the Derwent Consultancy for its generous support and to St. Mary's University College, Twickenham (UK) for hosting the conference.

We also want to thank Robin Baird-Smith for his encouraging interest in our project and for accepting the papers for publication by Continuum. We express our deep gratitude to Marie Fernandes, Carol Lourdas and Mark Murphy, whose generous work made the conference run smoothly and helped in the preparation of this volume.

Michael Hayes and Gerald O'Collins, S.J.   13 May 2008
St Mary's University College, Twickenham

List of Abbreviations

AAS	*Acta Apostolicae Sedis*
DV	*Dei verbum*
EV	*Evangelium vitae*
GS	*Gaudium et spes*
LG	*Lumen gentium*
NA	*Nostra aetate*
UR	*Unitatis redintegratio*
UUS	*Ut unum sint*
VS	*Veritatis splendor*

Chapter 1

John Paul II and the Development of Doctrine

Gerald O'Collins, S.J.

In a papacy that lasted for over 26 years (October 1978–April 2005), John Paul II left behind an enormous legacy. It included well over 70,000 pages of teaching, found in encyclicals, apostolic exhortations, apostolic letters, homilies, addresses, letters and other published texts. His teaching took up a very wide range of themes: from the self-revelation of God, through the sacramental life of the Church, relations with other Christians and the followers of other religions, questions of social and sexual morality and on to basic elements in the Christian spiritual life.

As one would expect, this teaching often recalled and applied traditional teaching of the Catholic Church. At times, however, John Paul II broke new ground and developed some fresh lines of thought and practice for Catholics and, indeed, for other Christians. In this chapter I want to single out and explore several themes which prove, at least partly, innovative and will contribute to a healthy development of doctrine.

In particular, what the late Pope said about divine revelation, human experience, suffering and the role of the Holy Spirit deserves retrieval. His teaching on these themes can vividly illuminate and nourish belief and behaviour for Catholics and other Christians and sometimes for those who follow other religions. Some of these themes (for instance, the universal role of the Holy Spirit for the salvation of human beings) have drawn the attention of commentators, but other themes (for instance, John Paul II's uninhibited appeal to 'experience') have been, in effect, ignored.

In an interview for Polish national television that was broadcast on 16 October 2005, the anniversary of the election of John Paul II in 1978, Pope Benedict XVI said: 'I consider it my essential and personal mission not so much to produce many new documents but to see to it that [John Paul II's] documents are assimilated, because they are a very rich treasure, the authentic interpretation of Vatican II.' One could add that at times the teaching of John Paul II represented an official reception of the texts of Vatican II that was not only faithful but also creative. Let us begin with one striking example – in the area of divine revelation. This illustrates how he received and developed doctrine, thereby leaving a legacy that can in turn be received and developed by others.[1]

Divine revelation and human faith

Divine revelation aims at arousing or strengthening the faith of human beings. In other words, revelation and faith are reciprocal terms and realities. God reveals and human beings believe. Revelation is not reducible to faith, but without the human response of faith, divine revelation does not happen. Let me first recall four themes from Vatican II which provide the background for the creative fidelity of John Paul II's teaching on revelation.

(1) The Constitution on Divine Revelation, *Dei verbum* (the Word of God), understood revelation to be *primarily* the self-revelation of God, to which human beings respond not only with an intellectual assent but also with the commitment of their whole person (no. 5). In the history of revelation/salvation, this divine self-communication reached its fullness with the incarnation, life, death and resurrection of Jesus Christ, followed by the outpouring of the Holy Spirit (no. 4).

Through personally encountering the Son of God and receiving the Spirit, the first Christians came to know more truth (for example, that God is tripersonal). Such revealed truths make up the 'deposit of faith' or 'treasure of revelation' (nos. 10, 26), transmitted through tradition and the inspired scriptures. But revelation remains primarily an encounter with the 'Mystery' or deep and inexhaustible truth of God manifested in the person of Jesus Christ.

(2) The dense opening chapter of *Dei verbum* uses the terms 'revelation' and 'salvation' more or less interchangeably. The 'economy' or

history of revelation is inseparably the history of salvation, and vice versa. The text of the Constitution shuttles back and forth between the two terms (for example, in no. 2).

(3) *Dei verbum* speaks of the divine self-disclosure not only in the past tense, as something completed with Christ and the gift of the Spirit, but also in the *present* tense. Revelation is a dynamic, present event that calls now for human faith: 'The obedience of faith . . . must be given to God as he reveals himself' (no. 5). The Constitution associates revelation as it happened then and as it happens now in the Church: 'God, who spoke in the past, continues to converse with the spouse of his beloved Son' (no. 8).

(4) But there is also a 'not yet' of revelation which the New Testament highlights. Drawing on 1 Tim. 6.14 and Tit. 2.13, *Dei verbum* points to what is still to come at the end of all history: the definitive 'glorious manifestation of Our Lord, Jesus Christ' (no. 4).

On all four points John Paul II followed Vatican II with fidelity and also with creativity. That creative reception showed itself most of all when he introduced the theme of experience. Let us look at four texts: his first encyclical *Redemptor hominis* (the Redeemer of the Human Person) of 1979, his second encyclical *Dives in misericordia* (Rich in Mercy) of 1980, his apostolic exhortation *Catechesi tradendae* (Handing on Catechesis) of 1979, and the encyclical of 1998, *Fides et ratio* (Faith and Reason).

Like Vatican II, John Paul II understood revelation to be, in the first place, the *self*-revelation of God through the whole Christ-event, which comprises everything from his incarnation to the resurrection and the gift of the Holy Spirit. He followed the lead of Vatican II by respecting the precedence of the revealed *Mystery* or Truth (also in upper case and in the singular) over the particular revealed mysteries or truths (in lower case and in the plural). Thus *Redemptor hominis* spoke 65 times of the 'Mystery of Redemption', the 'Paschal Mystery' and so forth, but never of the (revealed) 'mysteries', and only once of 'the truths [plural] revealed by God' (no. 6).

Right from that first encyclical, John Paul II also indicated that the divine revelation and the 'Mystery of Redemption' are inseparable (for instance, no. 9). By a clear margin, his favourite biblical source was John's Gospel, which he quotes or to which he refers 48 times. (Paul's Letter to the Romans comes in second, with 24 references and quotations.)

John Paul II appreciated how, in John's Gospel, Christ is inseparably the Light of the world (revelation) and the Life of the world (redemption) and 'full of grace [redemption] and truth [revelation]' (Jn 1.14).

The Pope also presented the divine self-revelation (and redemptive activity) not only as completed in the past but also both as a dynamic, *present* activity and as something to be definitively consummated in the *future*. Thus he wrote: the 'revelation of the Father and outpouring of the Holy Spirit, which stamp an indelible seal on the Mystery of Redemption, explain [present tense] the meaning of the cross and death of Christ. The God of creation is revealed [present] as the God of redemption'. Citing Rom. 8.18–19, John Paul II recalled the divine love which is 'always looking for "the revealing of the sons of God", who are called to the glory "that is to be revealed [future]"' (no. 9). He went on to write of 'the Mystery of Christ', hidden for ages in God, 'to be revealed in time [past] in the man Jesus Christ, and to be revealed continually in every time [present]' (no. 11).

Redemptor hominis also shows how ready John Paul II was to recognize the human *experience* of the divine self-revelation. Here he went beyond *Dei verbum*, which introduced sparingly the language of 'experience' (nos. 8, 14). This and other documents of Vatican II still reflected a certain unease about the language of 'experience'. One can ascribe that inhibition to the long shadow cast by the condemnation of 'Modernism' in the decree *Lamentabili* and the encyclical *Pascendi* of 1907. In condemning 'modernists', St. Pius X and his collaborators showed a certain blindness to historical developments in Christianity, but were right on other scores. Some 'modernists' were going astray in overemphasizing religious experience. Misuse of this category should not, however, lead to ruling it out or downplaying its value. Yet for many years that was the case in Catholic circles in many countries. Seminarians, in particular, were trained to be suspicious of 'experience', as if it were private, emotional and dangerously subjective.

But with his background in the phenomenology of Edmund Husserl, Max Scheler and others of this philosophical school that aims at describing the way things, as they actually are, manifest themselves, John Paul II had no such aversion to 'experience' and the language of 'experience' as such.[2] In *Redemptor hominis* he used the noun 'experience' four times and the verb 'experience' twice. In *Dives in misericordia*, he introduced 'experience' as a noun twelve times and as a verb five times.

One can easily justify the Pope's terminology. If the divine self-revelation does not enter our experience (to arouse or strengthen our faith), it simply does not happen as far as we are concerned. Non-experienced revelation makes no sense.

Of all the texts that John Paul II left us on revelation, easily the fullest is *Dives in misericordia*, which took as its theme 'the revelation of the mystery of the Father and his love' (no. 1). In the 1980s commentators latched onto the central theme of 'mercy' or else onto the encyclical's contribution to Trinitarian teaching. Where *Redemptor hominis* focused on the Son of God, *Dives in misericordia* focused on God the Father. The Holy Spirit was to be the central theme of a 1986 encyclical *Dominum et vivificantem* (Lord and Giver of Life). What commentators regularly overlooked was the importance of *Dives in misericordia* as a source for teaching on revelation. The language of the entire document repeatedly recalls this central theme. Over 80 times it uses the verb 'reveal' or the noun 'revelation'. Other revelational terms like 'manifest', 'make known' and 'proclaim' turn up constantly.[3] Where *Redemptor hominis* reflects on the condition of human beings to whom Christ is revealed and who are saved by Christ, *Dives in misericordia* highlights the revelation of the divine mercy that 'responds' to our primordial needs and remains a living, *present* reality.

To be sure, *Dives in misericordia* begins by portraying the divine revelation as something completed in the past: 'It is God who is rich in mercy whom Jesus Christ has revealed to us as Father; it is his very Son who . . . has manifested him and made him known to us' (no. 1). Yet the same encyclical repeatedly proclaims the present nature of this revelation, referring, for instance, to the cross that 'speaks and never ceases to speak of God the Father, who is absolutely faithful to his eternal love for human beings' (no. 7). The 'genuine face of mercy has to be ever revealed anew' (no. 6). John Paul II named the reason for the Church's ongoing existence as being 'to reveal God the Father who allows us to "see" him in Christ'. He prayed that 'the love which is in the Father may once again be revealed at this stage of history and that, through the work of the Son and Holy Spirit, it may be shown to be present in our modern world and to be more powerful than evil, . . . sin and death' (no. 15). No other document published by the late Pope has more to say on the theme of revelation in Christ, the living Word of God who spoke to us in the past and who continues to address us in the present.[4]

The same approach to revelation as being both a past and a present reality had already turned up in the 1979 apostolic exhortation, *Catechesi tradendae*. John Paul II wrote of 'the revelation that God has given of himself to humanity in Christ Jesus' (no. 22). A 'simple revelation of a good and provident Father' is something, however, that happens now when 'the very young child receives the first elements of catechesis from its parents and the family surroundings' (no. 36). In a telling question about catechesis for the young, the Pope presented divine revelation as something which has happened and which continues to happen:

> In our pastoral concern we ask ourselves: How are we to *reveal* Jesus Christ, God made man, to this multitude of children and young people, *reveal* him not just in the fascination of a first fleeting encounter but through an acquaintance, growing deeper and clearer daily, with him, his message, the plan of God that he has *revealed* [past tense], the call he addresses [present tense] to each person, and the kingdom that he wishes to establish in this world [future]. . .? (no. 35; italics mine).

That same apostolic exhortation also presented faith as a journey toward 'things not yet in our possession', while 'as yet we see only "in a mirror dimly"' (no. 60).

The text which John Paul II quoted here from 1 Cor. 13.12 would turn up again in his 1998 encyclical, *Fides et ratio* (Faith and reason). 'The believing community', he wrote, must

> proclaim the certitudes arrived at, albeit with a sense that every truth attained is but a step towards that fullness of truth which will appear with the final revelation of God: 'For now we see in a mirror dimly, but then face to face. Now I know in part; then I shall understand fully'. (no. 2)

In other words, any theology of revelation should respect the fact that the definitively full revelation of God has not yet taken place.

Earlier I outlined four themes from Vatican II's Constitution on Divine Revelation. It would, however, be a mistake to look only to *Dei verbum* for the Council's teaching on revelation. The other 15 conciliar documents fill out the Council's teaching on God's self-disclosure, even if they have normally been neglected as sources for a comprehensive view of revelation.[5] John Paul II himself was repeatedly drawn, especially in the early years of his pontificate, to cite a paragraph from the Constitution on the Church in the Modern World, *Gaudium et spes* (Joy and Hope) about the light that 'the mystery of the incarnate Word' threw on 'the mystery of human beings' (no. 22). In his penultimate encyclical, *Fides et ratio*, the Pope returned to this theme of Christ revealing the otherwise 'insoluble riddle' of human existence. John Paul II aligned himself with those who think in terms of a correlation between the *questions* raised by the human condition and the *answers* provided by Christ the Revealer: 'Where might the human being seek the answer to dramatic questions such as pain, the suffering of the innocent and death, if not in the light streaming from the mystery of Christ's passion, death and resurrection?' (no. 12).

Characteristically John Paul II concentrated here on the questions raised by human suffering. Few Popes had ever had such a direct experience of so much human suffering, and he set himself to discern that experience in the light of the scriptures. No previous Pope had ever developed so much teaching on the theme of suffering and, in particular, suffering with Christ and in the light of Christ.[6]

Suffering

Over and over again John Paul II took up the theme of suffering and the mysterious value it possesses for those united with Christ. In a 1980 discourse to senior citizens in Munich, he linked the trials of the elderly and dying with the crucified Christ. On that occasion he said:

> I do not want to belittle the anxieties of old age, your weaknesses and illnesses, your helplessness and loneliness. But I would like to see them in a reconciling light, in the light of our Saviour . . . In the trials of old age he is the companion of your pain, and you are his companions on the way of the cross . . . through your suffering you cooperate in his salvation.

He spoke of 'becoming old' as 'a slow taking leave of the unbroken fullness of life'.[7]

These words proved to be a prophetic sketch of what he himself was to experience in the final stages of his life, when the inroads of Parkinson's disease left him weak, helpless and, finally, speechless. As his health began its very public decline, he witnessed personally to the revealing and redeeming power of Christ's suffering that shines through those who devoutly let Christ incorporate their sufferings in his passion. The paradox of Christ's power actively present in human weakness (2 Cor. 12.9–10) was re-enacted in the last years and death of John Paul II.

The attempt on the Pope's life on 13 May 1981 prompted a remarkable radio broadcast from his hospital bed the following Sunday, when it was still not clear that he would survive. In a message addressed, in particular, to those gathered in St. Peter's Square for midday prayer (the *Regina Coeli* or 'Queen of heaven'), John Paul II said, slowly and in obvious pain:

> Praised be Jesus Christ! Beloved brothers and sisters, I know that during these days and especially in this hour of the *Regina Coeli* you are united with me. With deep emotion, I thank you for your prayers and I bless you all. I am particularly close to the two persons wounded together with me. I pray for that brother of ours who shot me and whom I have sincerely pardoned. United with Christ, priest and victim, I offer my suffering for the Church and the world. To you, Mary, I repeat: 'Totus tuus ego sum (I belong entirely to you).'[8]

The Pope recovered and was led by his close brush with death to write an apostolic letter, *Salvifici doloris* (Of suffering that saves) about those who unite their human sufferings to the salvific suffering of Christ.[9]

It is Christ, John Paul II declared, who

> *reveals* to the suffering brother and sister this wonderful interchange, situated at the very heart of the mystery of the redemption. Suffering is, in itself, an experience of evil. But Christ has made suffering the firmest basis of the definitive good, namely the good of eternal salvation.

The Pope drew together three values that have been conferred on suffering: Christ is present in all suffering; he reveals through it the deepest truth of redemption, and he acts through it to transform human existence. John Paul II wrote:

> [S]uffering cannot be transformed and changed by a grace from outside, but [only] *from within*. Christ through his own salvific suffering is very much present in every human suffering, and can act from within that suffering by the power of his Spirit of truth (*Salvifici doloris*, no. 26).

John Paul II set out the universal value that Christ's passion and death have given to human suffering wherever it occurs. Each human being 'is called to share in that suffering through which the redemption was accomplished . . . and through which all human suffering has been redeemed'. By 'bringing about the redemption through suffering, Christ has also raised human suffering to the level of the redemption'. This means that, whether they are aware of it or not, all human beings in their sufferings can also become 'sharers in the redemptive suffering of Christ' (*Salvifici doloris*, no. 19). In other words, 'the weaknesses of all human sufferings are capable of being infused with the same power of God manifested in Christ's cross' (no. 23). As the Pope was to write a few years later in his 1995 encyclical *Evangelium vitae* (The Gospel of Life), 'suffering, while still an evil and a trial in itself, can always become a source of good. It becomes such if it is experienced for love and with love through sharing' (no. 67).[10]

Among the striking new features that John Paul II introduced into the Jubilee Year of 2000 was the ecumenical commemoration of those who in the twentieth century had heroically witnessed to the faith. The ceremony was held on 7 May 2000 at the Coliseum, a place that vividly evokes the witness of faith given by early Christian martyrs. The ceremony brought together Anglicans, Catholics, Orthodox and Protestants to acknowledge the heroic example of countless men and women who bore witness to Christ in all parts of the world and so left an extraordinary example to the present and future generations of Christians. In his 1994 apostolic letter *Tertio millennio adveniente* (The Arrival of the Third Millennium), John Paul II had prepared the way for the celebration of May 2000: 'in our own century the martyrs have returned, many of them nameless, "unknown soldiers", as it were, of God's great cause. As far as possible, their witness should not be lost to the Church.'

He added with reference to the coming celebration: 'This gesture cannot fail to have an ecumenical character and expression. Perhaps the most convincing form of ecumenism is the ecumenism of saints and martyrs. The *communio sanctorum* (communion of saints) speaks louder than the things that divide us' (no. 37). A year earlier the Pope had reflected on the witness of martyrdom in the 1993 encyclical *Veritatis splendor* (The splendour of Truth) (nos. 90–93). In the 1995 encyclical *Ut unum sint* (That they may be one), he took up again the theme of martyrdom in an ecumenical context (nos. 1, 74).

When he spoke at the Coliseum in May 2000, John Paul II remarked:

> The experience of the martyrs and the witnesses to the faith is not a characteristic only of the Church's beginnings but [also] marks every epoch of her history. In the twentieth century, and maybe even more than in the first period of Christianity, there has been a vast number of men and women who bore witness to the faith through sufferings that were often heroic.[11]

The ceremony itself included a number of long testimonials written about or by such witnesses who had suffered in different parts of the world and who had belonged to a variety of Christian communities.

By the end of his life John Paul II had canonized or declared to be saints 482 men and women and 'beatified' – a stage before possible canonization – a total of 1,338. The majority of those canonized and beatified had died a martyr's death, and very many of these suffered in modern times: such as the 103 Koreans whom the Pope canonized during his visit to Seoul on 6 March, 1984, the 459 beatified and 12 canonized who were martyred during the Spanish Civil War (1936–39) and the 120 canonized on 1 October 2000, who had been martyred in China between 1648 and 1930.[12]

In what he said, wrote and did, John Paul II proved thoroughly innovative about Christian martyrdom. Right from the first centuries, to be sure, a number of Popes taught and did things to help Christians to appreciate and learn from the examples of courageous martyrs. St. Damasus (Pope 366–84), for instance, saw to it that the tombs of martyrs were adorned and had a church erected on the *Via Ardeatina* at the catacombs of two martyrs, Sts. Marcus and Marcellianus, as well as building a church to honour St. Laurence (a deacon martyred in 258), the titular church of San Lorenzo in Damaso. But John Paul II gave martyrdom a fresh visibility and value – not least by highlighting its ecumenical significance and doing so in the course of celebrating the great Jubilee of 2000. His own life, and not least the 1981 attempt on his life, disclosed characteristics of the modern martyrs whom he consistently wanted to recall and honour.

The Holy Spirit

In several ways John Paul II's creative fidelity contributed to a development of doctrine on the Holy Spirit. His 1986 encyclical *Dominum et vivificantem* (Lord and Giver of Life) was the first papal encyclical to be devoted to the Holy Spirit since Leo XIII's *Divinum illud* (That Divine [Office]) of 1897. In *Dominum et vivificantem* John Paul II introduced new terminology into official teaching by calling the Holy Spirit 'the Self-communication of God' 12 times. Over lunch a few years later I thanked him for introducing that term, which has a fairly rich background in modern German theology, both Catholic and Protestant. 'I didn't take it from Karl Rahner,' he said with a smile, obviously thinking that as a Jesuit I had that great Jesuit theologian in mind. He then explained his intention: 'I wanted to use some fresh language that might help build bridges with Orthodox Christians.' He thought of the difficulties which Greek, Russian and other Orthodox Christians have with the way that Catholics talk (or fail to talk) about the Holy Spirit's place in the eternal life and historical mission of the tripersonal God. Sensitive to the complaints from the Orthodox about Catholics making the Holy Spirit subsidiary in the Trinity, the Pope stressed the importance of the Spirit and, in particular, reached out to the Orthodox with some new language.

Three years before Communist regimes across Europe 'officially' fell in 1989, through his encyclical the Pope looked ahead in the hope of healing an ancient rift and promoting vigorous collaboration between Catholics and Orthodox in building a more Christian Europe. Sadly that was not going to happen. Ugly religious clashes were to occur in what was then the USSR and over 200,000 people died in the breakup of Yugoslavia.

In a remarkable address to the aboriginal peoples of Australia a little later in 1986, John Paul II developed the theme of the mysterious presence and activity of the divine Spirit in the culture and religions of those peoples.[13] That theme was very much in line with what he had written in *Dominum et vivificantem* about the Holy Spirit being active not only in the life of the Church but also in the whole world. According to God's plan of salvation, the 'action' of the Spirit 'has been exercised in every place and in every time, indeed in every individual' – an action that, to be sure, is 'closely linked with the mystery of the incarnation and the redemption' (no. 5). At the end of the year, in an address to the Roman Curia on 22 December 1986, the Pope took up again the universal activity of the Holy Spirit: 'every authentic prayer is called forth by the Holy Spirit, who is mysteriously present in the heart of every person.'[14] Here he echoed and extended a dictum which went back many centuries and was used 18 times by St. Thomas Aquinas ('every truth, no matter who says it, comes from the Holy Spirit').[15]

Four years later in the encyclical *Redemptoris missio* (the Mission of the Redeemer) John Paul II insisted that, while manifested 'in a special way in the Church and her members', the Spirit's 'presence and activity' are, nevertheless, 'universal'. He understood the Spirit to operate 'at the very source' of each person's 'religious questioning'. He went on to write: 'the Spirit's presence and activity affect not only individuals but also society and history, peoples, *cultures and religions*' (no. 28; italics mine).[16] These were two momentous statements.

First of all, the Holy Spirit is actively operating in and through the questions which sooner or later arise for everyone: where do I come from? Where am I going? What is the meaning of life? What are suffering, sin and death, and what do they mean? What will come after my death? Who is the God in whom I live and move and have my being (see Acts 17. 28)? As far as John Paul II was concerned, the Holy Spirit is actively present and operating not only when anyone prays authentically but also whenever anyone faces the profound religious questions of life.[17] No human being exists outside the powerful presence of God the Holy Spirit. The Spirit is the mysterious companion and religious friend in the life of every human being.

Second, the late Pope appreciated how the presence and activity of the Holy Spirit also affect wider human 'society' and all human 'history, peoples, cultures and religions'. In other words, the Spirit acts in and through the cultures and religious traditions of our world. This activity of the Spirit is inseparable from the salvation which Christ has brought about; it is an activity which aims at bringing all people, sooner or later, to Christ. But in the meantime the Spirit is present and operative in and through all that is true, good and beautiful in various cultures and religions around the world.

Conclusion

This essay has singled out three areas in which Pope John Paul II proved innovative in developing Catholic doctrine. (1) He maintained the teaching of Vatican II on divine revelation being primarily the self-revelation of God that reached its unsurpassable fullness with the whole Christ-event and the outpouring of the Spirit, that remains a vital, present reality, and that will be consummated at the end of human history. He went beyond the Council by using the language of experience and helping to show how God's revelation enters human experience. (2) No previous Pope had ever developed so much teaching on the redemptive and revelatory value of suffering and martyrdom. (3) John Paul II took Catholic teaching forward by his insistence on the presence and activity of the Holy Spirit in all individuals, cultures and religions.

Obviously one could recall from the teaching of the late Pope further items, where he also left an important legacy. He broke new ground, for instance, in a discourse pronounced in 1980 when he made reference to 'the People of God' of the First Covenant, 'which has never been revoked (cf. Rom. 11.29)'.[18] This official recognition of the enduring value of the covenant God made through Moses has proved a highly significant step in Jewish–Catholic dialogue and relationships.

This chapter does not pretend to give an exhaustive account of all that John Paul II contributed to the reception of Vatican II and the development of doctrine. It has aimed to explore three areas in which he left valuable teaching that continues to call for assimilation and will help Catholics (and, indeed, other Christians) in their life of faith.

Note. Denis Edwards has drawn my attention to the way in which the themes I have examined in the papal teaching of John Paul II enjoy rich parallels in the theology and preaching of Karl Rahner (1904–84): (1) The human experience of the divine self-communication, and

(2) human suffering. As for the third theme, what the late Pope taught (in his 1990 encyclical *Redemptoris missio*) about the Holy Spirit operating 'at the very source' of each person's 'religious questioning' can easily evoke what Rahner wrote about the 'supernatural existential, or the way in which, as a result of Christ's redemptive work, God has positively preconditioned human beings even before they exercise their freedom in accepting (or rejecting) divine grace. In his first encyclical (*Redemptoris hominis* of 1979) John Paul II moved somewhat close to this language by writing of 'the inward mystery of the human being' (no. 8) and of the way in which, right from the very moment of their conception, 'Christ has united himself for ever' with all human beings. Hence even before they make any free decisions, they share in Jesus Christ and 'the mystery of the redemption' (no. 13).

One might ascribe two of these three parallels to the fact that John Paul II and Rahner were both exposed to common philosophical and theological currents (for the theme of human experience of the divine self-communication) and to the same grim history of Europe (for the theme of suffering). Moreover, Juan Alfaro (1914–93), a friend and collaborator of Rahner, admitted to me that he was consulted by John Paul II when the Pope was preparing *Redemptor hominis* for publication. Alfaro (who had a passion for John's Gospel) may have been responsible not only for the remarkable use of that Gospel in the encyclical (see above) but also for the echo of Rahner's supernatural existential in the two passages I mentioned (nos. 8, 13).

Notes

1. On the development of doctrine see the bibliographies provided by J. H. Walgrave, 'Doctrine, Development of', *New Catholic Encyclopedia*, vol. 4 (Washington: Catholic University of America, 2nd edn., 2003), pp. 803–09; J. Drumm, 'Dogmenentwicklung', in W. Kasper and K. Baumgartner (eds.), *Lexikon für Theologie und Kirche*, vol. 3 (Freiburg: Herder, 3rd edn., 1995), col. 295-98. On the reception of doctrine and, in particular, the reception of Vatican II, see O. Rush, *Still Interpreting Vatican II. Some Hermeneutical Principles* (Mahwah, NJ: Paulist Press, 2004).
2. Since his doctoral studies involved St. John of the Cross, the future Pope was also able to appropriate the *experience* of love expounded by the mystics.

3. Here I rely on the versions of the encyclical in English, Italian and other modern languages. The official Latin version that appeared in *Acta Apostolicae Sedis* 72 (1980), pp. 1177–1232, uses a variety of elegant variations for 'reveal' and 'revelation', and in doing so introduces some lesser known Latin terms. An official Latinist at the Vatican, Fr. Reginald Foster, did the translation. I know this because I challenged him over introducing various elegant variations into the papal text and he cheerfully admitted that he was the translator. 'Reggie', I told him, 'in a hundred years time someone will work on the Latin text and credit John Paul II with a massive development in the basic terminology for revelation.'

4. On revelation as past and present, see G. O'Collins, *Retrieving Fundamental Theology* (Mahwah, NJ: Paulist Press, 1993), pp. 87–97.

5. See ibid., pp. 63–78.

6. In his major document on suffering, the 1984 apostolic letter *Salvifici doloris* (see no. 9 below), John Paul II has nothing to quote from previous official teaching on suffering. On the theme of suffering in the life and teaching of John Paul II, see E. Stourton, *John Paul II. Man of History* (London: Hodder, 2006), pp. 39–70.

7. 'Address to Senior Citizens in Munich (19 November 1980)', in *The Pope Speaks* 26 (1981), pp. 257–64, at 260, 262.

8. Tape recorded message broadcast in St. Peter's Square (17 May 1981), in *Origins* 11: 2 (1981), p. 17.

9. *Acta Apostolicae Sedis* 76 (1984), pp. 201–50; *Origins* 13: 37(1984), pp. 609–24; *The Pope Speaks* 29 (1984), pp. 105–39.

10. One is reminded here of how St. Thomas Aquinas stressed that love inspired Christ in his passion and death (e.g. *Summa theologiae*, 3a, 48, 3 resp.).

11. 'Address at the Coliseum (7 May 2000)', in AAS 92 (2000), pp. 677–79; *Origins* 30: 1(2000), pp. 4–5.

12. The 120 were made up of 87 Chinese and 33 foreign missionaries; they included laypersons, priests, seminarians, women religious and six bishops. The majority died in the 1900 Boxer Uprising.

13. 'Address to Aborigines and Torres Strait Islanders of Australia (29 November 1986)', in AAS 79 (1987), pp. 973–79; *Origins* 16:26 (1986), pp. 473–77.

14. AAS 79 (1987), p. 1089; *Origins* 16:31 (1987), p. 563.

15. Like his contemporaries, Aquinas thought the saying came from St Ambrose of Milan. In fact, it went back to an anonymous fourth-century author now known as Ambrosiaster and his comments on 1 Cor. 12.3 (PL [*Patrologia Latina*] 17, col. 245B; CSEL [*Corpus Scriptorum Ecclesiasticorum Latinorum*] 81, par. 2, 132).

16. *Redemptoris missio* is found in AAS 83 (1991), pp. 249–340, at 273–74; in *Origins* 20:34 (1991), pp. 541–68, at 549; in *The Pope Speaks* 36 (1991), pp. 138–93, at 151.

17. *Nostra aetate* (no. 1) and *Gaudium et spes* (no. 10) both remark on the basic questions that arise for human beings, but without attributing this profound questioning to the activity of the Holy Spirit.

18. AAS 73 (1981), pp. 78–82, at p. 80. On 'the covenant never revoked', see J. Dupuis, *Toward a Christian Theology of Religious Pluralism* (Maryknoll, NY: Orbis, 1997), pp. 228–33; see also the chapter in this volume by Sr. Margaret Shepherd.

Chapter 2

John Paul II: the Man and His Ideas

Edward Stourton

On 25 February 2008 *The Guardian* carried a story under the headline 'Burnt diary yields horror of Warsaw ghetto'. It referred to twenty pieces of blackened and badly damaged paper which were retrieved from behind a radiator in a bombed out apartment in Warsaw in 1945. The woman who found them – and had looked after them for half a century – revealed to her children on her deathbed in 1998 that they were all that was left of a diary kept by one of her childhood friends, a young woman called Debora who had been killed during the Warsaw uprising. The children passed on the papers to the Holocaust Museum in the United States and, after a long process of trial and error, conservationists there found a way to read them by using a combination of ultraviolet light and digital image manipulation.

Debora's diary includes an account of what it was like to hide with several other people in a shelter under the veranda of her family's apartment while it was searched by German soldiers. Debora hears one of the soldiers say to her mother: 'Is there a shelter here? If we find one you will be shot on the spot'. The soldiers eventually leave but no one comes to open the shelter – and there's no handle on the inside. And Debora writes: 'You can already cut the air, the stench is terrible, we scream and hit our heads against the wall . . . I realise that death like this will be terrible.' Eventually one of the girls in the shelter goes mad and starts banging her head against the trap-door – and, in what must have seemed a near miraculous manner, it opens. Debora goes to look for her mother, and discovers that she has been shot trying to stop the soldiers raping another girl in the apartment block. The diary records 'on the floor lies the cold corpse of my mother, shot through the mouth from which a thin ribbon of blood flows.'

The piece caught my eye because the idea of retrieving that vivid testimony from a few bits of burnt paper provides such a suggestive metaphor for the process of trying to recreate a sense of what it was like to live in the Poland that Karol Wojtyla knew as a young man. It was such a singular experience that it is almost beyond our imaginative reach – certainly for a generation like mine who grew up without experiencing anything remotely comparable. When I was writing my biography of John Paul II, I found researching that period of his life like stripping back veils of gauze and still being left with a slightly fuzzy picture at the end – although every so often an anecdote or a fact would shed a clear beam of light on a very hard-edged reality.

But it was worth the effort because the war years provide the key to understanding a number of salient intellectual characteristics which marked Karol Wojtyla the priest and bishop and later John Paul II the Pope. And if he was a figure who sometimes left the modern world puzzled, that is perhaps precisely because he was formed by a youth that is so difficult for us to imagine.

In this chapter I shall try to set out the areas where I believe it is fruitful to look for a link between Karol Wojtyla's wartime experience and his ideas. I am not going to follow that link into the detail of his thinking; he was a theologian and a philosopher, as the papers being given at this conference so eloquently testify, and I am neither of those things. And I am not – I hope – going to stray too far into what you might call cod-psychology; there has been a great deal of amateur psychology produced about the big events of Karol Wojtyla's childhood, and I think much of what has been written – on the subject, for example, of the impact of his mother's early death – is entirely speculative and seeks to take us into territory that is not only unknown but unknowable. My approach is that of a journalist; I shall at least attempt to stick to those areas where there is some objective evidence. A few basic facts to provide the context.

The wartime story

The city of Krakow, where Karol Wojtyla was living at the outbreak of the Second World War, fell very quickly to the German *Blitzkreig* campaign which began on 1 September 1939. Though this certainly will not have felt like a blessing at the time, in one way it was; this beautiful place was spared some of the physical damage that might have been inflicted by a prolonged siege. Stalin sent his forces into eastern Poland on 17 September, in keeping with the terms of the notorious Molotov-Ribbentrop Pact agreed between Moscow and Berlin, and Poland was then divided into three; large areas of the north and west were simply annexed by Germany, and the east was occupied by and absorbed into the Soviet Union. The central and southern areas of the country – including the city of Krakow – were designated a kind of German colony under the title of the *General-Gouvernment*. Hans Frank, who had served Hitler as his lawyer, was installed in Krakow's Wawel Castle as the governor-general and declared:

> From now on the political role of the Polish nation is ended. It is our aim that the very concept of Polak be erased for centuries to come. Neither the Republic nor any other form of Polish state will ever be reborn. Poland will be treated as a colony and Poles will become slaves in the German Empire.

German rule was enforced with far more savagery in the *General-Gouvernment* than it was in Western nations like France and Belgium, and Krakow was not liberated until January 1945. So the occupation there lasted longer than almost anywhere else. The first gas chambers began operating at the nearby town of Auschwitz in May 1942, and at the height of the 'Final Solution' the crematoria there were working at a capacity of 20,000 bodies a day. It really was the heart of darkness.

The bare bones of Karol Wojtyla's wartime story are these. He and his father – a widower by this stage of course – had moved to Krakow in 1938, and Karol junior had completed the first year of his university studies when war broke out. He was – famously – serving mass in Wawel cathedral when the first German bombers attacked, and he and his father fled east to avoid the German advance, a journey during which they were strafed on the road by a German fighter plane. When the news reached them that the Russians had crossed the border and were heading towards them, they gave up hope of escape and returned to Krakow, where they settled back into their two-room basement flat. The future Pope began work as a manual labourer in the quarry of the Solvay Company just outside Krakow in September 1940, and in February the following year his father, Karol senior, died suddenly at the relatively young age of 62, leaving the future Pope without any surviving members of his immediate family. Around this time Karol junior joined the cultural wing of the underground movement known as *Unia,* and he became involved in the production of clandestine performances of patriotic Polish plays. In October 1942 he presented himself as a candidate for the priesthood to Krakow's Prince Metropolitan, Archbishop Adam Sapieha, and began studying in secret for ordination. After the Warsaw uprising in August 1944, he was – in common with the other secret seminarians being trained under Sapieha's guidance – smuggled into the Archbishop's palace, where he remained until the liberation of the city 5 months later.

That story could, of course, have read very differently. Karol Wojtyla could have tried to leave the country, as many other young men did, and he could have decided to fight; by the spring of 1940 there was a Polish army of 80,000 outside Poland, and elements of armed resistance to the German occupation began inside the country very early on – within weeks of Poland's defeat.

But the 20-year-old Karol Wojtyla did not flee the country – perhaps because of the duty of care he felt towards his father – and he did not fight. Indeed, he wrote to a friend back in his childhood home of Wadowice: 'I am not a cavalier of the sword, but an artist.' Wojtyla's response to finding his world turned upside down was an intellectual one; he began to think, very hard, about the meaning of the experience he was enduring. To the same correspondent he wrote in December 1940:

> Would you believe that I am virtually running out of time! I read, I write, I study, I think, I pray, I struggle with myself. At times I feel a great oppression, depression, despair, evil. At other times as if I am seeing the dawn, the aurora, a great light.

He also wrote a play called *Job* in which he used the biblical story as a way of reinterpreting the traumatic experience of the Nazi occupation. On the title page he declares:

> The Action Took Place in the Old Testament
> Before Christ's Coming.
> The Action Takes Place in Our Days

In Job's Time
For Poland and the World.

So we have his own explicit testimony that he was trying to internalize
and rationalize the experience of living in what I have called the heart
of darkness – to use it to further his own intellectual development.

I have already said that I believe that it is very difficult for us to imagine the experience of occupation, and one of the factors most difficult
for us to grasp is surely the capriciousness with which terror or death
might erupt into the life of any Pole living in Krakow during that
period. The idea that we have a legal system which protects us against
the whimsical or vengeful exercise of state power is something we take
for granted. When we see evidence of a state abusing that, we are –
rightly – shocked; that is illustrated by our reaction to the way the
United States has used what is called extraordinary rendition and to the
practice of detention without due process in Guantanamo Bay. It is
also why there has been such resilient parliamentary resistance here in
the UK to the extension of the time during which terrorist suspects
may be held without charge. Under the Nazi occupation in Krakow
there was no such system of protection. Quite the reverse, in fact; the
idea that you could be punished at random – not because you had done
anything wrong or illegal but because you happened to be standing on
the wrong street corner at the wrong time – was part of the machinery
of terror which helped the occupiers maintain their control.

As a young man of fighting age Karol Wojtyla would have been a
natural target for the occupying authorities. In the aftermath of the outbreak of the Warsaw uprising in 1944, 8,000 men and boys were taken
into custody in Krakow in a single day. Karol Wojtyla was hiding in his
basement flat while German soldiers searched the rooms of the house
above, and seems to have been saved only by the sloppiness of their
search. He certainly lost friends to Nazi terror tactics. In *Gift and Mystery*, the book he wrote to commemorate the fiftieth anniversary of
his ordination, he recalls his mixed emotions about being ordained in
Adam Sapieha's private chapel:

During the occupation I would often go there in the morning, to
serve mass for the Prince Metropolitan. I also remember that another
clandestine seminarian, Jerzy Zachuta, would come with me. One day
he did not appear. After Mass I stopped by his house in Ludwinow

and learned that he had been taken by the Gestapo during the night. Immediately afterwards, his name appeared on the list of Poles who were to be shot.

Karol's friend Mieczyslaw Malinski provides further evidence of the way the fear of being picked up by the secret police preyed on people's minds. Like Karol Wojtyla, Malinski was recruited to join a prayer group called the Living Rosary. In an interview with me in 1997 he recalled that, when he was approached in the street by the group's founder for the first time , 'my immediate reaction was that he was from the Gestapo and had come to arrest me.'

So for a young man in the Krakow of the war years, survival really was a lottery. I suspect that many of us would have been drawn to a bleak and nihilistic set of conclusions about the human condition, if we had been forced to live with the daily uncertainty about whether we were going to be picked up and executed for no good reason. The logic of living in a world where your fate appears entirely detached from any system of law or justice must surely drive you towards the conclusion that the universe is a cruel and amoral place ruled by chance, not love or a grand design.

Providence and the Catholic Church

John Paul II reacted in precisely the opposite way. He turned to the traditional Catholic idea of Providence as a means of making sense of the apparently senseless conditions in which he found himself. Here he is looking back at his wartime experience in 1994:

> I was spared much of the immense and horrible drama of the Second World War . . . I could have been arrested any day, at home, in the stone quarry, in the plant, and taken to the concentration camp. Sometimes I asked myself: so many young people of my age are losing their lives, why not me? Today I know it was not mere chance. Amid the overwhelming evil of war, everything in my personal life was tending towards my vocation.

Pope John Paul II's sense of Providence was extraordinarily robust. It famously guided his interpretation of the meaning of the attempt on his life in 1981 – he of course attributed his survival to the guiding hand of Our Lady of Fatima – and it seems to have been a significant factor in the self-belief needed to take on Communism as he did. The way his confidence in Providence not only survived but was nurtured by his experience of a world cut loose from any anchor in morality is impressive. But I have to confess that I also find something hubristic and frightening about it. Writing as Pope years later, John Paul II comes close to suggesting that the whole of the Second World War, with its attendant horrors, was a kind of providential preparation for his papacy. Here is another extract from *Gift and Mystery* – the italics are John Paul II's own:

> *[M]y priesthood, even at its beginning, was in some way marked by the great sacrifice of countless men and women of my generation.* Providence spared me the most difficult experiences; and so my sense of indebtedness is all the greater, both to people whom I knew and to many more whom I did not know; all of them, regardless of nationality or language, by their sacrifice on the great altar of history, helped make my priestly vocation a reality.

The second significant factor which distinguishes Karol Wojtyla's experience decisively from our own is that he came to his adult understanding of the Church at a time when the Church in Poland was persecuted. Catholics here today may moan a bit about the assertive secularism of our government in twenty-first-century Britain, but the bruising it sometimes inflicts on Catholic sensibilities – over such questions as gay adoption – seems to result from absent-mindedness more than anything else. The Nazi assault on the Catholic Church in occupied Poland was altogether more deliberate and brutal; the occupiers quite rightly concluded that Catholicism was integral to Poland's sense of national identity, and since they wished to crush that identity Catholicism was a logical target.

It is striking how many of the earliest reports of atrocities in German-occupied Poland came from Catholic sources. In the spring of 1940 the religious publishers Burns and Oates published a book called *Poland, Yesterday, Today, Tomorrow* which was designed to raise public awareness in Britain about behaviour which Cardinal Hinsley, in his introduction, described as 'the barbarism of Genghis Khan'. It included a litany of stories of clergy being attacked and often killed. Here is an example of the kind of the thing it records:

> The Bishop of Posnan was interned and all his clergy were forbidden to say Mass; many of the clergy were shot in the market square. In Tarun the heavy work of reconstructing the bridge over the Vistula was carried out by the forced labour of prominent Polish citizens of the town, who were treated with ruthless barbarity. A Catholic prelate was compelled to take part in this work, and being old and exhausted fell into the river; workmen tried to save him, but the SS Nazi guards stopped them, and themselves shot their victim dead in the river.

And so, grimly, it goes on. And we know Karol Wojtyla had direct experience of this kind of thing, because in the summer of 1941 the Salesian priests who ran his local parish were all arrested by the SS. It is estimated that by the time the war was over 3,646 Polish priests had been sent to concentration camps, of whom more than 2,600 were killed.

The news filtering through about the way the Church was being treated in the Soviet zone of Poland was scarcely more encouraging. The Catholic media – *The Tablet* in London and *Osservatore Romano* in Rome – soon began to carry stories of churches being desecrated and used as stables or cinemas. In January 1940 the Polish Press bulletin in London published a document it said it had acquired from the city of Lvov; it was a programme laid out by a group calling itself the Soviet Union of Militant Godless, and it urged that 'All churches and ecclesiastical establishments on Polish territory occupied by Soviet troops must be liquidated,' and that 'All clergymen and other religious persons must give up religious practices.'

So wherever Karol Wojtyla looked he saw a suffering Church – and that context framed the two life-defining religious experiences he went through during the war years. The first was his membership of the prayer group I have mentioned above – the Living Rosary.

The Rosary and the seminary

The Rosary was centred around the Wojtylas' local parish church, St. Stanislaw Kostka, and it was led by one of the most influential but peculiar figures of Wojtyla's early life, a reclusive mystic called Jan Tyranowski – or 'the Master' as his acolytes called him. Tyranowski supported himself by working as a tailor but his real passions were prayer and the theology of *St. John of the Cross*. He would hang around the parish church trying to spot ardent young men whom he judged suitable for his prayer group, and those who were recruited would be invited to his tiny one bedroom apartment for spiritual instruction.

As Pope, John Paul II remained devoted to Tyranowski's memory; he described him as 'one of those unknown saints, hidden like a marvellous light at the bottom of life, at a depth where night usually reigns,' and said that 'in the example of a life given to God alone, he represented a new world that I did not know. I saw the beauty of the soul opened up by grace.' Others were less enthusiastic. Miecyslaw Malinski, Karol's close friend who was to go on to become his fellow seminarian and priest, found Tyranowski irritating: 'There was something bossy about his manner, and I kept wondering what he really wanted of me.' Two salient characteristics stand out in Malinksi's description of the way the Rosary was organized: secrecy, which of course made perfect sense in the context of Nazi attacks on the Church, and discipline. He later said that 'Every moment of every day was organised for activity or relaxation,' with each day's prayers, readings and thoughts recorded in notebooks.

The value of secrecy and discipline was of course reinforced by the second big religious event in Karol Wojtyla's life during the war years – his membership of Archbishop Sapieha's clandestine seminary. In the early days of the Occupation, the German authorities allowed seminaries to remain open, although they tried to dictate what was taught in them. They later decreed that no new students would be allowed to enrol, and it was this which prompted the Archbishop's decision to train new priests secretly.

Karol Wojtyla was part of the first cohort of recruits to what we might call today a 'virtual' seminary, in the sense that it did not exist as a physical building. The young men who joined continued to live and work as they had before, studying as and when they could. Karol Wojtyla had moved to another division of the Solway Company by this stage, and he did much of his reading at night in the boiler room of the purification plant there. His university had re-established itself as a kind of underground academic network; so there were informal tutorials and lectures in private homes too.

But all this changed with the mass round-up of young men which the Germans carried out in August 1944 to forestall any possibility that the Warsaw uprising would be repeated in Krakow. Archbishop Sapieha judged that his precious young charges were no longer safe, and brought them together in his own residence. For the remaining months of the occupation they lived under his protection, disguised as full-fledged priests of the archdiocese. Discreet arrangements were made to remove their names from the staff lists of companies like Solway.

I cannot, I am afraid, produce a passage in which John Paul II explicitly declares that he learnt how to run the Universal Church through the lessons learnt in wartime Krakow, and perhaps I am in danger of breaking my own rules of evidence here. But it is surely not too fanciful to see echoes of these very intense wartime experiences in the Church model he followed as Pope. The Church in Krakow under German occupation stood in opposition to the world around it – it had to. Discipline is everything when you are locked in an existential struggle – dissent a dangerous luxury. The authority of a figure like Archbishop Sapieha – aristocratic and iron-willed as he was – is an invaluable asset to a Church enduring persecution. Secretiveness is a virtue in those circumstances – and the discretion of a group like *Opus Dei*, a focus for so much suspicion among liberal Western European Catholics, would not seem in the least bit sinister to someone schooled in a group like the Living Rosary. And the example of Jan Tyranowski, eccentric as he was by worldly standards, offered evidence that holiness can be found in unexpected places.

Nationhood and culture

The third area I want to explore is John Paul II's understanding of nationhood and national culture – concepts which, again because of the singular nature of Poland's wartime experience, came to have a very particular resonance for the young Karol Wojtyla.

The Nazis' *General-Gouvernement* was of course an arrangement for governing without any legal basis. The Molotov-Ribbentrop Pact stated, in setting out the agreed 'spheres of influences' which the Soviet Union and Germany would enjoy over Poland, that 'The question of whether the interests of both parties make desirable the maintenance of an independent Polish State . . . can only be definitely determined in the course of future political developments'. So Hans Frank's Krakow-based fiefdom was simply an *ad hoc* arrangement for running things while the big boys decided whether Poland would exist at all. Dr. Frank made his views plain enough in the passage I have quoted earlier. 'Every vestige of Polish culture is to be eliminated'. He declared on another occasion:

> Those Poles who seem to have Nordic appearances will be taken to Germany to work in our factories. Children of Nordic appearance will be taken from their parents and raised as German workers. The rest? They will work. They will eat little. And in the end they will die out. There will never again be a Poland.

Poland of course was used to this kind of thing. For most of its modern history partition by great powers had been the norm rather than the exception, and the period of independence which followed the end of the First World War had lasted for a mere two decades. Polish writers had, as a result of this national experience, produced a significant body of literature dedicated to the survival of 'Polish-ness' during those periods when the country itself had been obliterated. The high-priest of what became known as 'Polish Romanticism' was the playwright and poet Adam Mickiewicz.

Writing in the early nineteenth century, during an earlier period of partition, Mickiewicz developed a spiritual theory of history which drew heavily on the Christian theology of redemption. Just as personal suffering could prepare the soul for the glory of salvation, he believed, the suffering of a nation could prepare it for a messianic role in world affairs. Poland, he wrote, was the nation loved by Christ, peopled by those who 'believe, who love, and who have hope'. Its subjugation was merely a step towards the day when, as the 'Lazarus among nations', it would be reborn to fulfil its destiny as the country with the 'heritage of the future freedom of the world'.

Karol Wojtyla had been taught the Polish romantics by his father, who was an autodidact and enthusiast for Polish literature and history. Mickiewicz remained one of the future Pope's literary heroes throughout his life; one of his most dramatic sermons on his first visit to Poland as Pope began with a quotation from the poet. The Mickiewicz message was of course a powerfully consoling one in the circumstances of occupation, and very early on we find Karol Wojtyla turning to him and the other great literary figures of the nineteenth century as he tries to make sense of his country's subjugation to Nazi rule. 'So this is Poland,' he wrote to a mentor in his home town of Wadowice in November 1939;

> I see her as you see her, but until now I did not see her in her full truth. I could not get the sense of the atmosphere of ideas that would be worthy of enveloping the nation of Mickiewicz, Slowacki, Norwid and Wyspianksi . . . I think that our liberation lies at the gate of Christ. I see an Athenian Poland, but made more perfect than Athens by the boundless immensity of Christianity.

The works of Mickiewicz and his fellow nationalist romantic Julius Slowacki featured regularly in the repertoire of the Rhapsodic Theatre, the clandestine company formed by Wojtyla and a group of like-minded thespian friends to stage Polish classics as a gesture of defiance against the German authorities. There were twice weekly rehearsals, often held in the basement flat where Karol had lived with his father, and the company's director described them as 'Romantic rehearsals, deepening our Polish consciousness, our resolution to survive and reach the shores of freedom'. The plays were performed discreetly in private homes, and there is an enjoyable anecdote about the future Pope declaiming the dying words of Pan Tadeusz, the hero of Mickiewicz' poem of the same name, when a German truck passed the windows blaring the news of a great German victory on the Eastern front. Those present recalled that Wojtyla simply raised his voice above the megaphone and completed his oration *con brio*.

It is easy to smile at some of these stories – and at the somewhat adolescent tone of Karol Wojtyla's passionately intellectual letters to friends during this period. But in the Krakow of the early 1940s staging Polish plays with a nationalist message was a genuinely dangerous thing to do, and for those involved the theatre was a very serious business indeed. At a time when Poland had ceased to exist – in the physical sense of a Polish territory run by a Polish government within recognized national borders – they believed that they were preserving the spirit of Poland as it was expressed in Polish culture. The great emphasis John Paul II placed on culture as a source of identity in his later writings must surely be directly related to this experience.

The fourth area where there is a very clear connection between the life lived by the young Karol Wotiyla's and the mature ideas of John Paul II the Pope relates to his relationship with Jews and his view of anti-Semitism. His lifelong friendship with Jews he first knew as a child and a young man are well-known as a matter of public record, and there is also a wealth of independent evidence from Wadowice and Krakow that his attitude to Jews was marked by a kind of obstinate sense of decency that went beyond personal affection. We know, for example, that when school football games were played between teams of Catholics and Jews, Karol Wojtyla would often play for the Jewish side. We have the testimony of Ginka Beer, a young Jewish neighbour in Wadowice who was sent to Israel by her parents because of the rise of anti-Semitism in Poland in the 1930s, that 'there was only one family who never showed any racial hostility towards us, and that was Lolek and his dad.' And we have the comment of a university contemporary in 1938 that 'Karol Wojtyla would often accompany Anka Weber and played a particular role with regard to her. As I perceived it then, and as I perceive it now, he protected her, a Jew, from potential aggression.'

So it is evident that the future Pope was not simply free from anti-Semitic prejudice himself; he made a positive effort to stand up to it in others – in what was an increasingly anti-Semitic social context even before the German occupation. Wartime Krakow of course offered the most powerful lesson imaginable about where anti-Semitism can lead, but, frustratingly, I have not been able to find any evidence in Karol Wojtyla's letters or writing of the period to shed light on what he thought of this at the time. However, as Sr Margaret Shepherd records elsewhere in this collection, he was, as Pope, explicit about the connection between his memories of the way Jews were treated then and his approach to Christian–Jewish relations.

The collapse of Communism

My final point is, I confess, somewhat speculative. One of the great puzzles I encountered in writing my life of John Paul II was the difficulty of making an intelligent assessment of his part in the collapse of Communism. Sometimes he of course acted like a conventional diplomat or politician, and you can judge his actions during – say – the Solidarity strike or Poland's declaration of martial law just as you would judge the actions of any other leader. But the moment which really made a difference was, it seems to me, that extraordinary first papal visit to Poland in 1979, and defining why that made such a difference is a very difficult thing to do. The best – and crispest – judgement was given to me by President Carter's National Security Adviser Zbigniew Brzezinski: 'The dominant mood until then', he said, 'was the inevitability of the existing system. After he left the dominant mood was the non-inevitability of the existing system. I think that was a fundamental transformation.'

In other words John Paul II's triumph in 1979 lay in an act of imagination. Despite all the evidence that the Soviet domination of Poland and Eastern Europe had become the settled natural order of things, he was able to imagine that the world might be different. In the way he conducted that visit he made the rest of us think there was a real possibility that things might change. In doing that he was, I think, drawing on the most important lesson of all those he learnt as a young man in Krakow. The possession of power does not confer moral legitimacy, and even those regimes which seem most impregnable are, in the end, vulnerable if they are based on bad ideas.

Select Bibliography

The Making of the Pope of the Millennium, Kalendarium of the Life of Karol Wojtyla, edited by Father Adam Boniecki and published by the Marian Press in the United States in 2000 (first English edition) is an invaluable collection of first-hand testimony about John Paul II's early life.

Accounts of conditions in wartime Poland can be found in *God's Playground: A History of Poland* by Norman Davies (Oxford: Oxford, 1981), *Poland in the Twentieth Century* by M. K. Dziewanowski: (New York: Columbia University Press, 1977) and, (for a contemporary picture) *Poland, Yesterday, Today, Tomorrow*, by Gertrude Golden (London: Burns and Oates, 1940).

I have treated this period in some detail in *John Paul II: Man of History* by Edward Stourton (London: Hodder and Stoughton, 2006), and there is valuable research in *His Holiness: John Paul II and the Hidden History of our Time* by Carl Bernstein and Marco Politi (London: Bantam, 1997).

Chapter 3

John Paul II and Hans Urs von Balthasar

Brendan Leahy

In considering the theological legacy of Pope John Paul II it is no surprise that von Balthasar comes to mind as a possible theological influence on the Polish Pope. As someone 'intensely loyal . . . to the person
of John Paul II'[1] von Balthasar has been described as fitting into the
Pope's 'agenda' of reform.[2] In 1997 Margaret Hebblethwaite commented
that 'commonly dubbed "the Pope's favourite theologian"' von Balthasar
had moved from being 'an institutional misfit excluded from Vatican II,
to the court theologian of today's Vatican'.[3] Yes, at first glance it does seem
that von Balthasar's thought may have influenced Pope John Paul II's
writings.[4]

That Pope John Paul II and Hans Urs von Balthasar held each other
in high esteem is clearly evident in the warm and significant references
made by the Pope to the Swiss theologian and vice versa. To push the
claim further, however, and maintain von Balthasar's theology influenced the Pope is warranted only indirectly and in a limited sense.

In this chapter I propose that in terms of material content, there
are some grounds for saying that von Balthasar exercised an influence
on the Pope's theology. Nevertheless, I believe John Paul II's theology
was shaped primarily through encounter with other teachers and different experiences. I shall point to some distinct aspects of the Swiss
theologian's theology that dart across the horizon of this intuitive, charismatic Pope's writings and actions. Moreover, the chapter affirms that
von Balthasar was undoubtedly considered an exemplary theologian
and proposed as such by the Pope.

Mutual esteem

Let's start with the mutual esteem. In 1984 John Paul II presented von Balthasar with the first Paul VI International Prize for theology expressing his warmest greetings to the theologian and noting the 'significant results' that resulted from his toilsome effort in research.[5] On that as on other occasions the Pope invited von Balthasar to lunch. At a conference in 1985 marking the ecclesial mission of Adrienne von Speyr, the Pope once again thanked von Balthasar for his 'enormous theological work'.[6] Two years later, addressing the Roman Curia on 22 December 1987, he explicitly cited von Balthasar, itself an unusual departure from the tradition of not quoting living theologians. Further evidence of papal appreciation of the theologian's contribution to theology can be gleaned in the fact that von Balthasar was re-appointed as a member (and by all accounts an active one) of the International Theological Commission right up until his death in 1988.

The year 1988 was to be a significant one in terms of the Pope's expression of regard for von Balthasar. It was the year his reflections on the Stations of the Cross were chosen as the basis for the Good Friday *Via Crucis* ceremony. It was also the year he was mentioned in the encyclical letter, *Mulieris dignitatem,* and the year he was named Cardinal shortly before his sudden death in June. In his telegram to Cardinal Ratzinger on the death of Hans Urs von Balthasar, Pope John Paul II spoke of the sense of loss 'of a great son of the Church, an outstanding man of theology and of the arts, who deserves a special place of honour in contemporary ecclesiastical and cultural life'. The Holy See, he said, held this theologian, in 'high esteem'.[7]

For a long time after von Balthasar's death, the Pope continued to refer to the theologian. In addressing participants at a meeting in 1992 of a group of the International Review, *Communio,* the Pope referred to him as one of the 'eminent theologians of Catholicity' and again quoted him.[8] The Pontiff also made reference to him in 1994 in his book, *Crossing the Threshold of Hope.*[9]

This multiplicity of references would certainly indicate the late Pope's high esteem for von Balthasar's writings. As a Pope who saw himself promoting an authentic implementation of Vatican II, John Paul II esteemed von Balthasar for providing a true theology corresponding to the directions of that Council. Just 2 weeks before his death the recently named Cardinal reported a comment the Pope had made to him: 'I'm not making you cardinal for Switzerland but for the Church of the world, for your theology.'[10] Indeed at his funeral Cardinal Ratzinger interpreted the Pope's nomination of von Balthasar as Cardinal as an affirmation that von Balthasar 'is right in what he teaches of the faith, that he points the way to the sources of living water – a witness to the Word which teaches us Christ and which teaches us how to live'.[11]

It is also easy to find many positive references to Pope John Paul II in the writings and comments of Hans Urs von Balthasar. Early on in the pontificate von Balthasar came to the Pope's 'defence' in the context of the Hans Küng controversy, praising him for taking positions on, and safeguarding fundamental questions of, Christian faith, for moving out from his desk in the Vatican to visit strategic points around the world, for working in continuity with his predecessors.[12] He also spoke very approvingly of the 'genial suggestion' by the Pope to gather people together for prayer in Assisi in October 1986.[13]

Commenting on the Pope's 'extraordinary personality', he observed 'there exists no more attentive a listener than our Pope.'[14] And on his teaching authority he observed:

> I think his teachings expressly contain theses which are central to the understanding of our faith: the body, for instance, the human person, the community and the wonderful things he has to say on human labour and divine mercy. What is developed here is rooted directly in revelation, and should be pondered by every Christian, not in order to construct a closed system with his encyclicals, but to obtain from his great intuitions a point of departure from which new reflections on divine revelations may emerge. I consider his thoughts concerning the body of the highest importance, because the subject has always been, and still is, surrounded by forms of Platonism and spiritualism, which disparage the body and everything material in favour of a pure spirituality.[15]

It is clear that von Balthasar admired the Pope greatly and not least for keeping a focus on the Conciliar vision of the Church as communion, a vision rooted in the deep springs of divine revelation.[16]

Theological affinities

It is not difficult to rehearse reasons why Pope John Paul II would have esteemed von Balthasar. There are affinities in thought and emphases. In tracing points of affinity we need to be mindful of Avery Dulles' observation that 'Karol Wojtyla's theological achievement is not primarily in the field of academic research and abstract theory . . . Nor has he undertaken to compose a multivolume theological summa like those of . . . Hans Urs von Balthasar.'[17] Nevertheless, as an academic and bishop Karol Wojtyla produced two scholarly dissertations and hundreds of articles and, as Pope, his enormous output as pastor was expressed in a huge number of encyclicals, other letters, homilies and addresses. Bearing in mind the difference in genre and purpose of the writings of the Pope and von Balthasar, any attempt to trace similarities of theological concern and approach can only be presented in broad brush strokes.

Both were schooled initially in the world of the humanities, John Paul II in Polish poetry and theatre, von Balthasar in music and German literature.[18] However, the humanistic background influenced them in different ways. It was above all the hardship of his Polish homeland that experienced the ravages of the Second World War and the ensuing Communism that brought Karol Wojtyla to affirm true beauty as a glimmer of the Spirit of God that transfigures matter, opening the human soul to the sense of the eternal.[19] That sustained him in his view of the human person and solidarity in the context of Communism. It shaped his engagement with culture even in its darkest aspects.[20] The Swiss theologian, on the other hand, was influenced by his studies in the humanities to go beyond the neo-scholasticism that he found so arid during his time of study as a young Jesuit. He went on to write a theological aesthetics (influenced by Karl Barth's *Dogmatics*[21]) and Theo-dramatics.

Both Pope John Paul II and von Balthasar underlined the importance of the theme of sanctity in the theological enterprise and as a source of theology. Encounter with some of the great saints influenced and shaped their theological vision – Ignatius of Loyola in the case of von Balthasar, John of the Cross in the case of the young priest Karol Wojtyla. They both understood saints not only as inspirational figures but as theological sources. Pope John Paul II did his doctoral research at the Angelicum on John of the Cross.[22] No Pope has canonized and beatified as many saints and blesseds. It is Pope John Paul II who declared Teresa of Lisieux a doctor of the Church and named three women patron saints of Europe. No recent theologian has been so attentive to saints, and in particular women saints, as von Balthasar.[23] Both believed in the integration of spirituality and theology with von Balthasar advocating what he called a 'kneeling' theology. He also saw the principle of sanctity emerging in a new 'lay' way in the mediation between the Church and the world.[24] The Pope too viewed the universal call to holiness and the role of the laity as of primary importance in renewing the ecclesial and social fabric.[25]

The motif of the triune God of love, the love of the three divine persons in a relational existence of mutuality, is very strong in the writings both of von Balthasar and of Pope John Paul II.[26] The Pope's first three encyclicals revolve around the three Persons of the Trinity. All of von Balthasar's writings are imbued with the Trinitarian theme. In both of them we see a Trinitarian Christology that impacts on their view of ecclesial communion, and a personalist theological anthropology that accentuates the relational identity of personhood. Bishop Wojtyla was clearly influenced by the theological integration of Trinity and Christology and anthropology that he witnessed emerging during Vatican II, the event that deeply shaped his theology.[27] In *Dives in misericordia* (n.2) he writes that the linking of God (theology) and what it is to be human (anthropology) is the main challenge of our time and was the main focus of Vatican II. He expanded his reflection on the metaphysical sense and mystery of the person in terms of solidarity and communion in the light of the Council's Trinitarian focus. For von Balthasar it was the Church fathers, Origen, Gregory of Nyssa and Maximus the Confessor as well as Russian writers such as Sergius Bulgakov that formed his Trinitarian vision. In his multi-volumed trilogy, *Glory of the Lord, Theo-Drama* and *Theologik*, he will seek to show how the Paschal Mystery reveals something of the inner (and *ad extra*) Trinitarian operations.

Linked to the previous theme, it has been commented that there is a strict analogy between the position of Karol Wojtyla and that of post-conciliar theologians like Hans Urs von Balthasar regarding the relationship of nature and grace. Rocco Buttiglione, for instance, claims that both developed similarly the theme of the nature–grace relation.

He points out that they underlined the analogy of faith by appropriating to Catholic theology some of Karl Barth's fundamental theology.[28] It's not clear that the Pope did appropriate Karl Barth's theology, but it is the case that he was influenced by the developments of the mid-twentieth century that underlined how Christ comes to bring humanity to its fullness not only in terms of a future or separate eternal life but also as a hundredfold of fulfilment of our natural desire for God in this life. He viewed the human project as the recovery and the full reorientation of our natural existence towards God that finds its highest meaning in Christ. It is true that von Balthasar too is one of the major writers on this Christo-centric theme in the mid-twentieth century.

Pope John Paul II would have appreciated von Balthasar's theology 'from above' rather than 'from below', an approach which risks measuring God in terms of humanity alone. Yet von Balthasar's recognition that theology must avail of philosophical mediation if it is to penetrate and express fully the riches of its own would have also pleased the Pope. In their research both were influenced by Thomas Aquinas but they also went further afield looking for ways to complement Thomistic philosophy with other currents available to them. Both turned to phenomenology, mediated through Max Scheler in the case of Wojtyla and through Heidegger (and his studies in the humanities) in the case of von Balthasar. Aidan Nichols writes that 'while Pope Wojtyla's philosophy is Thomas catalysed by Scheler and thus strongest in the ethical domain, Balthasar's is Thomas fructified by Goethe and Schelling, and therefore especially concerned with cosmology in its relation to subjecthood and interiority'.[29] Von Balthasar comes to terms with German idealism in particular, Pope John Paul II with the ethical challenges of Communist ideology. This explains also the greater degree of social categories in Wojtyla's writings than von Balthasar's.[30] Pope John Paul II indeed underlined the link between Catholic social thought and the civilization of love in a way we don't find in von Balthasar.[31] While the Pope would have agreed with von Balthasar in underlining the Christian's role as 'the guardian of that metaphysical wonderment which is the point of origin for philosophy and the continuation of which is the basis of its further existence',[32] he would go further in promoting a personalist anthropology that gives prominence to the notion of participation in solidarity in politics and economics. It is true that both Pope

and theologian underlined freedom at the centre of their Christo-
centric view of personhood.[33]

In his theological research von Balthasar exercised a style of exegesis
that clearly has a strong theological character. Exegesis is to be integrated into the entire enterprise of theological defence of the Word's
power and dignity.[34] A review of Pope John Paul II's use of Scripture in
his encyclicals reveals a method of 'wholeness'.[35] His tendency to cite
from the Johannine writings is a link with von Balthasar who established together with Adrienne von Speyr a community of consecrated
lay people and diocesan priests called 'The Johannine Community'. For
both the Pope and von Balthasar dogmatic questions are important to
exegetical research.[36]

The love of both Pope and theologian for Tradition needs also to be
mentioned. Von Balthasar is one of the best known twentieth-century
theologians engaged in the *Ressourcement,* the retrieval and renewal
of the whole Tradition, Patristic, Medieval and post-Reformation, for
a contemporary penetration of the Christian faith as it opens in its
catholicity to the world in a renewed radiant face.[37] In trying to propose
an alternative to neo-scholasticism von Balthasar wrote a series of
monographs on figures such as Irenaeus, Augustine, Denys, Anselm,
Bonaventure, Dante, John of the Cross, Pascal, Hamann, Soloviev,
Hopkins and Péguy. He learned from Scheeben, Karl Adam, Romano
Guardini and Erich Przywara. For Balthasar it is never a sealed tradition. Pope John Paul II also saw himself reclaiming Tradition.[38] Again
he saw this as something dynamic. Henri de Lubac can be considered a
major influence. On the thirtieth anniversary of the opening of the
Council, the Pope commented on how this great event of the Church
like all councils springs up, as it were, 'from the subsoil of the Church's
history, right from the beginning'.[39] His desire to pitch Vatican II in a
theological framework that took into account the bimillennial Tradition of the Church can be seen in the *Catechism of the Catholic Church*
or his comments in *Fides et ratio* to the effect that in 'engaging great
cultures for the first time the Church cannot abandon what she has
gained from her inculturation in the world of Graeco-Latin thought'.[40]

In terms of Church, both saw Mary as the perfect disciple, the partner
who co-operates with Christ and whose presence continues to be operative in the life of the Church. Both wrote extensively on the nuptial

mystery. Their ecclesiological writings reveal engagement with anthropological issues of the character of human life, human difference and human sexuality. Both viewed human life, from conception to natural death, demanding attentive contemplation and response of nurture and love. Mary was pivotal in their reflections. At this point, however, we have reached a theme where there is more than theological affinity between von Balthasar and the Pope. It is at this point we move into direct influence.

Gauging the extent of the influence

To gauge the extent, if any, of von Balthasar's influence on Pope John Paul II, it is useful to distinguish between the formative influences on the young student, priest and bishop Karol Wojtyla prior to 1978 (year of the Papal election) and influences that came to bear on the Pope during the 27 years of papacy that followed. In a strict sense, the focus of this essay is the papacy but obviously we cannot ignore any contact he might have had with von Balthasar's thought prior to his election as Pope.

Trawling through books or articles Karol Wojtyla wrote before 1978, and attending to comments made subsequently in interviews regarding his formative theological influences during that period, we can see that von Balthasar was not a major formative influence up to that point.

In *Sign of Contradiction*,[41] a book written on the basis of talks given at the 1976 Vatican retreat and one that perhaps, as none other, reveals the main lines of the mature theologian-bishop's theological reflections just 2 years before he became Pope, we find many of his favourite themes. *Gaudium et spes*, 22 (the truth that only in the mystery of the incarnate Word does the mystery of man take on light) is quoted. The importance of being a teacher of truth and servant of love is underlined. The Marian theme abounds. The paschal mystery is frequently referred to with the Trinitarian motif in relief. Henri de Lubac is praised for 'brilliantly' analysing the tragedy of atheistic humanism (p. 16). But there's not one reference to von Balthasar. There is also no mention of von Balthasar in *The Acting Person*[42] or *Sources of Renewal*[43] or *Love and Responsibility*.[44]

That's not to say he was unaware of von Balthasar. It is certainly possible to surmise that as a young doctoral student from November 1946 onwards Karol Wojtyla would have been at least familiar with von Balthasar's name and his place on the margins of the 'nouvelle théologie' debate. His doctoral moderator at the Angelicum, the renowned Professor Réginald Garrigou-Lagrange (1877–1969), was extremely negative towards this new development in theology and wrote his first critical article 'La nouvelle théologie où va-t-elle?' precisely in the year Wojtyla came to Rome. George Hunston Williams goes so far as to say that the debate 'caused a vortex of consternation within the Angelicum and constituted the intellectual agitation Wojtyla sensed at the Angelicum'.[45]

In 1975 a well-known figure in France for upholding the Church in a period of crisis, Gérard Soulages, visited Cardinal Wojtyla in Cracow. Mr. Soulages was admired as a man of faith and a sort of Amos by no less than Jean Guitton, professor of philosophy at the Sorbonne. The Cardinal was impressed with him. In his conversation with the future Pope, Soulages expressed his opinion that the Church had been through many crises but that this was the most grave of all. He referred to Hans Urs von Balthasar as having said the same thing.[46]

So much for the possible pre-1978 impact of von Balthasar on the future Pope. But did the theologian have a direct influence on the Pope after his election in 1978? We've already seen that the Pope certainly refers to von Balthasar with great warmth of esteem. But there's no direct evidence that von Balthasar influenced the Pope to a significant degree. Several biographies of Pope John Paul II do not even mention the Swiss theologian.[47] Those that do mention him make only marginal points. We find little reference to von Balthasar in works treating Pope John Paul II's magisterial teaching.[48] In the *Cambridge Companion to von Balthasar*, Pope John Paul II is mentioned only once in a footnote.[49] Commentators do not number von Balthasar as one of the Pope's mentors.[50]

While it's true that there is no direct evidence 'above the radar', as it were, it is not hard to imagine that von Balthasar may have indirectly wielded a discreet influence 'below the radar' in ways that might not immediately be quantifiable. Karol Wojtyla had come to know Henri de Lubac at Vatican II and kept in touch with the French Jesuit.[51] De Lubac regarded von Balthasar as perhaps the most cultured man of our times.

It can only be presumed he shared his impression of von Balthasar with the Polish bishop, Cardinal and then Pope.

In a masterly interview published in 1982, André Frossard asked the Pope if in the midst of all his activity he managed to get time for reading. His response was significant. He clarified how in the past as a researcher he didn't seek erudition but rather what seemed essential to the progress of his research. 'The time for assimilation and reflection counts for more'. As Pope he had, of course, less time at his disposal and yet he could say that in a way he read more because of the valuable work of his collaborators who kept him up to date on essential publications. He also revealed that at that time he was reading 'beaucoup plus de théologie que de philosophie'.[52]

What theology might that have been? His remark about the collaborators is not without significance in answering that question. A very close collaborator who met with him regularly on Friday evenings for more than 20 years of his pontificate was Cardinal Ratzinger who co-founded with von Balthasar the International Theological Review, *Communio*. Later as Pope Benedict XVI, Joseph Ratzinger acknowledged how he knew the distinguished Swiss theologian whom he 'had the joy of meeting regularly'.[53] It would make an interesting interview question to Pope Benedict XVI to ask him how much he spoke of von Balthasar's theology with Pope John Paul II. It can be fairly surmised that von Balthasar's insights were sometimes or even frequently brought to the Pope's attention.

Inspirational influence

Avery Dulles talks of Karol Wojtyla making use of 'a vast panoply of sources'.[54] It can be argued that, to at least a limited degree, von Balthasar belongs to that panoply. I am grateful to Prof. Jared Wicks for recounting an episode that indicates how in the years of his pontificate Pope John Paul II read von Balthasar's *Der antirömische Affekt*. It seems that when the then prefect of the Congregation for the Doctrine of the Faith, Cardinal Franjo Šeper, introduced von Balthasar to the Pope as one of the members of the International Theological Commission, the Pontiff remarked to the Swiss theologian that he was reading *Der antirömische Affekt*.[55] Either in the course of conversation with von Balthasar himself or in contact with his close collaborator Cardinal Ratzinger, it does seem that Pope John Paul II picked up some specific aspects of von Balthasar's work that dart across the horizon of this intuitive, charismatic Pope's writings and actions. In the final section of this chapter, I'd like to propose three such themes that inspired Pope John Paul II.

Marian profile

One aspect that I believe we can attribute to von Balthasar is his reference to the Church's 'Marian principle'. Rino Fisichella comments that 'the Marian principle cuts right across the teaching of Pope John Paul II'.[56] This reference to the 'Marian principle', an expression that the Pope adopts from von Balthasar, can be traced to an article written by von Balthasar in *Neue Klarstellungen*[57] and quoted by the Pope both in his 1987 address to the Roman Curia and in the 1988 encyclical *Mulieris dignitatem*.

Admittedly, the Marian theme itself in Pope John Paul II's thought and writings cannot simply be attributed to von Balthasar. It is well known that the classic work of Louis-Marie Grignon de Montfort (1673–1716), *True Devotion to the Blessed Virgin Mary* had an enormous impact on the young Wojtyla. Reading this book became a truly 'decisive turning-point' in his life. He discovered a Marian devotion that was based completely on Jesus Christ, the Incarnation and Redemption. It has been said, moreover, that 'Vatican II made him conscious of the "ecclesiotypical" vision of Mary'.[58]

Avery Dulles links Pope John Paul II and von Balthasar 'in maintaining that Marian devotion is not outdated and that the Second Vatican Council did nothing to authorize Marian minimalism'.[59] Indeed 'following Hans Urs von Balthasar, the Pope holds that the Church lives both by a Petrine principle of apostolic ministry and by a Marian principle of life and fruitful receptivity. Of the two, the Marian principle is primary'.[60] Aurelio Fusi also refers to von Balthasar in his work on Marian themes in John Paul II's ecclesiology.[61]

It is this notion of the Church as a multi-dimensional reality with various different profiles or principles that seems to be a feature in von Balthasar's ecclesiology that appealed to the Pope. In his symbolic personalist ecclesiology, the Swiss theologian spoke of the many continuing missions in the Church symbolized by Peter (Pope, bishops, institutional dimension), John the Baptist (martyrdom), John the Evangelist (contemplative love, the counsels), James (tradition), Paul (novelty, charisms). In particular von Balthasar saw the Church revolving around two principles of unity – the Petrine and the Marian. Cardinal Ratzinger confirmed that Pope John Paul II 'made his own' von Balthasar's notion of the Marian and Petrine dimensions of the Church.[62]

This can be seen, for instance, in an address he delivered to the Roman Curia just a few days before Christmas 1987. In it, he spoke of the Church's two profiles – the Marian ('subjective' holiness and the actualization of the life of the Word, the sacraments and community) and the Petrine ('objective' means of sanctification such as the sacraments effected by bishops and priests). He described how all that goes on in the life of the Church revolves around these two profiles but he particularly underlines the Marian:

> This Marian profile is also – even perhaps more so – fundamental and characteristic for the Church as is the apostolic and Petrine profile to which it is profoundly united . . . The Church lives on this authentic 'Marian profile', this 'Marian dimension' . . . The Marian dimension of the Church is antecedent to that of the Petrine . . . Mary . . . precedes all others, including obviously Peter himself and the Apostles . . . The link between the two profiles of the Church, the Marian and the Petrine, is profound and complementary. This is so even though the Marian profile is anterior (to that of the Petrine) not only in the plan of God but also in time, as well as being supreme and pre-eminent, the richer in personal and communitarian implications.[63]

Some months later, he returned to this theme in his apostolic letter, *Mulieris dignitatem*.[64] In his 1995 letter to priests for Holy Thursday, he recommended they reread *Mulieris dignitatem* and also in 1995 he wrote on this theme in his letter to women. In 1998 during a catechesis on the signs of hope in the Church he commented, 'At the dawn of the new millennium, we can joyfully discern that "Marian profile" of the Church which epitomizes the deepest meaning of conciliar renewal.'[65]

It seems to the present writer that John Paul II's appreciation of the Church's Marian profile explains much of his teaching on lay people in the Church, his encouragement of the new ecclesial movements, his promotion of the dignity of women in the Church and the world, his view on ecumenism and his enormous outreach to the world.[66]

An interesting inkling of how this notion of a Church consisting of many different profiles, figures or principles impacted on the Pope's thinking can be gleaned from a table conversation between him and Chiara Lubich, foundress of the Focolare Movement. She tells of how one day at lunch with the Pope she asked him if in the future the president of the Focolare Movement (with its variety of vocations including lay people, consecrated men and women, priests, religious and bishops) should always be a woman. He replied with enthusiasm 'And why not? On the contrary'!. Making reference to von Balthasar's theology, he went out to explain to her his vision of the Church having many different profiles or principles with the Marian profile of the Church as an all-embracing dimension of the Church.[67]

In ways it is a key also to his reading of the man–woman relationship as embodying the polarity of reciprocity at the heart of the Church. Indeed, influenced possibly also by von Balthasar, he views the Church's charism–institution polarity within the interplay between the Marian–Petrine profiles.[68] And this was a key to reading the Church as communion. Not least it was a handle for a way towards a fuller understanding of the role of women in the life of the Church, something yet to be fully teased out.[69]

Hell

In his book, *Crossing the Threshold of Hope*, Pope John Paul II noted how the problem of hell has always disturbed the 'great thinkers' in the Church, beginning with Origen and continuing with Mikhail Bulgakov. He mentions Hans Urs von Balthasar at this point.[70] It is worth noting that dealing with the same theme and making very similar points in *Sign of Contradiction* (composed before becoming Pope) he makes no reference to von Balthasar on this topic.[71] It seems he came to know of his thought later.

Von Balthasar is well known and sometimes criticized for his views on the issue of hope for the salvation for all.[72] The Pope knows the ancient councils rejected the theory of a final *apocatastasis*, a universal regeneration and salvation, but in his comments in *Crossing the Threshold of Hope* he also acknowledges, and here we can see perhaps see the influence of von Balthasar, that the Church has never made any statement to the effect that some will definitely go to eternal punishment. The 'silence of the Church' regarding this subject is the only appropriate position for Christian faith.

As the reader moves through these pages, he or she can almost hear the Pope in dialogue with von Balthasar on the issue, wondering 'isn't final punishment in some way necessary in order to re-establish moral equilibrium in the complex history of humanity?' And yet it would seem that the Pope is taking up a point already made by von Balthasar, when he says that 'even when Jesus says of Judas, the traitor, "It would be better for that man if he had never been born" (Mt 26:24), his words do not allude for certain to eternal damnation.'[73]

Pope John Paul II inclines like von Balthasar to hope that all may be saved, but ultimately it seems that it is the influence of John of the Cross that bears greater weight on the Pope. The Spanish mystic spoke of the place of God's purifying love and purgatory.[74] It seems the Pope wants to place greater emphasis on this than did von Balthasar is his writings on the topic.

Interestingly, in the *Redemptoris Mater* chapel in the Vatican Apartments, beautifully renovated by the Jesuit Marko Ivan Rupnik at the request of Pope John Paul II on the fiftieth anniversary of his priestly ordination, there is no depiction of any human being in hell.

The Holy Spirit

In 1986 Pope John Paul II published the third of his Trinitarian encyclicals, *Dominum et vivificantem*.[75] Von Balthasar wrote a commentary on it.[76] He notes the sources of the encyclical letter – the Gospel, previous encyclicals, ideas from Vatican II and ideas coming from the Pope's own heart. But it is possible to surmise that von Balthasar himself was in some way a source for the Pope's reflections.

It's a theme to be worked out further. But briefly, it is possible to point to themes that clearly resonate with von Balthasar's writings: God's Trinitarian logic, the theme of freedom, the suffering of God,[77] the drama of increasing resistance to God's offer, the theme of prayer as an experience in the Spirit leading us into participation in the Trinitarian dialogue.

Conclusion

Both Pope John Paul II and Hans Urs von Balthasar were great figures of the twentieth century, each with his own distinctive mission, one as bishop and Pope, the other as a major theologian. The Pope was above all very faithful to the agenda set by Vatican II, an agenda that had shaped his theological outlook. The theologian was above all very faithful to the Ignatian charism and his encounter with Adrienne von Speyr's mission that provided the prism through which he could reread the vast cultural, philosophical and theological insight he had gained through his studies. Both came into prominence particularly in the last 25 years of the twentieth century. Their paths crossed and they admired each other's fidelity to the mission assigned to them by God. The Pope seems to have picked up some pointers from von Balthasar. But the panoply of formational influences that shaped Karol Wojtyla both before and after becoming Pope reminds us that for all the convergence of their thought and interests, von Balthasar was but one influence on Pope John Paul II. That takes away nothing, however, from the great esteem in which he held the Swiss theologian and the degree to which he proposed von Balthasar as a model theologian at the service of the Church.

Notes

1. John O'Donnell, *Hans Urs von Balthasar* (London: Geoffrey Chapman, 1992), p. 2.
2. See Juan Arias, *L'enigma Wojtyla* (Rome: Borla, 1986), pp. 229 and 263.
3. Margaret Hebblethwaite, 'Balthasar's Golden Touch', *The Tablet* (20 September 1997), pp. 1208–1209, at p. 1208.
4. Philip Zaleski, 'The Saints of Pope John Paul II', *First Things* 16 (March, 2006), pp. 28–32.
5. See his address in *Istituto Paolo VI, Premio Internazionale* (Milan: Istituto Paolo VI, 1984), pp. 9–13, at 10.
6. See ISTRA, *La Mission Ecclesiale di Adrienne von Speyr: Atti del II Colloquio Internazionale del pensiero cristiano* (Milan: Jaca Book, 1986), pp. 186.

The Pope asked von Balthasar to hold the symposium on Adrienne von Speyr and subsequently gave 'express permission' for her posthumous works to be published. See Hans Urs von Balthasar, *Our Task* (San Francisco, CA: Ignatius, 1994), p. 9.

7. The text of the telegram is printed in *Communio* 15 (1988), p. 511.

8. Address to a Group of the International Review, *Communio*, 29 May 1992.

9. Pope John Paul II, *Crossing the Threshold of Hope* (London: Jonathan Cape, 1994), p. 185.

10. Claudio Mesionat, 'Prevedo la persecuzione' (interview with von Balthasar) in *Il Sabato* (11 June 1988) and reprinted in Hans Urs von Balthasar, *La Realtà e la Gloria* (Milan: Edit, 1988), p. 206.

11. See the text of his funeral homily, in Karl Lehmann and Walter Kasper (eds), *Hans Urs von Balthasar: Figura e Opera* (Casale Monferrato: Piemme, 1991), pp. 451–59, at p. 458.

12. 'In difesa di Wojtyla', in *Il Sabato* (24 November 1979) reprinted in *La Realtà*, pp. 27–33.

13. 'Io e Assisi' in *Il Sabato* (8 November 2006) and reprinted in *La Realtá*, pp. 95–96.

14. Test Everything, Hold Fast to What is Good: An Interview by Angelo Scola (San Francisco, CA: Ignatius Press, 1989), p. 60.

15. *Test Everything*, pp. 79–80.

16. Mesionat, 'Prevedo la persecuzione', pp. 203–206.

17. Avery Dulles, The Splendor of Faith: The Theological Vision of Pope John Paul II (New York: Crossroad, 1999), p. 183.

18. John McNerney, Footbridge towards the Other: An Introduction to the Philosophy and Poetry of John Paul II (Edinburgh: T&T Clark, 2003).

19. Cf. Pope John Paul II, *Letter to Artists* (4 April 1999), no. 16.

20. See John McNerney, Footbridge towards the Other.

21. See Fergus Kerr, 'Foreword: Assessing this "Giddy Synthesis"', in Lucy Gardner, David Moss, Ben Quash and Graham Ward, *Balthasar at the End of Modernity* (Edinburgh: T&T Clark, 1999), pp. 1–14.

22. Karol Wojtyla, *Faith According to St. John of the Cross* (San Francisco, CA: Ignatius Press, 1981). For Garrigou-Lagrange's comments on this thesis that he supervised, see the Italian translation of Wojtyla's thesis, *La Fede secondo S. Giovanni della Croce* (Rome: Angelicum-Herder, 1979).

23. Of particular relevance here is his belief in the mission of Adrienne von Speyr to whom he owed so much. See Hans Urs von Balthasar, *First Glance at Adrienne von Speyr* (San Francisco, CA: Ignatius Press, 1981), p. 13. See also his essay 'Theology and Sanctity', in Hans Urs von Balthasar, *Explorations in Theology. I: The Word Made Flesh* (San Francisco, CA: Ignatius, 1989), pp. 181–209.

24. See Hans Urs von Balthasar, 'Riflessioni per un Lavoro sui movimenti laicali nella Chiesa' in Inos Biffi, Georges Chantraine, Angelo Scola, Antonio Sicari, Hans Urs von Balthasar, Benedetto Testa, Franco Follo, Angela Chiasserini, Angelo Busetto. *I Laici e la Missione della Chiesa* (Milan: Istra, 1987), pp. 85–106.
25. See Pope John Paul II, Post-Synodal Apostolic Exhortation, *Christifideles Laici* (30 December 1988), no. 34 and 36.
26. John McNerney writes that 'there is a close parallel between the work of Wojtyla and von Balthasar in that the latter conceives of being as intelligible only as love.' See John McNerney, *Footbridge towards the Other*, xv, fn. 11.
27. See, for instance, Cardinal Karol Wojtyla, *Sources of Renewal: The Implementation of the Second Vatican Council* (San Francisco, CA: Harper & Row, 1979), esp. pp. 53–65.
28. Rocco Buttiglione, *Karol Wojtyla: The Thought of the Man who Became Pope John Paul II* (Grand Rapids, MI: Eerdmans, 1997, p. 198.
29. Aidan Nichols, *Say it is Pentecost* (Edinburgh: T&T Clark, 2001), p. 211. See also James J. Buckley, 'Balthasar's Use of the Theology of Aquinas', *The Thomist* 59 (1995), pp. 517–545.
30. Thomas Dalzell, The Dramatic Encounter of Divine and Human Freedom in the Theology of Hans Urs von Balthasar (New York: Peter Lang, 2000).
31. Russell Hittinger, 'Making Sense of the Civilization of Love: John Paul II's Contribution to Catholic Social Thought', in Geoffrey Gneuhs, *The Legacy of Pope John Paul II: His Contribution to Catholic Thought* (New York, Crossroad, 2000), pp. 71–93.
32. Hans Urs von Balthasar, Glory of the Lord: A Theological Aesthetics. Vol. 5: The Realm of Metaphysics in the Modern Age (Edinburgh: T&T Clark, 1991), p. 646.
33. See Gerald A. McCool's essay 'The Theology of John Paul II' and John M. McDermott's response, in John M. McDermott (ed.), *The Thought of Pope John Paul II* (Rome: PUG, 1993), pp. 29–53 and pp. 55–68. See Hans Urs von Balthasar, *Theo-Drama: Theological Dramatis Theory. II: Dramatic Personae: Man in God* (San Francisco, CA: Ignatius, 1990), pp. 189–334.
34. See, for example, Hans Urs von Balthasar, *Glory of the Lord: A Theological Aesthetics. Vol. I: Seeing the Form* (San Francisco, CA: Ignatius, 1982), pp. 74–79.
35. See Terrence Prendergast, 'A Vision of Wholeness': A Reflection on the Use of Scripture in a Cross-Section of Papal Writing", in John M. McDermott, *The Thought of Pope John Paul*, pp. 69–97.
36. Brian McNeil, 'The Exegete as Iconographer: Balthasar and the Gospels', in John Riches, *The Analogy of Beauty* (Edinburgh: T&T Clark, 1986), pp. 134–146.

37. See Thomas Norris, 'The Symphonic Unity of His Theology: An Overview', in Bede McGregor and Thomas Norris (eds.), *The Beauty of Christ: An Introduction to the Theology of Hans Urs von Balthasar* (Edinburgh: T&T Clark, 1994), pp. 213–252. See also Kevin Mongrain, *The Systematic Thought of Hans Urs von Balthasar: An Irenaean Retrieval* (New York: Crossroad, 2002).

38. See Tracey Rowland, 'Reclaiming the Tradition: John Paul II as the Authentic Interpreter of Vatican II', in William Oddie (ed.), *John Paul the Great: Maker of the Post-Conciliar Church* (London: CTS, 2003), pp. 27–48.

39. Pope John Paul II, 'Address to the Roman Curia on Vatican Council II', *L'Osservatore Romano* (23 December 1992), p.6.

40. *Fides et ratio*, n.72.

41. Karol Wojtyla, *Sign of Contradiction* (Middlegreen, Slough: St. Paul Publications, 1979).

42. Karol Wojtyla, *The Acting Person* (Boston, MA: Reidel, 1979).

43. Karol Wojtyla, Sources of Renewal (Vatican City: Libreria Editrice Vaticana, 1979).

44. Pope John Paul II, *Love and Responsibility* (London: Collins, 1981).

45. George Hunston Williams, *The Mind of John Paul II: The Origins of his Thought and Action* (New York: Seabury Press, 1981), p. 101.

46. Ibid., p. 243.

47. Among those biographies that do not mention von Balthasar, see Tad Szulc, *John Paul II: The Biography* (New York: Scribner, 1995); Giovanni Reale, *Karol Wojtyla: Un Pellegrino dell'Assoluto* (Milan: RCS, 2005); Peter Simpson, *On Karol Wojtyla* (New York: Wadsowth, 2001).

48. There is no mention of von Balthasar in works that deal with the Pope's thought: Philippe Portier, *La Pensée de Jean-Paul: La Critique du Monde Moderne* (Paris: De l'Atelier/Editions Ouvrières, 2006); Graziano Borgonovo and Arturo Cattaneo, *Giovanni Paolo Teologo: Nel Segno delle Encicliche* (Milan: Mondadori, 2003); Kenneth D. Whitehead (ed.), *John Paul II – Witness to Truth* (South Bend, IN: St. Augustine's Press, 2001); Jaroslaw Kupczak, *Destined for Liberty: The Human Person in the Philosophy of Karol Wojtyla/John Paul II* (Washington: CUA, 2000); Geoffrey Gneus, *The Legacy of Pope John Paul II: His Contribution to Catholic Thought* (New York: Crossroad, 2000); Kenneth L. Schmitz, *At the Centre of the Human Drama: The Philosophical Anthropology of Karol Wojtyla/Pope John Paul II* (Washington: CUA, 1993); Costantino Esposito (ed.), *Karol Wojtyla e il Pensiero Europeo* (Milan: ISTRA, 1984); Paul Johnson, *Pope John Paul II and the Catholic Restoration* (New York: St. Martin's Press, 1981).

49. David Moss and Edward T. Oakes (eds), *Cambridge Companion to von Balthasar* (Cambridge University Press, 2004), 64, fn. 4.

50. See John Coulson, 'The Pope's Mentors', *The Tablet* (May, 1982) pp. 506–08, In his excellent work, *Twentieth-Century Catholic Theologians* (Oxford: Blackwell, 2007), Fergus Kerr makes no mention of any influence of von Balthasar on Pope John Paul II.

51. See Henri de Lubac, *At the Service of the Church* (San Francisco, CA: Ignatius, 1993). See also Hans Urs von Balthasar, *The Theology of Henri de Lubac* (San Francisco, CA: Ignatius, 1991).

52. André Frossard, *'N'Ayez Pas Peur!': Dialogue avec Jean-Paul II* (Paris: Laffont, 1982), p. 48.

53. Message for the Centenary of the birth of Hans Urs von Balthasar, 6 October 2005. See http://www.vatican.va/holy_father/benedict_xvi/messages/pont-messages/2005/documents/hf_ben-xvi_mes_20051006_von-balthasar_en.html (accessed on 28 January 2008)

54. Dulles, *The Splendor of Faith*, p. 184.

55. Hans Urs von Balthasar, *Der antirömische Affekt* (Freiburg im Breisgau: Herder, 1974); *The Office of Peter and the Structure of the Church*, trans. Andrée Emery(San Francisco, 1986).

56. See Rino Fisichella, *L'impronta trinitaria delle encicliche di Giovanni Paolo II*, in Graziano Borgonovo and Arturo Cattaneo (eds), *Giovanni Paolo Teologo: Nel Segno delle Encicliche* (Milan: Mondadori, 2003), pp. 34–43, at, p. 35.

57. Hans Urs von Balthasar, *Neue Klarstellungen* (New Elucidations) (San Francisco, CA: Ignatius, 1986). It is possible that the Pope read other articles from this volume.

58. Edward O'Connor, 'The Roots of John Paul II's Devotion to Mary', *Marian Studies'*(1988) pp. 16–39, pp. 78–114, at p. 112. See Cardinal Wojtyla, in *Sources of Renewal* 'Mary in the Mystery of Christ and the Church' (pp. 100–113) and 'The Meaning of Holiness. Mary as a Figure of the Church' pp. 189–200. See also Frederick Millner, 'The Marian Orientation of Spirituality in the Thought of Pope John Paul II', *Heythrop Journal* 17 (1990), pp. 566–579.

59. Dulles, *Splendour of Faith*, p. 43.

60. Dulles, *Splendour of Faith*, p. 115.

61. Aurelio Fusi, Richiami Mariani nel Pensiero Ecclesiologico di Giovanni Paolo II (Rome: PUG, 1997).

62. See Elisabeth Gössmann, *Il Tempo della Donna* (Brescia: Queriniana, 1990), p. 15.

63. Address to the Cardinal and Prelates of the Roman Curia (22 December, 1987); *L'Osservatore Romano* (23 December 1987).

64. Apostolic Letter of the Supreme Pontiff John Paul II on the Dignity and Vocation of Women on the Occasion of the Marian Year, *Mulieris*

dignitatem (15 August, 1988), no. 27, fn. 55 [AAS 80 (1988) II, 1653–1729 at 1718].

65. General Audience Catechesis (25 November 1998).

66. See an article I wrote on this topic, 'Totus Tuus: The Mariology of John Paul II', in William Oddie (ed.), *John Paul the Great: Maker of the Post-Conciliar Church* (London: CTS, 2003), pp. 69–93. See also in the same volume, Ian Ker, 'The Radicalism of the Papacy: John Paul II and the New Ecclesial Movements' pp. 49–68 and Léonie Caldecott, 'Sincere Gift: The New Feminism of John Paul II' (pp. 109–129).

67. See Franca Zambonini, *Chiara Lubich: A Life for Unity* (New City: London, 1992), pp. 142–145 and Jim Gallagher, *A Woman's Work* (London: Harper Collins, 1997), pp. 202–211. See John Saward, 'Mary and Peter in the Christological Constellation: Balthasar's Ecclesiology', in John Riches (ed.), *The Analogy of Beauty*, pp. 105–133.

68. For development of this theme see the articles by David Schindler, 'Institution and Charism' (pp. 53–76) and Piero Coda, 'The Ecclesial Movements, Gift of the Spirit: A Theological Reflection' (pp. 77–105), in Pontifical Council for the Laity, *Movements in the Church* (Vatican City: Libreria Editrice Vaticana, 1999).

69. See his 'Letter to Women', in *Origins* 25 (1995), pp. 139–142.

70. Pope John Paul II, *Crossing the Threshold of Hope*, pp. 178–187, at p. 185.

71. Pope John Paul II, 'The Glory of God is Man alive', in *Sign of Contradiction*, pp. 173–183.

72. See Hans Urs von Balthasar, *Dare We Hope 'That all Men be Saved' with a Short Discourse on Hell* (San Francisco, CA: Ignatius, 1988). See a critique of von Balthasar's thought in Alyssa Lyra Pitstick *Light in Darkness: Hans Urs von Balthasar and the Catholic Doctrine of Christ's Descent into Hell* (Grand Rapids, MI: Eerdmans, 2007).

73. Pope John Paul II, *Crossing the Threshold of Hope*, p. 186.

74. See Pope John Paul II, *Sign of Contradiction*, pp. 163–171.

75. Encyclical letter on the Holy Spirit in the Life of the Church and the World, *Dominum et vivificantem* (18 May 1986).

76. See his commentary, in Giovanni Paolo II, *Lasciatevi Muovere dallo Spirito* (Brescia: Queriniana, 1986), pp. 101–127.

77. On this theme see Gerard O'Hanlon, *The Immutability of God in the Theology of Hans Urs von Balthasar* (Cambridge: Cambridge University Press, 1990).

Chapter 4

John Paul II and His Ecclesiology

John McDade S.J.

I

Hans Urs von Balthasar is widely regarded as the most influential Catholic theologian of the post-Conciliar period. In the early 1970s, Balthasar, Henri de Lubac, Joseph Ratzinger, Louis Bouyer and others founded the international theological revue *Communio*, in order to promote a more balanced, centrist and 'authentically Catholic' reception of the Council than was taking place through *Concilium* which they judged to be infected with ideological and secular agendas out of keeping with the genuine Catholic tradition. The influence of this *Communio* movement has been considerable, with Cardinal Ratzinger's subsequent position as head of the Congregation for the Doctrine of the Faith and the influence Balthasar's writings have exercised on papal teaching: the Vatican rejection of the ordination of women, for example, derives in part from a Balthasarian account of gender-symbolism, and his influence can be easily seen in sections of the *Catechism of the Catholic Church*. (He is said to be Pope John Paul II's favourite theologian.[1]) *Communio* theology is now the form in which current Catholic orthodoxy is being expressed: hence the relevance of this paper on Balthasar's account of the office of Peter and its exercise of authority.

II

'The Pope is head. Who else is known by all? Who else is recognized by all, with the power to infiltrate the whole body because he holds the main branch which infiltrates everywhere? How easy it would have been for this to degenerate into tyranny! That is why Christ gave them this commandment: "But it shall not be so with you" (Lk. 22.26). (Blaise Pascal, Pensées, L569)'

The English title of Balthasar's work, *The Office of Peter and the Structure of the Church*, ignores the point of the original German title: *Der antirömische Affekt* (The Anti-Roman Attitude).[2] The work was originally published in 1974 (in the pontificate of Paul VI) to offer a theological reflection on the 'deep-seated anti-Roman attitude within the Catholic Church', 'the strangely irrational phenomenon of the anti-Roman attitude among Catholics' (p. 16), an attitude that has 'not only sociological and historical grounds but also a *theological* basis' and that 'has to be overcome again and again by the community of the Church' (p. 9). 'Throughout Church history, and today more explicitly than ever, there has been an evident *contest* within the Church herself, mostly against the Petrine principle.' (p. 314). Balthasar presses the Church to examine the bias in its nature against its central focus of authority.

In Balthasar's view, the papacy is misrepresented if it is pictured at the top of an ecclesial pyramid: he regards this as a legacy of Imperial Rome and a reaction to the encroachments of medieval emperors. Such an image distorts the relation of the papacy to the rest of the Church, because the Pope is not 'above' the Church in any serious sense, nor is the Church 'under' him ('but it shall not be so with you.' (Lk. 22.26). Only Jesus stands above the Church as its Lord (p. 308). Equally, Balthasar has little time for attempts to remove the *scandalon* of the Petrine Office by softening it into an Orthodox 'honorary primacy' based upon the autonomy of particular churches (77). Instead, the papacy is one of the elements within the complex identity of the Church: it is both a *primary* feature of the Church as 'the guarantor of concrete unity in the concrete centre of the Church' (p. 127), and *relative*, 'one of several indispensable elements in the ecclesiastical structure' which, by their very relationship to one another constitute the Church's identity (p. 21). Hence both Protestantism and Papolatry are unacceptable, because they dissolve the differentiated character of the Church, one by excising episcopal and papal authority from the structure, the other by exalting the Pope above everything else. Balthasar quotes the sharp comment of Johann Adam Möhler (1896–1938) on their common source in an exaggerated egoism:

Protestantism is papism carried to the extreme, that is, complete egoism *in principle*. In papism each gives himself unconditionally to *one* person: in Protestantism, each *one* is in a position to oppose all others (insofar as he makes of himself the principle of interpretation of revelation) (p. 172).

Balthasar prefers to speak of the 'multi-dimensional reality of the Church' (p. 26) the 'force-fields that bear upon the church' (p. 22), the 'network of tensions in the Church' (p. 24). In the Church, there are 'more fundamental tensions' than that between primacy and collegiality, or 'monarchy' and 'democracy' (sociological parallels from secular society that are dismissed by him as inadequate to the *mysterium*). In his view, the *necessary* tensions in the Church are neither the symptoms of spiritual shortcomings nor flaws which can be remedied by structural change: they are constitutive of the Church because the Church is inherently *a complex, multi-dimensional network of principles* which, in their interaction, constitute the reality of the Church founded by Christ. (Balthasar rejects the idea that the original form of the Church was a charismatic community of equality, only later corrupted by patriarchal patterns of government. Instead, the Church, as shaped by Christ in its period of origins, is differentiated and invested with centres of authority, adjudication and service.)

Balthasar presents an account of the Church in which Mary, Peter and the other figures around Jesus form a network of principles which, in their mutuality, interaction and tension, form the Church which relates to its Lord. Balthasar approves of Congar's definition of Catholicity as 'the dynamic universality of the principles which yield her unity' (p. 323), and proposes an ecclesiology of symbolic archetypes as a way of identifying these constitutive principles and missions which form the *Catholica*.

III

Balthasar's approach is simple: the 'larger unity' of the Church corresponds to the 'constellation' of persons around Jesus in the New Testament, a constellation of 'real symbols' which designate particular missions within the Church, forming the dimensions of *the Catholica* (p. 309). The historical Jesus stands within a 'constitutive human group';

withdrawing him from this differentiated network makes him (and Christology) 'hopelessly abstract' (p. 136). The Church is born in the relationships Christ establishes in 'the period of origins' (p. 158), and their symbolic pattern forms the subsequent pattern of the Church in which the Risen Jesus continues to give missions: it is this subsistent pattern of continuity between 'then' and 'now' which makes them constitutive *principles* of the Church in every age.

An analogy can be drawn between Balthasar's ecclesiological approach and that adopted by Carl Jung in his account of the process of individuation. For Jung, all the elements which surface in a dream are aspects of the self which press for attention: becoming 'individuated' as a person means coming to acknowledge the self in all the aspects of its fullness. Just as the self is complex, composed of different dynamic aspects, all of which emerge from and contribute to a process of integrated personality, so the Church has internal dimensions, all of which belong together in a dynamic interchange and tension. These dimensions come to light in the figures who are archetypal dimensions in the 'individuation' of the Church. (Significantly, one of Balthasar's essays is entitled 'Who is the Church?' rather than 'What is the Church?', because he favours imagery of the Church as Virgin/Spouse/Mother – a 'person' rather than an 'assembly' – in relation to God.)

Balthasar identifies a number of individuals in the New Testament and amplifies their symbolic significance as foundational archetypes within the Church: Mary, Joseph, Mary Magdalene, Martha and Mary, the Jews who were sympathetic to him (Nicodemus, Joseph of Arimathea, Simon of Cyrene), Judas Iscariot, John the Baptist, Peter, the Twelve, Paul, the Beloved Disciple, James. The diagram on page 55 gives an idea of the resulting picture of the *Catholica*.

Mary is at the centre of the Church because her faith represents 'the all-inclusive, protective and directive form of all ecclesial life' (208), 'the model of all being and acting' in the Church (p. 206). Think of the form of her faith radiating through the other dimensions which do not have the paradigmatic quality of Marian holiness. The Church, after all, begins in the chamber at Nazareth in the faith of the Virgin, 'through which the Son of God becomes man' and by which 'he also forms the truly universal Church' (p. 207). The first of the redeemed, she is the 'archetype of the Church', the body image of the Church's holiness, realized in advance through her conception without sin and fulfilled in her assumption into resurrection life. In her is seen 'the nuptial encounter between God and the creature'. 'The entire Church is Marian', Balthasar says, quoting Charles Journet (p. 205), because 'Mary disappears into the heart of the Church to remain there as a real presence which, however, always gives place to her Son' (pp. 158–59). For von Balthasar, the radiant heart of the Church is *lay, faithful and holy*, characterized by contemplative receptivity in relation to God, and symbolized by the femininity and virginal maternity of Mary: as she is, so is the Church.

ARCHETYPES WITHIN THE IDENTITY OF THE CHURCH

PETER
(*Pastoral Office*)

THE TWELVE (*Collegiality*)	**PAUL** (*Adaptation to Cultures/Mission*)
THE BAPTIST (*OT Witness; Prophetic Martyrdom*)	**JUDAS** (*Betrayal*)
OUTSIDERS (*Sinners & Weak*)	**CHILDREN** (*Unlettered*)

MARY
(*Lay holiness*)

NICODEMUS (*Searchers*)	**WOMEN AT TOMB** (*Generating Resurrection Faith*)
JOSEPH (*Fatherhood/Work*)	**MARTHA & MARY** (*Domestic Church/Hospitality*)
BELOVED DISCIPLE (*Love/Contemplation*)	**JAMES** (*Tradition & Law*)

A brief comment on Balthasar's use of male–female symbolism: this can pose problems in a society uncertain about these terms in its own cultural life, but his fundamental distinction is between 'a feminine element . . . [which] makes a person *secure* in nature and in being,' and a masculine element by which a person 'pushes forward into things in order to change them by implanting and imposing something of its own'.[3] At the level of individual identity, then, it corresponds to *who you are and what you do*. Mary symbolizes the Church in its core identity: simply by being herself in perfect union with God's self-gift in Christ, she expresses the identity of the Church. Within this over-arching Marian pattern, the other dimensions arise as active expressions of its selfhood, just as personal identity flows into action. Hence, for example, Balthasar can think of Papal infallibility as arising within the trustworthiness of what is known in the Marian Church: 'What Peter will receive as "infallibility" for his office of governing will be a partial share in the total flawlessness of the feminine, Marian church'.[4] In the same spirit, one might say that the women at the tomb on Easter morning who generate the Church's faith in the Resurrection speak of what Mary already knows of God's power and love. Similarly, John's contemplative discipleship, James' sense that Christ is the fulfilment of Jewish observance and Paul's preaching of the universal efficacy of faith in Christ are particular expressions of what is comprehended in Mary's faith.[5]

Peter has a distinctive role, set within the network of missions in the Church:

As shepherd who has to pasture the *whole* flock, he has a right to claim authority (in doctrine and leadership) and to demand unity. This prerogative is his alone. But it does not isolate him from the others who have founding missions and who, in their own way, have no less a continuing life and representation in the church (p. 158).

In his office Peter, Balthasar argues, 'must take his bearings by the all-encompassing totality of the Church, which expresses itself concretely in the dynamic interplay of her major missions and in the laws inherent in her structure' (pp. 314–15). While Balthasar develops this, several alternative configurations are excluded as inadequate: he rejects a neo-scholastic division of the Church into a 'teaching' (*ecclesia discens*) and a 'listening' part (*ecclesia docens*), preferring a 'much more nuanced scale of ministries in the Church' (p. 236). Yet even the New Testament triads of 'apostles, prophets, teachers' (1 Cor. 12.28) and 'evangelists, pastors, teachers' (Eph. 4.11) are insufficient in Balthasar's view to account for the scale of differentiation within the *Catholica*. Nor does he accept the typological division of the universal Church into 'Petrine' (Catholic), 'Pauline' (Protestant) and 'Johannine' (Orthodox) Churches (p. 146). Paul and John are not to be thought of as principles 'tending in opposite directions' from Peter: *communio* is not incompatible with collegiality and primacy. But the office of Peter is not the defining feature of the Catholic Church, as though a Pauline stamp were

characteristic of Protestantism and Johannine contemplation the feature of Orthodoxy:

> ['T']he communion of the *Catholica* cannot be characterized exclu-
> sively by the Petrine principle and thereby placed in opposition to
> other Christian communions and communities. (pp. 145–46)

It is precisely the task of the Church to realize its Catholicity in ways
which bring together the Petrine, Pauline, Johannine and other dimensions within a concrete unity. Petrine authority is at the service of
the other dimensions of the Church, and it flourishes when it promotes
the functioning of the other missions and dimensions within the
Church. When it marginalizes itself from them – for example, by acting
as though they had no proper status within the life of the Church – or
when it is marginalized by them (a not uncommon attitude in some
parts of the Western Church) – the *Catholica* becomes as dysfunctional
as a family in which the father has no role.

The authority linked with the Petrine office is *one* of those principles,
but it is not the centre of the Church's identity: faithful union with
Christ, embodied in Mary, not Peter, is the archetypal centre of the
Church. Balthasar recognizes that it is 'difficult to keep the office of
Peter in balance within the integral unity of the Church', because the
Petrine office has frequently drawn energy to itself at the expense of
other principles. He aims to restore a better balance to the Church's
image of itself and speaks of the particularly Catholic concern of
'balancing *Petrus with Maria-ecclesia*', thereby enabling the Roman
aspect to stand in a right relationship to the more fundamental Marian
dimension and to the other principles in the Church. The more the
Petrine office asserted itself, from Gregory VII onward, he says, the
more difficult it has been to keep sight of the Marian, and the other,
equally valid, dimensions and missions in the Church which counter-
balance juridical authority within the *mysterium* (p. 184). He is aware
of the difficulty of the task:

> [H]ow can the office of Peter, without negating itself [i.e., without
> abandoning the trajectory of Papal authority expressed in Vatican
> I and Vatican II], come down from the top of the pyramid where it
> is usually pictured, and where, for so long, it has seen itself? (p. 127)

By displacing the Petrine office from the 'centre' or 'top' of the Church, Balthasar aims to restore a balance to ecclesiology which an over-juridical, Ultramontane approach to papal authority has inhibited. By placing the papacy within the 'larger unity' of the Church – 'relativising' it, as he puts it, without marginalizing it – he thereby restores to the heart of the Church the dimension of lay holiness and faith embodied in Mary and sets the papacy within a network of other, equally valid principles and missions. Participation in the 'all-embracing form' of Mary's faith, not the act of obedient acceptance of Peter's authority, is found the deepest dimension of the Church's identity. Balthasar argues that one nourishes the other – the Church is both Marian and Petrine – and that they are not to be opposed. But one must clarify which is *central*, in order to avoid an exaggerated estimate of papal authority:

> While this office [of Peter] is definitely not the centre, it must be rooted and maintained *in* the centre to become the criterion, the concrete point of reference for unity (and without it unity would fall apart), thus leading beyond itself to *the* centre, Christ, and liberating people for Christian freedom. (p. 287)

IV

> If the Church is regarded as one, then the Pope, as its head, repre-sents the whole; if it is regarded as multiple, then the Pope is only a part. The Fathers sometimes looked at it in one way and sometimes another, and thus spoke in different ways about the Pope.
>
> But in the laying down one of these two truths, they did not exclude the other.
>
> Multiplicity which is not reduced to unity is confusion. Unity which does not depend on multiplicity is tyranny.' (Blaise Pascal, *Pensées*, L604, P204)

The structuring of the Marian Church emerges later, during Jesus' ministry when he appoints Peter and the Twelve to apostolic authority in his name, and is completed when the Risen Christ calls Paul to apostolic service. Within the complex, multi-dimensional network of principles in the Church, Balthasar identifies a smaller network which bears upon the exercise of authority - what he calls 'the Apostolic Foursome' represented by Peter John, James and Paul the 'four who dominate the field of force of the developing Church' (p. 309). Each principle in the Foursome represents a clearly defined mission within the Church, necessarily involved with each other. Here there is a particular interaction among the principles which determines how the Petrine/collegial mission is to be conducted. Petrine authority, of course, is to be exercised in the collegial authority invested in the Twelve ('a symbolic, solemn founding of the New Israel' (p. 139)): there has to be a 'breathing together' (*conspiratio*), if Petrine authority is to function with a respect for collegiality and if collegial authority is to have a concrete centre of unity.

THE FOURFOLD OFFICE

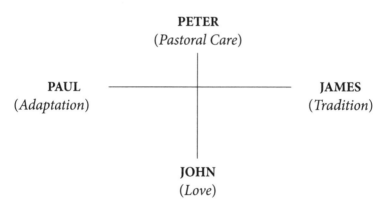

PETER
(*Pastoral Care*)

PAUL
(*Adaptation*)

JAMES
(*Tradition*)

JOHN
(*Love*)

Petrine authority is called upon to respect the demands of other principles: these may be thought of as 'checks' on unrestrained Petrine power. But the Petrine ministry sets a framework within which each principle can function most effectively. Each principle, like each human being, has its own particular way of going wrong: the Johannine, Jamesian and Pauline, no less than the Petrine. (Only the Marian gets it right.) Separated from the others, each principle in the Fourfold Office can become distorted: Johannine love can weaken to a 'universal humanitarian benevolence'; Pauline flexibility can become a fashionable assimilation to cultural mores; the tradition of James can give rise to an 'anxiously integralist, reactionary clinging to obsolete forms'; and the distortions to which the Petrine ministry is subject need 'no further mention here' (pp. 328–329). The whole point of Balthasar's account is that these *equal but differentiated* foundational principles must affect one another if there is to be genuine Catholicity. (Remember Congar's definition of Catholicity as 'the dynamic universality of the principles which yield her unity'.)

A Brief Outline of the Features of Each Principle:

- Peter exercises the *pastoral office*. The scandal of Peter is that he is given 'singular participation in Jesus' authority', which obliges him to 'participate especially in Jesus' spirit of service and his readiness to suffer' (p. 142). A sinful man, he is to hold the keys of the kingdom and feed the sheep and lambs of Jesus the Good Shepherd. In his weakness he is appointed as the Rock/Shepherd, who is to exemplify Christ's own position as the cornerstone (Eph. 2.20) and the true shepherd (Jn 10.11). His denial of Christ places him closest to Judas in his betrayal, yet he is called to strengthen the faith of his brethren and be the unifying principle within the Church. The authority given to Peter is 'social and universal, affecting the entire flock' (p. 62).
- John, the Beloved Disciple, exercises the *office of love*, the dimension of reciprocal love between Christ and his Church, an office exercised by the saints of the Church who always 'represent the link between the Marian and the Petrine Church' (p. 225). Balthasar sees Johannine love as fulfilling a mediating role, first of all, between Christ and Peter's pastoral office. When Peter is asked by Christ, 'Do you love me?', he is asked to share in Johannine love as a condition of his exercising the pastoral ministry ('Feed my sheep'). Peter is reminded by Christ that Johannine love will remain (in the Church) until Christ returns in glory: 'In the unfathomable mystery of Jesus' good pleasure, John retains his own mission, distinct from that of Peter.' John 21 contains 'a subtly composed symbolic doctrine of the Church in which the task of 'office' (Peter) and the task of 'love' (John) become . . . intertwined' (p. 142). John's second mediating role, between the (lay) Marian and the (institutional) Petrine Church, is signalled by his faithful discipleship at the foot of the Cross when, Peter having denied Christ, John becomes the son and

guardian of *Maria-Ecclesia*. 'The truly Johannine Church is . . . the one that stands under the Cross in place of Peter and on his behalf receives the Marian Church' (p. 225).

- James, the brother of the Lord, represents the dimension of *tradition and law* (Torah). The leader of the Jewish–Christian, Jerusalem community (the *ecclesia ex circumcisione*) – takes Peter's place after he leaves Jerusalem (Acts 12.17), representing continuity between the Old and New Covenants and the dimension of Torah-observance that Jesus came to perfect. James mediates between Jews and Gentiles at the first Council of Jerusalem, reconciling conservative Jewish Christians to the presence in the Church of 'those not under the law' (1 Cor. 2.20–1). He puts forward nothing less than 'the perfect law of liberty' (Jas 1.25). The Jewish writer Franz Rosenzweig in the early part of the twentieth century suggested that God's 'Star of Redemption' had Judaism at its core from which the rays of Christianity spread to the Gentile world. Rosenzweig argued that Christianity had to stay close to Jewish faith and observance or it would get lost in the gnosticisms of the pagan world. By making the principle of tradition and law constitutive of the Church, Balthasar echoes Rosenzweig in making the tie to Jewish tradition a bulwark against cultural assimilation and compromise.
- Paul represents the dimension of *universalism and inculturation*. The apostle of the *ecclesia ex gentibus*, he represents the Church's engagement with the cultures of the world, in which it is to find a home, becoming 'all things to all people . . . for the sake of the Gospel' (1 Cor. 9.22–23). He also represents charismatic vocation. He is outside the structure of the Twelve, yet is given a vocation which the hierarchical Church must acknowledge as willed by Christ, and a dynamic mission modelled on the 'type' of Christ (p. 144). He also represents the dimension of the creation and development of local churches—his 'anxiety for all the churches' (2 Cor. 11.28) and his 'travail till Christ be formed' in them (Gal. 4.19) – which are to find their place within the *Catholica*. He also symbolizes the dimension of freedom in the Spirit: the dialectic between James and Paul (Rom. 4.2–3 versus James 2.20–23) mirrors the dialectic in the Church between freedom from the Law and obedience to the Law until the return of Christ. Paul is, in short, the dimension of *apostolic energy* in the Church.

V

Pope. God does not perform miracles in the ordinary conduct of his Church. It would be a strange miracle if infallibility resided in one man, but that it should be in the many seems so natural that God's work is hidden beneath nature, as in all his other works. (Blaise Pascal, *Pensées*, L726).

The Petrine office is thus set in an indispensable relation to these other principles: the concrete centre of unity in the *Catholica* requires a living relationship with the principles of love/holiness, tradition and adaptation. It is important that the Petrine dimension, located in the *collegium* of the Twelve, is the only one to find visible, institutional expression (the papacy): there is no stable focus of holiness (how could there be?) and the principles of Jamesian tradition and Pauline adaptation have been in tension since the admission of Gentiles at Antioch, and continue to be so today.

The development of Liberation Theology in the 1970s and 1980s – best viewed, in my opinion, as a *prophetic spirituality* rather than as a 'theology' – is the most dramatic instance in recent years of the Pauline adaptation of Gospel principles to the demands of a particular situation, that of Third World poverty and injustice. There has been a traditionalist resistance to this development, but the role of Rome in handling the matter – issuing two documents from the Congregation for the Faith, one deliberately critical (1984) and the other deliberately appreciative (1980) – tends towards neither integralist condemnation nor naive approval. This Pauline development is filtering through all levels of the Church's life, including the social teaching of Pope John Paul II whose theological vocabulary shows that he has learned from the Liberationists.

Authority has a natural bias towards tradition and will always be cautious about the rate of change appropriate to a Church whose life is transcultural. The public perception is that the papacy of John Paul II is characterized by a stronger bond between Peter and James (tradition) than between Peter and Paul (adaptation), largely because 'adaptation' is often interpreted as accommodation to the culture of the secularized West, and moral teaching hits the headlines more than theological teaching. There is truth in this perception, but it is not the whole story.

It is clear that Pope John Paul II wanted to shape a Church which is strong at its centre (strong in identity, core beliefs, boundary markers, faith-experience and practice), because only then can the Church have the inner strength to promote values on which the good of all depends. Authority *ad intra* in his papacy was directed towards re-centring the Church in the post-Conciliar period and ensuring that potentially fissiparous cracks are repaired. *Ad extra*, in his relations with the non-Christian religions, the moral authority of the papacy was characterized by openness and a more imaginative theological vision than has been generally acknowledged: his encyclical *Redemptoris Missio* (1990), the remarkable *Dialogue and Proclamation* published by the Pontifical Council for Interreligious Dialogue (1991) and his speeches on Jewish–Christian relations were in advance of most of the rest of the Church. In these areas, he exemplified a creative engagement – genuinely Pauline, I think – with the spectrum to be found in the contemporary religious Areopagus.

The principles in the Fourfold Office should be directed, Balthasar judges, towards what he calls 'the *eschatological centre of gravity* of the Gospel of Christ', a dense phrase whose meaning is difficult to discern. (p. 329). I take it to mean that the Fourfold Office must aim at giving the most complete form of witness to God's unsurpassable self-gift in Christ, and must settle for nothing less than this. In which case, it is the Johannine principle, the ideal of holiness and unitive love for Christ, towards which the interaction of the other three principles must be directed. (John, after all, is the point of contact between Marian holiness and Petrine authority.) The goal of the Fourfold Office is the holiness of the Church. Consequently, *the Petrine office is to be directed towards enabling the Church to embody Johannine love and holiness, and it must do this with an eye on what comes both from the Jamesian principle of tradition and from the Pauline principle of adaptation.* Sometimes the Fourfold Office discerns easily what teaching to give in order to foster love and holiness, but not always:

[T]here are cases where it is extremely difficult to weigh the reasons for and against, particularly when one tries to keep in mind the 'eschatological centre of gravity', not only because some current situation did not exist in the period of biblical revelation, which means that conclusions have to be drawn from the spirit of a unique historical past and applied to a very different present, but also because Christ's Church contains a wide spectrum of human possibilities or obstructions, at the same time contributing to and detracting from a perfect human response to the perfect grace of God in Christ . . . A decision that is justifiable for those whose love is alive might be impractical for the lukewarm . . . on the other hand, a decision made to suit these latter could seriously endanger the balance of the Church's eschatological response, the ideal of those who love. (p. 329)

This was precisely the situation of *Humanae vitae*, he says, the most controversial instance of recent papal teaching, in which Paul VI opted to point the Church's teaching towards the latter (Johannine) ideal and, consequently, to offer the more difficult teaching on marital sexuality. Balthasar presents the case of *Humanae vitae* (1968) as a contemporary paradigm of the functioning of the Fourfold Office: 'though empowered and obliged to take the final, personal responsibility alone, the pope is directed to share in a dialogue with the other three partners of the "foursome"' (pp. 330–331). The problem, Balthasar says, has to do with the *form* of the teaching (an encyclical which bound the consciences of married Catholics) rather than its *content*: 'this resulted in a crisis for the more recent trend which had endeavoured to mask the exercise of authority' (p. 330). Balthasar challenges neither the decision made by Pope Paul VI to issue the encyclical nor its (non-infallible) content, but he wonders whether another, less decisive response might not have been as effective:

It might have been sufficient to point to the ideal as a 'normative goal' to satisfy the objective, eschatological idea of the Christian concept of selfless and self-renouncing love, the personal ideal of the committed, while at the same time both stimulating and reassuring those who were either too unable or too perplexed to follow this course. For who does not see the devastation created in the sexual area by the separation of pleasure from the risk of self-giving, as well as the tremendous weight of sociological arguments on the other side? (p. 330)

Yet what Balthasar outlines here as an alternative is what the encyclical set out to achieve. Using his own terms, one can say that while the papal teaching points the Church towards the Johannine ideal and affirms the Church's tradition on contraception, it is no less coloured by a nuanced Pauline response to the presence of both 'strong' and 'weak' members of the community and a pastoral strategy for directing them toward unity (Rom. 14; 1 Cor. 8.4–9.14). Although public comment on the encyclical often ignores this aspect, both in the encyclical and in the subsequent statements of Episcopal Conferences, this Pauline principle of acknowledging different capacities and insights within the Church was a central part of the Petrine and episcopal presentation of the teaching. A long quotation from Balthasar is apposite here:

> Peter too must be continually learning: he must not think that he can carry out his office in isolation (which could easily tempt him to overvalue it). He too must take his bearings by the all-encompassing totality of the Church, which expresses itself concretely in the dynamic interplay of her major missions and in the laws inherent in her structure . . . Revelation is entrusted to the whole Church, and all, under the leadership of Peter, are to preserve it, interpret it and produce a living exposition of it. And since the office of Peter is borne by fallible human beings, it needs everyone's watchful but loving cooperation so that the exercise of this office may be characterized by the degree of 'in-fallibility' that belongs to it. More precisely, this means that a pope can exercise his office fruitfully for all only if he is *recognized and loved in a truly ecclesial way, even in the midst of paraklesis or dispute.* (p. 315)

This quotation which bears meditation, not simply for what it says about how the papacy should behave, but also because it directs attention to the question of the appropriate response to Petrine authority. Like a tango, it takes more than one for authority to work well, but it only takes one to ruin it: either the one in authority or the one under authority.

VI

I will end with some comments on Abbé Laberthonnière who, according to Balthasar, 'in his meditations on the form of ecclesial authority . . . came up with the most profound and prophetic insights' on the exercise of authority and the response to authority (p. 262). Laberthonnière

(1860–1932), whose works were put on the Index in the post-Modernist purge, was a sharp-tongued critic of Roman authorities, whom he accused of promoting a 'lord-servant' relationship in the Church incompatible with the Christian concept of a self-giving God:

> You [Romans] always imagine that God created men to rule over them and to assert his rights as sovereign. You see God as a kind of potentate, and then you pass yourselves off as being delegated by him to implement his power and reign. Thus you stand the Gospel on its head. (p. 263)

A strong attack, of course, is in the best tradition of protest against Roman domineering. For Laberthonnière, the Church can be only 'a unity through *communio*' of free persons who, by their freely willed love, are moved to build a unified Church' (p. 262). Christian authority, he says, can never instruct 'from outside', nor can the truth be imposed; nor should the Christian submit himself to be led and instructed purely passively (p. 263). He denounces those in authority who withdraw into 'proud self-sufficiency' and boast that it 'only has to wait for others to come' to them. But then the conduct of authority in the Church splits into, on the one hand, 'authoritarianism and the lust for power', and on the other, into a servility filled with 'ambitious grovelling'.

Laberthonnière, is clear that the solution to the exercise of authority in the Church cannot be one-sided. There is simply no point in constantly demanding that those in authority behave better, if those under authority do not change at the same time: the responsibility for making Church authority authentically Christian is shared by all. Laberthonnière makes two penetrating statements, and then asks two questions as a way of clarifying the point of the second statement:

> In what spirit and in what manner should leadership and instruction be given, to be truly human and Christian? And, in turn, how should a person who is progressing in faith prepare himself to receive guidance and instruction? . . . How should people like us [who have not been given authority] act, so that, spiritually deepened by the acceptance of authority, we can contribute to the spiritual deepening of authority itself?. (p. 262)

I cannot prescribe what the answers to Laberthonnière's questions should be, since they bear upon each Catholic's core of spiritual responsibility. Levinas' aphorism, 'responsibility cannot be preached, only borne.' is exactly right here. But some comments are required: Laberthonnière's questions look for a dimension of spiritual deepening in the *acceptance* of authority which will bring about an analogous deepening in the *exercise* of authority, a relationship of reciprocity and mutuality in which, by my acceptance of authority, the conditions are created for authority in the Church to be exercised in a fruitful way. I have a spiritual responsibility in this regard which comes from my sense that salvation is mediated to me through this *mysterium*, and that in its direction and guidance I encounter a claim on my obedience grounded in Christ's authority and my obedience to him.[6] This aspect is central to how we are to live together, hierarchy and people, with a shared but differentiated responsibility to one another and to Christ. (Möhler's earlier comment on Protestantism and papism sharing a common source in a self-regarding 'egoism' is to the point here.) In the Church, I have obligations to help those in authority to promote the Church's holiness which I must acknowledge if my membership of this body makes any sense and if my identity as a Catholic Christian is to be spiritually and ethically mature.

For Balthasar, Laberthonnière's last questions are 'still with the Church', and it is 'the question of mutuality, of *communio*' (p. 265). This points, he says, towards how we should *help* one another: this simple category needs to come to the fore, if authority is not to be prompted to respond in 'pre-conciliar ways' in the contemporary Church. It points, too, towards the quality of *conversation* fostered in the Church, for which everyone has responsibility. Where there is deafness, people shout. Balthasar's insistence that a pope can exercise his office fruitfully only if he is '*recognized and loved* in a truly ecclesial way, even in the midst of dispute' (p. 315) points to the responsibility of those under authority to make it possible for those in authority to exercise it properly.

In Laberthonnière's opinion, the mutuality which exists among persons in the Church means that

Obeying has the same dignity as commanding; the existence of both is justified only if they lead to free brotherly union of minds and souls in love and truth in the bosom of the heavenly Father (p. 264; emphasis added).

This seems to me exactly right and evangelical in its insight: it is not a question of where 'power' lies in the Church, but of the elimination of the category of power from the attitudes of all in the Church. It will be eliminated by neither abrogating the claims of the Petrine Office, nor by transferring it democratically to synodical assemblies, although such bodies may well have a useful part to play in the governance of the Church. That obedience has the same dignity as commanding is also the single point which disturbs any possible parallel we may want to draw between the Church and secular organizations: there are, after all, no 'greater' persons and 'lesser' persons in the Church since the only dignity which lasts into eternity is holiness.

If obeying is no less than commanding, then the dignity of the Christian who responds maturely to authority is far from servility, but is a responsibility freely undertaken for the good of all, as an expression of devotion to Christ. If commanding is no greater than obeying, it will be humble in its manner. When Laberthonnière speaks of 'a "unity through *communio*" of free persons who, by their freely willed love, are moved to build a unified Church', he is pointing to this spiritual responsibility on the part of all, coming from the core of their faith in Christ. There is, after all, a limit to the extent to which organizational analysis and change can improve the quality of the Church's life: a church of committees pleases only religious journalists.

Although Balthasar would distance himself from the anti-Roman stance adopted by Laberthonnière in his long confrontation with harsh authority, it seems to me he has immense sympathy for the tone of what Laberthonnière is calling for. Laberthonnière's statements about the spiritual maturity which should be sought both by those who exercise authority and those who respond to it are exact and profound: we help one another, not by creating an adolescent 'Church of Siblings' from which authority is banished or marginalized, but by fostering an attentive and humble maturity both in the exercise of authority and in our response to it.

Balthasar's constellation of ecclesial principles and the features of the Fourfold Office describes the Church in a way which enables Laberthonnière's questions to be asked properly and appropriate answers sought. If Balthasar is right that the centre of the Church is not Petrine but Marian, then the obedience of faith flowing from Marian experience flows into a mature spiritual response to the authority of Peter and the *collegium*. A sense that the core of the Church is *lay holiness* which precedes hierarchical structuring corrects to an exaggerated estimate of Papal authority and will condition how the Papacy conducts itself in the Church. If Petrine authority is to avoid destructive patterns of authoritarian isolation, it must acknowledge other, equally valid dimensions of the Church and serve them and listen to them with respect. At the same time, Balthasar's insistence that Petrine authority is an indispensable dimension of the Church, whose role is neither to be dissolved nor its claims softened, firmly sets Papal authority within the essential structure of the Church and requires courteous acknowledgement from the members of the Church. His account of the Fourfold Office is, I think, a helpful configuration of the factors which come into play in the proper exercise of authority in the Church. At the beginning of this chapter, I said that Balthasar 'presses the community of the Church to examine the bias in its nature against its central institutional focus'. He also, I think, provides the Church with an account of its identity within which authority can be properly set, judged, evaluated and valued.

Notes

1. Pope John Paul II takes the unusual step of citing him in his Apostolic Letter *Mulieris dignitatem*, (1998).
2. The references in the text are to Hans Urs von Balthasar, *The Office of Peter and the Structure of the Church* (San Francisco, CA: Ignatius Press, 1986).
3. An extract from Hans Urs von Balthasar, *New Elucidations* reproduced in *Communio*, 22 (1995), p. 165.
4. Ibid., p. 167.
5. I can only touch on the role of those principles which bear upon authority in the Church; but it is important to note the presence of 'sinners' within a communion called to holiness – omit them, and you create the Church of the righteous elect; the presence of Judas requires constant acknowledgement; the women at the tomb responsible for first proclaiming the resurrection to the Church is an important symbol of the role of women in the Church and the Josephite dimension of fatherhood and work has been an equally unexplored aspect of the *Catholica*.

6. Can we ignore the spirituality of obedience developed particularly in the religious orders which speak about an 'obedience of will and intellect' in response to the exercise of authority? The theme is obviously an expression of a particular charism, but it elucidates something fundamental in Christian life: a 'de-centring' of the self in faithful membership of the Body of Christ. How much of the resistance to authority comes from a view of the 'autonomous self', which regards obligations to authority and claims on obedience as intrusive impositions which must be discarded for the self to be free?

Response to Chapters 3 and 4 Brendan Leahy and John McDade S.J.

Peter and Mary: Some Rahnerian Reflections

Philip Endean S.J.

In response to Brendan Leahy's elegant, lucid paper, and to John McDade's exposition of the Balthasarian vision that may well inform John Paul II's understanding of Mary and the Church, it is my task to offer some comments in the light of Rahner's theology.

It is important not to overstate the differences between Rahnerian and Balthasarian theology. Admittedly, whereas John Paul II and von Balthasar clearly admired each other, anecdotes and interviews from the last years of Rahner's life suggest that Rahner distinguished sharply between his obedient respect for John Paul II as Pope and his reservations about some aspects of papal theology and policy.[1] But the similarities between what we might term the *Communio* and *Concilium* approaches to dogmatic theology are far more significant than the differences. Both emerge form a *nouvelle théologie* that came to prominence in Francophone and German-speaking Europe in the years following the Second World War. At Vatican II, the official Church rather abruptly abandoned its reservations about such writing – reservations that had led during the previous decade to morally dubious disciplinary measures against some major figures. Instead it took up some of the movement's central themes: revelation as divine self-communication; the consequent close links between doctrines of revelation and Trinity; the repudiation of what was called extrinsicism; the Church as charismatic as well as institutional; the affirmation that grace might exist beyond the Church's boundaries, and a correlative tendency (never expressed other than tentatively) towards denial that eternal Hell is conceptually possible. There are differences in accent and detail between the major theologians of the conciliar generation, but they converge in their general drift – a drift which, as both Brendan Leahy and Gerald O'Collins show, John Paul II to some extent appropriated. The substantive theological points in both papers could be documented from both Rahnerian and Balthasarian sources.

In passing, however, we might raise questions about how deeply John Paul II, coming as he did from Communist Poland, really sympathized with the *nouvelle théologie* developed in the relative comfort of the free West. Karol Wojtyla's thesis director in Rome was Reginald Garrigou-Lagrange, a stout opponent of the movement. Could it be that John Paul II's reading of Vatican II – however much other authors in this symposium may be right in saying that the experience of the Council influenced him – was always, from the beginning, one that downplayed any sense that it represented momentous theological change? Could it be that John Paul II's charismatic and intuitive gestures in evangelization beyond the Church's confines coexisted with a reflective theology of the Church's internal life untouched by the *renovatio accommodata* conventionally associated with the Council? If so, the very success of his papacy might imply a claim that the 'extrinsicism' of the old manuals is more defensible than mainstream Catholic theologians generally recognize – a claim reflected also in such trends as the current revival of pre-conciliar habits of worship. And the important and significant question about the theological legacy of John Paul II's long pontificate is about how we are to react to such a claim.

Such a question, however, is one that I cannot explore. Instead I propose to pick up von Balthasar's account in *Der antirömische Affekt* of the Petrine ministry within a Church that is fundamentally Marian in character – a point which Brendan Leahy suggests to be the strongest intellectual link between Balthasar and John Paul II, and which John McDade has expounded in a most attractive and stimulating way. Von Balthasar's account of different archetypes of holiness in the Church seems to help us address the agenda raised by Pope John Paul II in nos. 88–96 of *Ut unum sint*: the quest for how the Petrine ministry 'may accomplish a service of love recognized by all concerned', for a vision of primacy 'which, while in no way renouncing what is essential to its mission, is nonetheless open to a new situation'.[2] Now, von Balthasar is by no means the first Catholic thinker to situate the authority of office-holders amid other styles of Christian teaching that are of a different kind: Newman, von Hügel and many of von Balthasar's contemporaries moved in similar directions, even if von Balthasar's identification of the different charisms with major New Testament characters renders his version of such a move particularly vivid and attractive. Nevertheless, I want to argue that Pope John Paul II's aspiration will be satisfied only if we extend von Balthasar's account (or at least the version of it reported by McDade).

At one point in his paper, McDade notes the similarities between von Balthasar's ecclesiology and Jungian type theory. By writing of the Church as 'she', McDade can make a quick transition in his argument from Jungian theories primarily about the mature *individual* to theological claims about the *corporate* life of faith within the Church. In Jungian theory, the mature individual operates by preference out of particular functions and archetypes, but the balanced personality draws on a wider range. Obviously this account of individuation can be transferred fruitfully to organizations, but it remains primarily an account of how the healthy individual functions.

I suggest that we can read von Balthasar's use of archetypes sensibly only if we read it, just as much as Jungian type theory, as firstly an account of individual Christian maturity, and only secondarily as an account of roles in the Church. We need a more complex account of the individual believer than we find implied in (McDade's) von Balthasar. Each Christian may live predominantly as a Peter, a Paul, a Mary or a John, but nevertheless needs to be able to draw on a wider range of archetypes. Von Balthasar's articulation of a sub-Jungian ecclesiology implies a division of labour: Mary represents lay holiness; Peter is responsible for jurisdiction; James embodies tradition; Paul is a figure of adaptation. But such a vision makes sense only if all these figures draw on elements of *each* of these gifts, even if they may draw by preference on *one* of them. Mary can, at one point in the gospel, *enjoin* people, exercise her own authority over others, so that they do what Jesus tells them. Paul does not simply adapt; Paul draws deeply on the Jewish tradition in which he was steeped; James's representation of tradition occurs precisely in the context of his commitment to revolution in that tradition which Jesus had inaugurated; Peter, as *Ut unum sint* implicitly recognizes, must pray in best Marian fashion, opening himself up to the gift of mercy out of which he lives.

It follows, then, that von Balthasar's way of thinking about charisms in the Church can and should be extended. It is not just that Petrine jurisdiction operates amid other values and charisms. It is also the case that these charisms bring with them a genuine, if somehow less central, authority of their own, an authority which Peter, and reflective ecclesiology, must acknowledge. Mary does not merely pray and receive; there is an authority that comes from her prayerful listening that Peter is obliged to recognize. Unless this mutuality of authority is somehow articulated ecclesiologically, the case for a Petrine ministry is always likely to appear unpersuasive to many Christians.

Moreover, ecclesiology needs to deal with the fact that the members of the Church, including its office-holders, are not, by virtue of baptism or ordination, completely immune from sin or error. The promise is merely that the gates of Hell will not prevail against the Church; not that Hell's influence will be absent from it. To the extent that official Church teaching is conditioned by such influence, the fundamental Christian duty is not to obey but rather – with all due charity and prudence – to resist. Particular applications of this principle will always, in the nature of things, be disputed. Whenever authority takes a significant stand it is responding to an existing disagreement, and the authoritative pronouncement is unlikely to remove that disagreement. But the principle itself, that Christians must be the Pope's good servants but God's first, is surely undeniable. If we are to honour it, we need to move beyond conceptualities and psychological habits that leave little or no room for the idea of a sinful exercise of authority – a point which recent discoveries about the institutional denial of clerical sexual abuse surely put beyond dispute.[3]

Each of the archetypes in von Balthasar's interplay can fail: Mary's receptive holiness can become sentimental passivity (the biblical Mary at one point thinks that Jesus is out of his mind); Pauline adaptation, as McDade reminds us, can become lazy accommodation; James's upholding of tradition can become unthinking traditionalism; and Petrine authority can become despotic tyranny. Catholic theology has to find ways of articulating how such failure can never be ultimate.

Von Balthasar's interplay of charismatic forces opens up more persuasive ways of fulfilling this task. The different vocations may supply for each other's shortcomings. When Peter fails, Paul can and should tell him to his face that he is wrong.

Mary too can play her part in such situations. The receptivity of all to the grace of God can generate its own power. When authority is exercised unjustly, Marian holiness refuses to collude, rather as Shakespeare's Cordelia, in the name of love and truth, refuses to go along with manipulative and unjustified demands from her king and father. Rather, again like Cordelia fleeing to France only to return at the head of a reforming army, she might perhaps draw on memory, and on resources located at least temporarily outside the visible Church, in order to preserve and restore the Church's truth and holiness. The reverence and admiration with which Balthasarians speak of Marian holiness can obscure the corrective function it can and should exercise when necessary. Perhaps Peter is preserved from fundamental error, not only by prerogatives intrinsic to his own charism, but also through his dependence on the charisms of others – others who can, in extreme cases, supply for his individual failure. If Roman Catholicism could bring itself to think in such terms, both in its ecclesiology and its canonical procedures, then perhaps the scandal that other Christians take from some recent papal ways of operating might be reduced, and the Petrine office's indispensability appear more self-evident.

Let me finish by quoting two texts. Rahner never replied in public to the later von Balthasar's strictures on his theology. One quotation from a talk given to a private Jesuit meeting in 1973 can, however, be taken as a rejoinder:

> If we were to behave as if our being Christian gave us a 'world-view' in which everything fits together harmonically, we would, in the end, be setting ourselves up to be God. This is because the whole of reality is a symphony only for him. To make pluralism into a symphony – as good old Balthasar does – a symphony which we can hear as such – this is fundamentally impossible.[4]

If we have an expectation that the Church as it is now should always be harmonious, this prevents us from even recognizing the need for growth and conversion, processes that are always conflictual. Within von Balthasar's parallelogram of charismatic forces, Peter's authority remains unchallengeable; lay holiness is praised and encouraged, but it is not allowed any scope to make a real difference. If we accept such an ecclesiology uncritically, and set it alongside the immensely powerful charismatic presence of John Paul II, the result is a legacy in ecclesiology in severe need of rebalancing. Von Balthasar's vision of different charisms in the Church needs to be complemented by, indeed grounded in, a sense of how the integrated individual lives out of all the fundamental functions, even if different people have different habitual preferences. More importantly, the harmoniousness of the picture needs to be understood as expressing an eschatological ideal, emphatically not as a description of how things should be now. Obedience to God's truth comes before obedience to human authority, even religious authority; Jesus' obedience to his Abba was a conflictive business, even within the family of faith.

My other text is from the Jesuit *Constitutions*. At the end of his highly creative work of legislation, Ignatius is recapitulating what will help the whole body of the Society of Jesus grow. It is important, he says, that superiors of parts of the Society have much authority over the subjects, and that the general superior have much authority over the partial superiors. But at the same time, it is very important that the Society have much authority over the general, 'so that all, as regards the good, have full power; and should they act badly, they be completely under control'[5] Power for the good, and effective control over the bad, depend on a rich mutuality, a network of vigorous relationships. Ignatius is by no means the simplistic authoritarian he is often presented as being. But Ignatius goes further, and further than von Balthasar acknowledges. Crucially, the other members of the Society have an *authority* over the office-holder; he is obliged regularly and systematically to listen to them, and detailed provision exists in the *Constitutions* for him to be deposed in case of misconduct.[6] These latter provisions are naively impracticable, especially in modern conditions. But what remains important is the acknowledgement, first, that the head's authority and credibility are enhanced by the obligation laid upon him to listen, and secondly that the body must have some protection – though Ignatius adds 'may God never permit this' – against the danger that its head might behave abusively. The fact that there are obvious differences between the offices of Jesuit superior general and pope does not imply any dogmatic reason why authentic papal authority could not be strengthened and protected by analogous stipulations and safeguards.

The visionary agenda named by Pope John Paul II in *Ut unum sint* must, as the Pope himself says, be addressed by all Christians together. But von Balthasar's ecclesiology, whether or not extended along the lines I have been suggesting, might help us Roman Catholics make the contribution to that process which is primarily ours.

Notes

1. One example from a 1982 interview: 'I believe that the Pope's trips are not what the Church today really needs. It would be better if the Holy Father remained in Rome and exercised his leadership from there.' (*Faith in a Wintry Season: Conversations and Interviews with Karl Rahner in the Last Years of his Life,* edited by. Paul Imhof and Hubert Biallowons, translation edited Harvey D. Egan (New York: Crossroad, 1990). The version that was published in Italian is sharper:

   > I think it is one thing to obey, and another thing to applaud. A Christian's obedience should not be confused with conformism, as though they could not freely express their opinion (no doubt subject to correction), that the Pope's journeys are not what is wanted for the Church today, and that he would do better to stay in Rome and govern the Church without leaving command in the hands of the Polish troops that surround him. (*Karl Rahner Sämtliche Werke,* vol 31. *Im Gespräch über Kirche und Gesellschaft: Interviews und Stellungnahmen,* edited by Albert Raffelt, 406 (Freiburg: Herder, 2007)).

   Rahner goes on to say that he can only object when the CDF proclaims that the ordination of women is not possible, and say that dogmatically it is not impossible.

2. *Ut unum sint,* 95, quoting a 1987 homily.

3. It has been claimed that Rahner's 1947 essay, 'The Church of Sinners' (*Theological Investigations* 6, pp. 253–269) – a very tame piece of writing – is the first treatment of the topic. If that is true, it points to a serious intellectual lack.

4. Publication of this text is announced for volume 25 of Rahner's *Sämtliche Werke,* edited by Andreas R. Batlogg (Freiburg: Herder, 2008).

5. *Constitutions*, X.8 [820]. . . . importa grandemente el tener mucha auctoridad los prepósitos particulares sobre los súbditos y el general sobre los particulares, y por otra parte la Compañía cerca el general, . . . en manera que todos para el bien tengan toda potestad, y si hiciessen mal, tengan toda subjección.

6. See for example *Constitutions*, Examen IV.35–36 [92–93]; IX. 4.7 [774]; IX.5.4 [782].

Chapter 5

John Paul II and Moral Theology

David Albert Jones

Not all Popes are good Popes. There have been good Popes and bad Popes. This is evident from even a passing acquaintance with Church history. More subtly, someone may be a good man, but not a particularly good Pope, or may be a good Pope without being a particularly good theologian. For example, Pius X, of blessed memory, was a holy man, but in his response to what was then called 'the modernist crisis' he was neither a good Pope nor a good theologian.

I start with these qualifications because I wish to argue that at least within the field of moral theology, John Paul II was a good theologian. This judgement does not reflect an estimation of his personal holiness or an evaluation of the effectiveness of his papal ministry. Furthermore, even in relation to theology, this judgement is not concerned with other aspects of his theological legacy, which will be addressed in other chapters. This paper concerns the development of Roman Catholic moral theology at the end of the second millennium of the Christian era. At least in this context, and at least in this respect, John Paul II was a great theologian who leaves an important theological legacy. To establish this claim, it is first necessary to explore the current state of moral theology and the history of the discipline. In the light of this discussion, one aspect of the moral theology of John Paul II will be used to demonstrate his distinctive contribution.

Section I: the current state of moral theology

The need for renewal

The need for renewal in moral theology was widely recognised in the wake of Vatican II (1963–1965). The Catholic philosopher Elizabeth Anscombe once remarked that, in the late 1960s some sentence in a sermon would often begin, 'We used to believe that . . .' She always heard this phrase with an alarming sinking of the heart, expecting either some absurd lie; for example, 'We used to believe that there was no worse sin than to miss Mass on Sunday;' or much worse, of hearing something like, 'We used to believe that the Church was here for the salvation of souls.' Nevertheless, she acknowledged that there was a 'We used to believe . . .' which could be said 'with some truth and where the implied rejection wasn't a disaster' (Anscombe 1981:113). The example she had in mind was the relationship between faith and reason, which seemed to her to have been presented in a way that implied an extravagant view of rationality and a distorted account of the virtue of faith. This criticism has a direct analogy in the realm of moral theology. Moral theology in the period preceding Vatican II was scarcely 'theology' at all. In the main, it was an exercise in natural reasoning.

While the style of the reasoning shifted over then next 20 years or so, the lack of *theological* analysis within Catholic moral theology was something Richard McCormick could still highlight in the 1980s: 'Those who are concerned with concrete moral problems and a disciplined analysis of their solution say little about vision and character and the biblical–liturgical materials that nourish and sustain them. In other words, they act like moral philosophers' (McCormick 1981:295).

In addition to the lack of a properly theological method, there were several other weaknesses in much of the Catholic moral theology that immediately preceded Vatican II. The discipline was dominated by the production of handbooks of moral theology for the training of priests.[1] While these were not the only works of Catholic moral theology to be produced,[2] they helped shape and, to an extent, define the discipline. They were primarily produced in Latin for a seminary education that was conducted through the medium of Latin.[3] These twentieth-century manuals were the final flowering of a tradition that can be traced back to the thirteenth century.[4] The result was a moral theology that was 'confession oriented, magisterium-dominated, canon law-related, sin-centred, and seminary controlled',[5] to which one might add, excessively focused on rules, exceptions, and questions of conscience, insufficiently grounded in the Scripture and the Fathers, insufficiently concerned with grace, virtue and the gifts of the Spirit.

A tale of three councils

How did moral theology come to such a pass? While there may always be some element of arbitrariness in seeking to define the beginning of any intellectual tradition, the convoking of the Fourth Lateran Council (1215) was certainly a very significant event in the shaping of all subsequent Catholic moral theology.[6] A major concern of that Council was to promote a revival of pastoral care for the spiritual needs of ordinary Christians (*cura animarum*). The Council both expressed and facilitated the movement that gave rise to the preaching friars: the Dominicans and Franciscans, and later the Carmelites, Trinitarians and others. Not only was the Council concerned to defend the Church against the threat of heresy and to evangelize among the heathen, but also it sought to renew the Church by a re-evangelization of nominal Christians. Regular preaching was made mandatory and the systematic study of theology was to be promoted. Most significant for moral theology, the practice of regular oracular confession, already increasingly common, was buttressed by law: every Catholic over the age of reason was to confess his or her sins to a priest at least once a year.[7]

The work of hearing these confessions created a need for practical textbooks or *manuals* to inform and support confessors in their work. These texts reflected both the scholastic manner of presentation used in the developing schools and universities, and the revival and systematisation of canon law.[8] It was a contention of the Dominican historian Leonard Boyle that the greatest work of Thomas Aquinas, his *Summa Theologiae*, was written out of dissatisfaction with the form of these manuals.[9] The central moral section of the *Summa*, the *secunda pars*, was nested between consideration of God and creation in the *prima pars* and consideration of the incarnation, the sacraments and, presumably, the life of the world to come in the *tertia pars*.[10] Moral reflection requires as its context a grasp of the theological and metaphysical truths of creation and redemption. Actions should not be considered in isolation, but within a larger theological framework. Likewise, the sacraments cannot properly be understood without the context of Christology and eschatology.

If Boyle's contention is correct, then it was a cruel irony that even within Thomas's lifetime copies of the *secunda pars* started to circulate independently of the rest of the work. It was to remain the most popular section of the *Summa Theologiae* being copied many times more than the other sections.[11] Thus, from the very origins of the tradition of Catholic moral theology there was a danger that moral or practical considerations could be divorced from their proper doctrinal context. Instead of producing texts that presented the moral life as living out the doctrinal message of the gospel, the practical needs of confessors shaped handbooks that tended to focus attention on condemning or excusing various transgressions of the laws of God and of the Church.

Trent, the reformers and the Society of Jesus

The tradition of manuals for confessors, mixing scholastic theology, canon law and the treatment of individual moral cases, continued throughout the Middle Ages.[12]

Later, a significant development in the tradition was brought about through the influence of the Council of Trent (1545–1563). Like Lateran IV, Trent was also a pastoral council concerned with the spiritual and intellectual formation of priests and the pastoral role of the local bishop. Both expressed and promoted a religious reform movement that had given rise to new religious orders with an evangelical zeal for the salvation of souls.

The most significant influence of Trent upon the shape of moral theology was through the work of a new religious order, the Society of Jesus. The Jesuits were founded specifically to preach the gospel and minister to the spiritual good of Christians. 'Spiritual direction' became central to their work and this required rigorous formation in moral theology and confessional practice. The *Ratio Studiorum*, the plan of studies within the Society, also became the model for studies within the newly established seminaries for secular priests.[13] Grace and virtue ceased to be the focus of attention of moral theologians. The section on grace and the gifts of the Spirit, which had found a place in the tradi-tional schema (i.e. in the *Prima Secundae* of the *Summa Theologiae* of Thomas Aquinas) was replaced by a detailed study of the relations of divine law and liberty of conscience. Trent was also significant for its criticism of extreme versions of the doctrine of original sin and the total depravity of human nature, as these were expressed by the Protestant Reformers. This left many Catholic theologians keen to emphasize that human beings retain free will even after the fall, and that, even after grace, human beings are still bound to keep the commandments.

These were developments of great significance. While organization according to the Ten Commandments had the superficial attraction of structuring topics according to a Scriptural model, it really repre-sented a turn away from considering of the internal qualities of a good Christian character and towards the external fulfilment of requirements of the law. The well-springs of grace, inspiration and prayer, and the overflowing of asceticism and religious vocation, were abstracted out of the picture, and left only the limits of the law and the determination of what bare minimum would suffice to excuse from sin. The great interest taken in the sixteenth century and later in the affective, ascetic and spir-itual life was not integrated with the tasks of the moral theologian; rather, moral theology had as its focus the determination of what was licit according to the moral law. In this period 'moral theology became separated from dogmatic and spiritual theology and acquired the nar-row goal of training priests as judges in the sacrament of penance, with an accompanying minimalistic and legalistic approach concerned primarily with the sinfulness of particular acts' (Curran 1971:180).

Vatican II and *Humanae vitae*

Vatican II was destined to provoke a further transition and a reshaping of the whole discipline of moral theology, as, in their different ways, the Councils of Lateran IV and of Trent had done before. It is widely recognized that Vatican II had a massive impact on moral theology. This was not primarily through the few paragraphs that directly refer to and call for the reform of moral theology;[14] it was the fundamental theological moves of the Council and the whole mood or spirit of the age, which affected the Council, that had most immediate impact on moral theology. Moral theology, like all theology and all Church life, was called to be more open to revision and criticism through dialogue,[15] particularly with other Christians and even non-Christians.[16] It was called to be more aware of existential or experiential reality.[17] Most significant for our concerns, moral theology was called to be more attentive to Scripture.[18]

Charles Curran remarks that

> in the seventeenth and eighteenth centuries there was a call for a more scriptural approach to moral theology, but the attempts along this line failed because they were entwined in the polemics of the rigorist and the probabiliorists against the laxists and probabilists. (Curran 1971:180).

Whether or not this is a fair assessment of that earlier period, it is certainly the case that the task of renewing Catholic moral theology after Vatican II was immediately overshadowed by an analogous polemic.

Only 3 years after the close of the Council, Paul VI in *Humanae vitae* reiterated the Catholic Church's traditional condemnation of contraception. This might not have been anything unexpected. But expectations had been raised both by the convening of a commission of experts and laity to discuss the question, and by the leaked 'majority report'. More fundamentally the great changes that seemed to be happening all around in the 1960s and the message of the Council itself prepared Catholics rather for change than for continuity. There was a massive fallout from this encyclical and most lay Catholics failed to accept the teaching. This chain of events effectively discredited the 'manualist' moral theology prior to Vatican II and was undoubtedly one of the causes for the collapse of the discipline of regular confession among practising (i.e. church-going) Catholics. Mahoney is surely right to see the publishing of Paul VI's encyclical as a watershed in Catholic moral theology.[19] The question of the contraceptive pill, while far from central to the gospel message or to traditional moral theology, became a test case. After this point moral theologians began to diverge according to whether they accepted an increasingly revisionist moral theology which aimed to reflect better the actual experience of conscientious lay Catholics, or whether they sought a renewed method in moral theology which would be able to make more persuasive the traditional moral conclusions. In either case, whether in putting forward new conclusions or defending old ones, there was widespread agreement that the state of moral theology before Vatican II had been shown wanting and needed to be renewed.

The controversy surrounding *Humanae vitae* thus had undoubted historical significance for the development of Catholic moral theology and it would not be difficult to fit Karol Wojtyla, both before and after he became John Paul II, into this schema. In *Love and Responsibility* Wojtyla offered a new methodology for questions of human sexuality, including the question of contraception. As Pope he reiterated the traditional teaching on contraception in his *Familiaris consortio* (1981) and also in his Wednesday addresses later collected together as *The Theology of the Body*. Then, in *Veritatis splendor*, he condemned certain schools of moral theology whose adherents have dissented from the teaching of Paul VI on contraception. However, even this brief sketch is enough to show how narrow and how strained an interpretation of John Paul II this would generate. Even in works devoted to marriage and human sexuality, the subject matter is not reducible to the issue of contraception. Furthermore, neither of his most significant works on moral theology, *Veritatis splendor* (1993) and *Evangelium vitae* (1995), can plausibly be regarded as concerned focally with contraception.[20]

The issue of *Veritatis splendor* concerns moral theological method and the fundamental question of whether *any* acts can be characterized as intrinsically wrong prior to a consideration of their consequences. This is an important issue, whether or not contraception is placed among the acts which are always wrong. Indeed, while contraception is mentioned in *Veritatis splendor* in passing,[21] a more central example of an intrinsically wrong action is the taking of innocent human life. This is made explicit in *Evangelium vitae* especially in relation to abortion and euthanasia. The Pope is clear in this later encyclical that contraception and abortion differ categorically both in nature and in *moral gravity*:

> Certainly, from the moral point of view contraception and abortion are specifically different evils: the former contradicts the full truth of the sexual act as the proper expression of conjugal love, while the latter destroys the life of a human being; the former is opposed to the virtue of chastity in marriage, the latter is opposed to the virtue of

justice and directly violates the divine commandment 'You shall not kill.' (EV, 13).

Without wishing to minimize the importance of chastity for individual integrity and for society, and without denying the significance of the question of whether contraception need always be contrary to chastity, it is important nevertheless to refocus the debate. The enduring significance and theological legacy of Pope John Paul II, do not lie in relation to the issue of contraception. What then is the significance of John Paul II in the development of Catholic moral theology?

Section II: John Paul II and the renewal of moral theology

Acknowledging the person

John Paul II had a particular interest in moral theology. This needs to be stated as it does not follow necessarily from his role as Pope or from his ability as a theologian. Pope Benedict XVI is a very able theologian, and like John Paul II is one who might well have continued to be a professional academic theologian had he not been called to serve as a bishop. Nevertheless, as a theologian, Benedict XVI has much less interest in moral theology and much more interest, for example, in liturgy. Within the twentieth century the only other Pope who had a comparable interest in moral theology was Pius XII. Other Popes felt called upon to make statements on moral issues as they were needed or requested, but only in Pius XII and John Paul II do you find Popes who look for opportunities to reflect on moral theology, who do so from their own initiative, and who are interested in the fundamental principles of moral theology. Nevertheless, while Pius XII usefully enunciates many themes in the moral theology of his day, the extent of his own contribution to the discipline is debatable. He was not an original thinker. In contrast there are at least two areas where John Paul II makes a significant and original contribution to moral theology. The first relates to his 'personalism', the second to his use of Scripture in moral theology.

Karol Wojtyla was one of a number of Catholic thinkers in the mid-twentieth century who moved beyond the then predominant neo-scholastic form of Thomism and who sought engagement and inspiration from other strands of contemporary philosophy. As Karl Rahner sought to engage with Heidegger and with other forms of existentialist philosophy, or as Bernard Lonergan addressed himself to Kant and to empiricism, Wojtyla looked to Husserl and Scheler and to that movement in philosophy that is called phenomenology. His focus was the human person not only as experiencing but as acting: *The Acting Person*. This concern not only provided the material, or one might say the form, for his argument in *Love and Responsibility* but also exercised a strong influence on the way the Pope appealed to experience and to existential categories more broadly in his writings.

A complaint that was commonly made against the prevailing moral theology of the period leading up to Vatican II was that it attempted to draw conclusions about the human good from physiology. This is perhaps best exemplified in the argument against sterilization based on 'natural functions', an argument found both in the encyclical of Pius IX *Casti connubii*, (no, 71) and in certain writings of Pius XII (e.g. *Allocution to Midwives,* 12 October 1951). Many critics of *Humanae vitae* see in this later encyclical the same 'physicalist' error. Without prejudicing the debate as to whether Paul VI makes the same move as Pius XI, and whether that move rests on a fallacy, it is clear that John Paul II argues in a quite different way. His argument begins not with the physiology of procreation but with the human meaning of sexual union as nuptial. If John Paul II's approach is also flawed, it will be flawed for quite different reasons, for he certainly does not fall into the trap of reiterating widely rejected arguments from 'nature'.[22]

The shift towards the personal and the existential is evident in a number of twentieth-century thinkers, inside and outside the Catholic fold, and John Paul II is one of those who applied this in the area of moral theology. This is to his credit, and the particular form of his philosophical thought may yet leave a significant legacy. I have no wish to dispute this. Nevertheless, the remainder of this chapter will address the second of John Paul II's contributions, his use of Scripture, as this is more fundamental from the perspective of methodology, and I believe it will be the more enduring legacy.

The use of Scripture in Catholic moral theology

Vatican II was the fruit of a renewal movement that called on theologians, and on all the faithful to return to the sources (ressourcement), among which pre-eminent place goes to the sacred Scriptures. The Scriptures, taken together with the sacred tradition constitutes the 'supreme rule of faith' (*Dei verbum*, 21). The Scriptures both nourish and regulate the Church. The Council therefore urged that easy access to sacred Scripture should be provided for all the Christian faithful (DV, 22). As for theologians, they should engage energetically and with vigour in the work of exploring and expounding the Scriptures, 'for the Sacred Scriptures contain the word of God and since they are inspired really are the word of God; and so the study of the sacred page is, as it were, the soul of sacred theology' (DV, 24).

In another Vatican II document, this general injunction to theologians is applied specifically to *moral* theologians: 'Special care must be given to the perfecting of moral theology. Its scientific exposition, nourished more on the teaching of the Bible, should shed light on the loftiness of the calling of the faithful in Christ' (*Optatam totius* 16).

Servais Pinckaers has pointed out how this theme is further developed in a 1976 document from the Congregation for Catholic Education:

> In the past, moral theology exhibited at times a certain narrowness of vision and some lacunas. This was due in large part to a kind of legalism, to an individualistic orientation, and to a separation from the sources of revelation. To counter all this . . . it is necessary to clarify the method by which moral theology ought to be developed in close contact with Holy Scripture.[23]

Note that the Congregation openly acknowledges the commonly perceived flaws in Catholic moral theology in the time preceding the Council, in particular, that it was legalistic (concerned with laws, exceptions, and conscience) and that it was separated from the sources Revelation (and conducted more as a kind of moral philosophy than as theology).

In 1971 Charles Curran published an article surveying the use of Scripture in moral theology. While he opined that a 'biblical renewal' within theology had had a positive impact on moral theology, he was critical of the limitations of these approaches. Moreover, at a methodological level he put forward the view that there is nothing distinctive about Christian ethics[24] which is not 'common to the ethical enterprise', that is, 'in continuity with ethical methodology in general' (1971:198). Later he appeals to John Macquarrie in support of the view that 'on the level of ethical conclusions and proximate values, norms, and dispositions, there is nothing distinctive about the Christian ethic.' (1971:203). Curran's stance is characterized by Tom Deidun, seemingly with approval, as a concern to 'uphold the autonomy of that discipline' (1998:28). Deidun also cites Gerard Hughes as claiming that 'neither Scripture nor tradition could ever be the ultimate authority' for deciding any moral issue, since they are both subject to the discrimination of reason (Deidun 1998:28). To borrow a phrase from Kant, this would make at least moral theology 'religion within the limits of reason alone'.

In relation to Scripture, McCormick seems to suggest a middle way between 'sectarian exhortation' and 'unbiblical rationalism' (McCormick 1981:295). However, he puts no limits on his claim that 'Christian warrants are confirmatory' (1981:299), that is, they confirm what is 'in principle available to human insight (shareable by others than Christians)' (1981:297). Yet, if the *whole* of moral theology were 'in principle available' to those who are ignorant of the Scriptures, then clearly the Scriptures would have no essential role in Christian moral reasoning. If this were the case then it would be difficult to see how the Scriptures could have more than a very limited secondary role within moral theology, and indeed how moral theology qualifies as theology. The stance taken by Curran, Hughes, Macquarrie and McCormick should not be criticized too severely, for it is in continuity with the dominant Catholic approach to moral theology before Vatican II, perhaps as far back as Trent. They all represent variations on natural law thinking. However, what these theologians fail to do, and what much of Catholic moral theology has failed to do, is respond to the call of Vatican II to nourish moral theology through detailed study of the Scriptures.

In contrast, in his writing on fundamental moral theology and on specific moral issues, John Paul II turned to the Scriptures. He used the Scriptures not just as 'proof texts' for conclusions provided by the tradition or established by natural reason. He used the Scriptures to do work. He engaged in a sustained exegesis of Scriptural passages attentive to what they have to teach on moral issues. An Anglican moral theologian, Oliver O'Donovan, has appreciated the way that the Pope used Scripture, 'not quoted as a proof but teased out as a way of framing a question in scriptural terms' (O'Donovan 2005). O'Donovan particularly draws attention to 'the unforgettable treatment of the rich young ruler at the beginning of *Veritatis Splendor*, or of Cain and Abel in *Evangelium vitae*.' An evaluation of the contribution of John Paul II to the use of Scripture in moral theology should perhaps start then with an examination of these passages in these encyclicals, beginning with *Veritatis splendor*.

Veritatis splendor and the rich young man

The encyclical *Veritatis splendor* begins with a claim that the splendour of truth shines forth from all the works of the creator. With such a beginning we might imagine that the Pope would move from there to the grasp of the natural law that is placed in every human heart. This would be the more typical Catholic move. However, immediately after he has announced the theme of light, John Paul II identifies this light with Jesus Christ, 'the true light that enlightens everyone' (*VS* 1, quoting John 1.9). From the beginning John Paul II gives a Christo-centric account of the moral life. This is developed over the course of the first third of the encyclical through a reflection on the encounter between Jesus and the rich young man.

John Paul II uses this story to explore various aspects of the moral life. He starts with the fact of the young man coming to Jesus and asking what he must do to have eternal life. John Paul II notices that the man approaches Jesus because he is attracted by him or intrigued by him. He comes seeking an answer to a fundamental question of meaning, 'what good must I do to have eternal life?' (Mt. 19:16). From this and from Jesus' initial response, John Paul II draws the conclusion that Christian moral action begins with an encounter with Jesus and with an attraction towards 'the one who is good.' The commandments, which Jesus goes on to mention, have as their context this encounter and this attraction. For his understanding of the meaning of the commandments, and the relationship between the commandments given in the law and the way of the gospel, John Paul II turns to the Sermon on the Mount.

There we are told that the commandments remain binding, but they are understood in relation to their fulfilment in Christ. The fulfilment of the law for the follower of Christ must take the form of interiorizing the commandments and of understanding their fullest meaning.

These themes John Paul II continues to develop to the point in the story when the young man goes away sad and the disciples ask who can be saved. Jesus replies, 'With God all things are possible' (Mt. 19.26). John Paul II sees here the theme of the power of God's grace. He quotes with approval the phrase of Augustine that so enraged Pelagius: *Da quod iubes et iube quod vis* (grant what you command and command what you will, *Confessions*, X.29). It is not the command that comes first and then the power to fulfil it, still less is the command given without the power, rather it is the transforming Spirit that comes first, giving first the ability to live a new life, and then the command is given.

Of this first chapter which presents the moral life as a response to Christ's invitation, Richard McCormick says, 'Its biblical base is a breath of fresh air' (1994:484). He then quotes the theologian Ronald Modras as saying that it 'shows all the signs of not only being written by the Pope but of arising out of his own deeply personal introspective reflections on the gospel story' (McCormick quoting Modras 1994). Richard McBrien is far more muted in his praise, using the chapter only to have a side swipe at more conservative Catholics:

> The first chapter is a detailed outline of the biblical basis for Catholic moral teachings. It is a presentation that, for the most part, mainline Protestants, Anglicans and Orthodox could join with progressive Catholics in endorsing. Conservative Catholics looking for some reinforcement might feel disappointed. (McBrien 1993).

Nevertheless, not all commentators are well disposed towards this first section. Gareth Moore was one critic who attacked the use of Scripture in the first chapter of that encyclical. He alleged that *Veritatis splendor* 'distorts the natural sense of the passage' (Moore 1994:81), the main theme of which is 'the power of riches over those who own them' (Moore 1994:81). A similar point is made by Curran who claims that 'the parable [*sic*] does not deal with every person in general but with deals in particular with a rich young man . . . The thrust of the story. . . is the question of riches' (Curran 2005: 52). This also seems to be the reasoning behind the rather elliptical criticism of Deidun, who complains of John Paul II's 'refocusing of Matthew's account of the Rich Young Man [Matthew 19:16–22] on verses 17–18' (Deidun 1998:15). These are varieties of the more general criticism that John Paul II indulges in eisegesis, reading into the Scriptures what he wishes to get out.

Nevertheless, how far is this criticism justified? Is it true, as Curran claims, that the passage in the gospel relates only to this person in particular and is not addressed to 'every person in general'? If so, why then is it part of the Gospel story? If it had no relevance to others, then why would it be retold? In fact, on the reading that Curran and Moore offer, it is of relevance to every person, for it relates in general to the question of riches and the attitude one should have to them. Going further, even if we accept, for the sake of argument that the 'main thrust' of the story is the power of riches, is this all we can glean from the story? Is the story reducible to its punch line? While the story clearly does relate to the cost of discipleship it also involves discussion of the keeping of the commandments, a theme that is touched on several times in Matthew's Gospel. It does involve someone coming to Jesus as 'teacher' in search of 'eternal life'. The themes that John Paul II brings out from this passage are elements of a rich and multi-layered text, and are related to themes elsewhere in the Gospel and elsewhere in the Scriptures.

Thomas Stegman usefully distinguishes four characteristics of John Paul II's use of Scripture (in a different context but relevant also to *Veritatis splendor*) in terms of four interpretative principles:

(1) the unity of Scripture;
(2) Scripture's multivalent potential meaning;
(3) Christ as the hermeneutical key to understanding Scripture; and
(4) the importance of the creeds (and by extension, Church teaching) for the interpretation of Scripture (Stegman 2007:48).

This approach Stegman calls the actualization of Scripture, taking that term from the Pontifical Biblical Commission which used it to describe the appropriation of the Scriptures in the ongoing life of the Church.

Some are concerned that this kind of exegesis is not confined by any limitation, and that it leads to fanciful allegory in which anything is possible. However, actualization does have limits and a context and is measured against a wider context given by the whole of Scripture and the later tradition. This might generate a reading that is in tension with the surface or literal sense provided by historical–critical readings of the text (what can be retrieved, if anything, of the author's original intention and the context of the intended readers), but the literal sense is not disregarded. Rather the literal sense is taken in dialogue with a fuller sense provided by the larger context of the text. How this tension or dialogue is made fruitful is a difficult issue not just for moral theology but from theology in general. It is my contention that John Paul II makes a significant contribution here, by daring to take the Scriptures as his starting point even after the Catholic acceptance of the historical–critical method.

A second related criticism raised by Moore about the use of Scripture in the first chapter of *Veritatis splendor* is that John Paul II stresses 'one particular mode of biblical discourse among several, namely, the legal' (Moore 1994:81). This criticism is again echoed by Curran who claims that the encyclical 'makes primary the insistence on obedience to commandments' (Curran 2005:52). If these charges were true, then clearly this would amount to a serious distortion of the message of the Gospel. The Gospel is not primarily concerned with obedience to commandments. However, the starting point of John Paul II is not obedience to the commandments but the encounter with Christ and the search for meaning. While the commandments remain binding (and this is a feature which is true of the Gospel according to Matthew), the meaning of the commandments is found in the good that comes as a gift from God. Arguably, the main thrust of the whole of the first chapter of *Veritatis splendor* is that obedience to the commandments makes sense only in relation to the final end of human beings in the 'one who is good' and who is also the one who makes this possible. The basis of this chapter is not the commandments as unchanging expressions of reason or of nature; rather the commandments are looked at in relation to Christ as the fulfilment of human meaning and hence the fulfilment of the law (a prominent theme both in the Gospel according to Matthew and in the letters of Paul). I would suggest that those who criticize John Paul II for focusing on law and commandments are in fact reading their own adverse reactions to chapter two back into chapter one.

It is the second chapter, which is far less Scriptural than the first and which is directed towards analyzing current trends in moral theology, that has generated much hostility. In this section John Paul II is acting not only as teacher but also as judge and, as supreme pontiff, is attempting to settle certain disputed questions. The tension between John Paul II as theologian and John Paul II as Pope is something we will return to below.

Before moving on to *Evangelium vitae*, the second major moral theological work of John Paul II, it is worth considering some ecumenical reactions to *Veritatis splendor*. Gilbert Meilaender (1995) takes issue not just with the controversial chapter two but also with the treatment of theology in chapter one. He contrasts John Paul II's use of the parable of the rich young man with Karl Barth's analysis of the same passage. Both John Paul II and Barth see a greater significance in this passage than the question of riches. Both see in it a disclosure of the moral life. However, Barth extends his treatment to consider the reaction of the disciples and the way in which they are incomplete in their own conversion and need to rely on faith. Meilaender finds the virtue of faith and the need for forgiveness among the disciples notable by its absence in John Paul II's treatment. He accepts and welcomes John Paul II's acknowledgement of 'grace alone' but thinks that John Paul II should also acknowledge the truth of 'faith alone'. Despite the appeal to the Scriptures and the Christo-centric focus, Meilaender still faults John Paul II for failing to learn from the Reformation. However, another Lutheran David Yaego (1998) who compares the approach of John Paul II with that of Luther finds much in common. Both endeavour to avoid the twin pitfalls of Pelagianism and antinomianism. If John Paul II raises difficult issues for dialogue between Catholic and Lutheran, that is because he is concerned to talk about grace and to put the issue back on the agenda. Richard McBrien, no fan of *Veritatis splendor*, says that it should be understood as 'a follow-up to a previous papal document, *Reconciliato et Poenitentia* (1984)' (McBrien 1993). However, if Meilaender took these two documents together he would find addressed the theme he was looking for.

Evangelium vitae and Cain and Abel

As *Veritatis splendor* starts with an extended consideration of the story of the rich young man, *Evangelium vitae* starts with a consideration of the story of Cain and Abel. The theme of taking human life is addressed through the Scriptural account of the first and archetypal taking of life, the original fratricide. From this John Paul II draws several themes, that all killing is the killing of a brother, that we do have a responsibility for our brothers and sisters, and that whoever attacks human life in some way attacks God who gave it.

The story of Cain and Abel is not the only part of Scripture to be invoked in *Evangelium vitae*; indeed virtually every page contains some appeal to Scripture. At one point John Paul II returns to the theme of *Veritatis splendor*, that the encounter with the rich young man shows how the Gospel is both a gift from God and a task for human beings. '*The gift* thus *becomes a commandment* [to love], and *the commandment itself is a gift*' (VS, 52) Nevertheless, the Cain and Abel story is the most extended treatment of any one passage and provides the basis for what follows. It is again striking that John Paul II in talking of killing does not start with the commandment 'Thou shalt not kill' (Exodus 20:13), as Augustine and Thomas Aquinas did before him. Rather he uses the story of Cain and Abel in part because his interest is in theological anthropology, for which reason he naturally returns to the early chapters of Genesis rather than to the giving of the law in Exodus. In part he turns to the story of Cain and Abel as a passage that can provide insight not directly by giving commands or doctrine but by presenting a narrative through which values and truths are disclosed.

In relation to *Evangelium vitae* again John Paul II was attacked for failing to take account of critical method and for indulging in eisegesis. One example given by Curran is the way that John Paul II 'prepares the way' for his own opposition to capital punishment when he draws attention to the way that God puts his mark upon Cain so that no one would kill him. Curran comments: 'All have to recognize that one really cannot use this text to argue against capital punishment' (Curran 2005:50). Curran here implies that John Paul II uses this text as a proof text against capital punishment, yet the text in question is not cited in those sections of *Evangelium vitae* that discuss capital punishment. It is not used in a facile way as a demonstration. It is used, in Curran's apt phrase, to prepare the way. For help in this regard John Paul II turns to Saint Ambrose. He gives an extended quotation from Ambrose on this passage in which Ambrose concludes, 'God who preferred the correction rather than the death of the sinner, did not desire that a homicide be punished by the extraction of another act of homicide' (*De Cain et. Abel* II, 10, 38 quoted by EV, 9). Here we see at work the 'actualization' that Stegman refers to. John Paul II shows how this text has been used by Ambrose and thus has become reflected and refracted in the tradition.

This does not show that the text implies that capital punishment is impermissible (such a reading would have to cope with Gen. 9.6, not to mention the commanding of capital punishment by the law). Nevertheless, John Paul II's method is profound. He looks back to the beginning. He sees in the story of Cain and Abel the archetypal story of taking human life. This is surely true. He notes that in this archetypal story Cain is not punished with death but with exile, and is even protected. The murderer, and Cain is certainly the archetypal murderer, is not cut off altogether from the love of God or from that dignity that comes from God. Mercy predominates over justice, at least in this story, at least at that point. The use that Ambrose makes of this text is reasonable. It is quite appropriate to find inspiration in this story for a preference for correction over execution. It is not quite the same point as the story of the woman taken in adultery, but both stories face in the same direction, as it were, and both give a reason to forgo punishing. *Pace* Curran, it is not illegitimate to use this text as part of the context for thinking about capital punishment, especially if the point at issue is whether there is a necessity in justice to punishment and, if not, whether there might also be benefit in mercy instead to correct.

In what is otherwise a sympathetic account of *Evangelium vitae*, O'Donovan takes issue with John Paul II for not emphasizing the resurrection. The resurrection is mentioned, as is eternal life, but there is a tendency in the encyclical to elide the different senses of 'life' and to assume that valuing eternal life always translates as valuing this life, which of course it does not. Some attention to this deeply Scriptural theme would have enabled John Paul II to criticize more effectively the idolatry of this life and the denial of death which are features of our culture. Michael Banner cites with approval O'Donovan's central criticism: 'with only the categories of life-enhancement at his disposal [John Paul II] ends up reinforcing certain vitalist perceptions which are fuelling the cultural conflagration' (Banner 1999:46 quoting O'Donovan 1996:94). This is a valid criticism. John Paul II, who showed such a good example to others of a good death, focuses too much on the positive value of life as though, if he admitted the acceptance of death, he might open the way to killing. This criticism does not undermine the fundamental method of John Paul II in relation to Scripture but calls for a similar attention to a great range of texts and by a great number of theologians so that different insights taken from the Scriptures can be fruitfully integrated.

A more fundament criticism by Michael Banner (1999) of the encyclical *Evangelium vitae* was the way that its assertion of natural knowledge of human rights and the human good was in tension with this account of the Scriptural basis for these rights and with its characterization of a pervasive culture of death (which prevents people acquiring knowledge of the human good). He admits in a footnote (40, n. 33,) that, in conversation with O'Donovan, he had come to accept that this tension is not a logical contradiction. It is possible that cultural prejudice darkens judgement without altogether removing the possibility of moral insight or criticism of the culture. Similarly there is grace and the culture of life operative in the world constantly struggling against the culture of death. Nevertheless, Banner thinks that the maintenance of the category of natural law, along with the acceptance of the category of human rights, weakens the strength of the argument. He argues that John Paul II would be better off dropping natural law altogether, something he claims was done in *Veritatis splendor*.

However, at this point Banner asks more of John Paul II than a Catholic could concede, and fails to recognize just how far John Paul II goes in rooting moral theology in a Scriptural, Christo-centric theological vision. Banner's criticism here is similar to Meilaender's criticism of *Veritatis splendor* (which curiously Banner thinks is free from this error), and both are dependent on Barth.

From a Barthian perspective any acknowledgement of a continuing validity in natural reason to come to an understanding of the natural law is dangerously misguided. Those elements of John Paul II's theology which retain the theme of natural law or natural reason and which even seek new formulations of the same idea in terms of human rights, must be rejected absolutely. However, John Paul II, by retaining these elements but qualifying them (by reference to structures of sin, the culture of sin and the presence of God's grace in the world) presents what could be a bridge between Catholic and Reformed theology as recognized by Yaego (1998). It may be, as Banner points out, that there is a tension between the claim that natural reason can function and the claim that there are structures of sin that inhibit this, but Banner has not showed that this tension is destructive.

From a Catholic perspective, natural reason can and should be affirmed because this is part of the affirmation of the gift of creation which is wounded but not destroyed by the fall. One can agree with Banner that much contemporary moral language is inadequate and in need of criticism, one can further agree that the common language of human morality lies more in the future than in the present, and is something that we must help to construct. Nevertheless, these positions do not undermine either the reality of some human powers of reason, will and emotion to grasp some aspect of the human good, or the presence of some moral truths within the Western philosophical tradition and even in contemporary culture.

This digression has taken us beyond the use of Scripture by John Paul II, but it is relevant because it shows that John Paul II, has not repudiated the possibility of moral knowledge from philosophy. He has not repudiated philosophy but he has provided a theological account which encompasses philosophy, what MacIntyre has called 'a theology of moral philosophy' (1994:189). It is theology that provides the vision and the measure by which philosophies are judged, and it is the theological vision of the Gospel that provides the ultimate inspiration and the final measure, the life and the rule for Christian moral reflection (cf. *Dei verbum*, 21).

The theology of the body

Another area of John Paul II's moral theological reflection which must be mentioned is the development of a 'theology of the body', especially but not exclusively in his Wednesday addresses on the nuptial mystery. These again turn to the Scriptures and especially to the book of Genesis as their source and inspiration. The original unity of man and woman in the Garden is taken as a guide to the meaning of marriage and hence to the nuptial meaning of the human body. These works again comprise an extended reflection on Scripture as a source for moral understanding.

Within the constraints of this chapter I will not explore this corpus except to make a brief comment on John Paul II's use of another Scriptural passage, Ephesians 5. In this passage Paul relates a 'household code', (the ordered relations of husbands, wives, children, and slaves), to the love that exists between Christ and his Church. Paul does this by means of the idea of 'mutual subjection'. From this John Paul II draws the conclusion that the equality of mutual subjection is more fundamental than the inequality implied by the conventional subordination of wives to husbands. Curran takes issue with this, saying that John Paul II has read his understanding into the text (the question of eisegesis again). Against the view that the equality of man and woman, and indeed of slave and free, is the more fundamental principle, Curran asks rhetorically: 'Yet how many generations were necessary for such a precept to be realized in the history of humanity with the abolition of slavery?' (Curran 2005:55). In contrast one might ask why it was in the Christian tradition, and despite the powerful influence of Aristotle and the great commercial gain of the new slave trade, that slavery came to be abolished. Texts such as Gal. 3.20 (though not such texts in isolation) played an important role in Christian repudiation of slavery.

Curran says of John Paul II's exegesis, 'Here a liberal interpretation distorts the scriptural meaning', but this is to assume that it is principles outside the tradition of the Scriptures that are shaping the interpretation. In contrast John Paul II looking for a meaning that is found in the light of other passages and becomes evident only after much reflection in the tradition is still looking for a scriptural meaning. He is not content to say that the inequalities of the household codes are theologically basic or significant in a way that the fundamental equality of every human being in the sight of God is basic or significant. Elizabeth Schüssler Fiorenza on this passage from Ephesians laments that Paul failed to reshape the household codes radically enough to prevent them remaining as an oppressive force: 'this christological modification of the husband's patriarchal position and duties does not have the power, theologically speaking, to transform the patriarchal pattern of the household code, even though *this might have been the intention of the author* (1983:270, emphasis added). There is clearly a distance here between Schüssler Fiorenza and John Paul II, but it is less than the distance between those two and Curran. Schüssler Fiorenza and John Paul II take it that there is a tension between the language of mutual subjection and the conventional subjugation of women (and slaves). Schüssler Fiorenza thinks that Paul does not succeed in overcoming the practical subjugation. John Paul II takes Paul's equalitarian aims (which Schüssler Fiorenza also recognizes but which Curran denies) in the light of later tradition as the more significant feature and for that reason appeals to them.

An irony and a criticism that some will level at John Paul II is that his approach implies quite a strong sense of the possibility of the development of doctrine in the realm of moral theology, whereas he is well known as a conservative thinker. Now these two elements are not incompatible as someone can admit the great importance of change over time while being very cautious of actual proposed changes. In *Veritatis splendor* John Paul II explicitly acknowledges that doctrinal development has occurred in moral understanding (no. 28). This is a very important teaching and is itself a significant contribution of John Paul II. Where criticism of John Paul II is perhaps justified is in an apparent overconfidence about the unchanging character of very many particular doctrines, practices and moral precepts and also in his failure to give sufficient acknowledgement of the degree to which Christians have misunderstood things in the past. The story of the Christian repudiation of slavery cannot simply be portrayed as a glorious success but also must include recognition of failure and moral ignorance, error or insensitivity. This certainly does not apply equally to all parts of the Christian message neither in relation to faith or morals; there are some things that remain unchanged. Nevertheless, the possibility of present ignorance and future development is a necessary part of the humility of the moral theologian.

The tensions between Pope and theologian

This chapter started by noting the difference between being a good Pope and being a good theologian. A good theologian might not necessarily be an effective or inspiring Pope. A good Pope may not be an insightful or original theologian. On average we might suppose it better to have a good theologian as Pope, but there are tensions between the roles and this becomes evident, for example, in the style of writing.

One criticism of John Paul II in relation to his use of Scripture is that he does not draw upon recent developments in historical–critical scholarship. This is not altogether fair, as John Paul II does show awareness at various points of the results of historical–critical scholarship (e.g. in his exegesis of Genesis). Nevertheless, it is more difficult to show these links because of a particular feature of the papal style of writing. In stark contrast to academic writing, it is not usual in papal writing to refer explicitly to the work of contemporary scholars. While papal documents are replete with footnotes, these notes refer to official documents, to previous Popes or to ancient and medieval theologians, the fathers and doctors of the Church. This style is part of a deliberate attempt to emphasize continuity and authority, and not to be drawn too far into debates within academic circles. However, this unwillingness to acknowledge influences which must be present weakens the theological value of the work. There is a good reason for acknowledging influence and for weighing down the academic text with references to contemporary literature. Such references help situate a text within academic debate and also help clarify the basis of certain claims and certain forms of argument. If the influences are not made explicit, then it becomes less clear what degree of confidence can be given to some assertion, or whether some writer has been taken into account.

In particular when criticizing other views it is expected, in academic circles, to quote the authors themselves. This helps establish that the views attacked are actually held by named authors. They are held to account for their own words. In a previous age it was more common (though certainly not universal) for papal documents to identify the authors of mistaken views and quote them directly. However, this clarity about attribution goes hand in hand with theological censure. Certain authors stand condemned for their views. It is understandable why Popes have increasingly avoided naming their targets and have preferred to identify views as erroneous, rather than specific authors. However, this unwillingness to name and shame does leave greater problems as to whether the characterization of a particular view (for example 'proportionalism') corresponds to anything that anyone actually holds.

The second chapter of *Veritatis splendor* sets out a series of dichotomies, most notably the dichotomy between freedom and truth, and condemns a number of interpretations of Christian morality that are 'contrary to sound teaching' and 'incompatible with revealed truth' (no.29). It is unsurprising that it is this chapter that has generated most controversy and hostility. The reaction of Catholic moral theologians to these condemnations bears a direct relation to the school with which the theologian identified. Typically, those who self-identify as 'proportionalists' do not recognize themselves in the document (see for example McCormick 1994). Typically, those who oppose proportionalism recognize the other theologians in the document (see for example May 2004).[25] It is not my task here to adjudicate that dispute, though I will notice that the encyclical has been effective in discouraging the language of proportionality in Catholic moral theology. This has not prevented some theologians from taking revisionist positions on moral conclusions (such as abortion and homosexuality), but now these theologians are likely to appeal not to proportionality but to virtue theory or narrative. What is of more interest for this chapter is the tension between the role of judge and the role of theologian. It is part of the papal role to seek to settle disputes of doctrine between schools of theology, when one school is believed to have departed from the faith. However, this is a difficult role to combine with setting out a (necessarily particular) positive theological understanding of the point at issue.

In *Veritatis splendor* John Paul II asserts that he 'does not intend to impose upon the faithful any particular theological system, still less a philosophical one' (no.29). Rather he is presenting a vision of the moral life and then, in that context, condemning certain errors in fundamental moral theology. There are those who have questioned whether John Paul II does not in fact canonize one particular school, but I think that the Pope should be taken at his word and this then provides an interpretative principle for the document as a whole. The condemnations are intended to identify certain errors which theologians must avoid. These are intended as binding. The positive theological account of the moral life is offered as a means of understanding but is not presented as binding in the same way.

Alasdair MacIntyre has argued that *Veritatis splendor* is a major contribution to moral reflection and has urged 'that continuing philosophical conversation between Christianity and modernity to which Pascal and Kierkegaard, Newman and Barth and von Balthasar, have all been contributors'. Yet there is a danger that this will be missed because of concern to defend or to criticize those theologians who are condemned in the document. 'One way of missing the point of *Veritatis splendor* would be to tie its reading too closely to the work of those particular moral theologians whose writings may have been the occasion for its composition' (MacIntyre 1994:195). This would have been much easier if the document were not a papal document and hence was not trying to do two things at once: put forward a theological vision and set limits to the legitimate diversity of Catholic moral theology.

For all then that the papal role has given greater prominence to the theology of John Paul II, it has also inhibited that theology in some areas. Theology is developed and tested through dispute and the papal role has made it difficult for those within the Church to debate with him effectively, and has also distanced him from the style of academic writing and the benefits of that style. Ironically some of his most interesting interlocutors have been those who are not under any Catholic discipline who freely mix criticism and appreciation: theologians such as Banner (1999), Hauerwas (1994), Meilaender (1995), and O'Donovan (1996). In order to appreciate John Paul II as a theologian (without either excessive deference or excessive defensiveness) it seems better to try to forget that he was also Pope. Perhaps now that John Paul II is no longer Pope, the extent of his legacy precisely as theologian can become better appreciated. It is interesting that these non-Catholic commentators have recognized as a (perhaps the greatest) contribution of John Paul II to moral theology his use of Scripture. This does not mean that John Paul II makes no mistakes or is immune from challenge in relation to his use of Scripture; quite the contrary. It means that John Paul II had the courage to begin with Scripture and to use Scripture to do work. A failure to do so had been a weakness not for years but for many centuries in Catholic moral theology. Vatican II had called for a moral theology that would be firmly scriptural. In this area, as far as I am aware, John Paul II is without parallel. This is not to say that John Paul II made similarly important contributions to all areas of Catholic moral theology. To give one obvious example, John Paul II does not use *virtue* as a core category for his moral theology, and yet the rediscovery of virtue theory is one of the most interesting developments of the past 40 years. Nevertheless, in relation to the use of Scripture in moral theology John Paul II is a great theologian, measured not only against his own generation but by the measure of the last 1000 years of Catholic moral theology.

Notes

1. A good survey is provided by McKeever (1999). For more detail see Gallagher (1990).
2. Apart from the manuals there was a substantial amount of Catholic moral theology published as journal articles and also some books written not for seminary use but for a lay Catholic audience, for example, Slater (1925) or Vann (1937).
3. There were some manuals written in English such as those of Slater (1908), Koch and Preuss (1924), McHugh-Callan (1929) and, most prominently, Henry Davis (1935). However, even in English and American seminaries, the field was dominated by the Latin texts of such writers as Sabetti and Barrett (1924), Génicot and Salsmans (1927), Noldin and Schmitt (1927), Prümmer (1928), Merkelbach (1946) and Zalba (1958).
4. Prümmer gives a 24 page Brevis Catalogus Auctorum qui de theologia morali scripserunt.
5. McCormick (1999:47). Nevertheless, this tradition also contained a great deal of practical wisdom 'very pastoral and prudent, critically respectful, realistic, compassionate, open and charitable, well-informed' Ibid.
6. While he shows little sympathy for the reforming efforts of Lateran IV, Mahoney (1987, ch. 1) rightly stresses the importance of this Council and its legislation for the subsequent development of Catholic moral theology. Conversely, it is a strange lacuna in Servais Pinckaers' otherwise insightful survey (1995a, ch. 9) that in treating the period of high scholasticism he fails to mention the significance of this Council.
7. Canon 21; Tanner (1990:245).
8. There had been *Summae Confessorum* since the eleventh century, but the Council gave rise to a great proliferation of these, influential among which was the *Summa de Casibus* by the renowned Dominican canon lawyer St Raymund of Penyafort (*c.*1180–1275), though Leonard Boyle contended that the influence of this and even the influence of the *secunda pars* of the *Summa Theologiae* of Thomas Aquinas were indirect, being mediated primarily through the immensely influential *Summa Confessorum* of John of Freiburg. cf. Boyle (1974), (1982).
9. Boyle (1982).
10. Though the final section of *Summa* was never completed, by comparison with the commentary on the sentences and the *Summa Contra Gentiles*, it is possible to reconstruct the projected scheme of the whole.
11. Boyle (1982:29).
12. One of the more popular was the mid-fifteenth century *Summa Moralis* of St Antoninus of Florence (1389–1459). Among other areas of interest, this

work contained a detailed moral analysis of the banking system so significant in the life of that city. In the mid-sixteenth century the discovery of
the New World and a flourishing reform movement in Spain gave rise to a
revival of moral theology among the Dominicans in Salamanca, of whom
the most prominent figure was Francisco de Vitoria (1483–1546). This
revival combined commentary on the text on Thomas Aquinas with
detailed examination of particular moral questions or cases. The method
of case law or *casuistry* was not new but could already be seen in the works
of Raymund or Antoninus. Vitoria and later Dominicans of the Salamanca
school attempted to develop this method while integrating it into a
Thomistic framework.

13. The first detailed syllabus for moral theology produced according to
    this *ratio* was the *Institutionum Moralium* of Juan Azor (1563–1603)
    (cf. Pinkaers (1995a:260–261.)). He proposed a fourfold division of moral
    theology into the commandments, the sacraments, ecclesiastical censures
    and states of life. Thus it was according to the commandments, rather than
    according to the Cardinal and theological virtues, that moral theology was
    organized. Azor's introductory treatment of the principles of human
    action followed St Thomas very closely (*Summa Theologiae* IaIIae), except
    that there was no treatment of the gifts of the Spirit and the beatitudes
    and no treatment of grace, while an extended treatment of conscience
    made its appearance.
14. *Optatam totius* 16 (Tanner 1990:955–956).
15. *Gaudium et spes* 40–44 (Tanner 1990:1093–1099).
16. *Lumen gentium* 13–16 (Tanner 1990:859–862), *Unitatis redintegratio* 3–11
    (Tanner 1990:909–915), *Nostra aetate* (Tanner 1990:968–971).
17. *Gaudium et spes* 1–11 (Tanner 1990:1069–1075).
18. *Dei verbum* 21–26 (Tanner 1990:979–981).
19. Mahoney (1987, ch.7).
20. Bernard Häring alleges that 'the whole document is directed above all
    toward one goal: to endorse total assent and submission to all utterances
    of the Pope, and above all on one crucial point: that the use of any artificial
    means of regulating birth is intrinsically evil and sinful, without excep-
    tion, even in circumstances where contraception would be a lesser evil.'
    (Haring 1993:1378)

    This reading of the encyclical can only be regarded as an example of
    eisegesis by a theologian who was much involved in the debates following
    Humanae vitae and to whom contemporary debates in Catholic moral
    theology still seem to be viewed through this lens. McBrien, no fan of
    Veritatis splendor, admits that, 'he official teaching on birth control is not
    cloaked in the mantle of infallibility (indeed, contraception is mentioned
    only in passing)' (McBrien 1993).

21. Contraception is mentioned twice, in sections 47 and 80.
22. Again prescinding from whether such criticisms are apt and whether they do not themselves rest on a distinction of fact and value (going back to David Hume) that is unsustainable, see *Veritatis splendor*, pp. 47–48.
23. *On the Formation of Future Priests*, published 22 February 1976 by the Congregation for Catholic Education n. 96 quoted by Pinckaers 1995b.
24. Note that Curran uses the term 'Christian ethics' rather than 'moral theology'. There is an irony that while the established Catholic term is moral theology, the methodology used before and often still the methodology used after the Council is rarely theological. In contrast the established term in Reformed theology is 'Christian ethics', and yet there are far fewer Protestant theologians who would advocate the view that Christian ethics is simply generic ethics that happens to be done by Christians.
25. In this regard there is a curious historical irony as the line taken by defenders of proportionalism reflects almost exactly the line taken by the Jansenist Antoine Arnauld to the condemnation of Jansenism by Pope Innocent X in 1653 in *Cum occasione*. Arnauld asserted that, while he accepted the condemnation of the five propositions, and hence rejected those propositions, he did not agree that these propositions were actually contained in the works of Jansen, or if they were found there, it was in another sense than in the condemnation. The condemnation of Jansenism was, of course, welcomed by the Society of Jesus.

Bibliography

Anscombe G.E.M. (1981) 'Faith', in Anscombe G.E.M. *Ethics, Religion and Politics: Collected Philosophical Papers*, Vol. III, Oxford: Basil Blackwell, pp. 113–120.

Banner, M. (1999) 'Catholics and Anglicans and Contemporary Bioethics: divided or united?', in L. Gormally (ed.) *Issues for a Catholic Bioethics*, London: the Linacre Centre, pp. 34–57.

Boyle, L. (1974) '*The Summa Confessorum* of John of Freiburg and the popularization of the moral teaching of St. Thomas and of some of his contemporaries', in Mauer, A. (eds) *St. Thomas Aquinas 1274–1974 Commemorative Studies*, Toronto: Pontifical Institute of Mediaeval Studies.

Boyle, L. (1982) *The Setting of the Summa of St Thomas Aquinas*, The Etienne Gilson Series 5, Toronto: Pontifical Institute of Mediaeval Studies.

Curran, C. (1971) 'The Role and Function of the Scriptures in Moral theology' reprinted in C. Curran and R. McCormick (eds) (1984) *Moral Theology No. 4: The Use of Scripture in Moral Theology*, New York: Paulist Press, pp. 178–212.

Curran, C. (2005) *The Moral Theology of John Paul II*, London: T & T Clark.

Deidun, T (1998) 'The Bible and Christian Ethics', in B. Hoose (ed.) *Christian Ethics: An Introduction*, London: Cassell, pp. 3–46.

Davis, H. (1935) *Moral and Pastoral Theology*, 4 vols, London: Sheed and Ward.

Gallagher, J. A. (1990) *Time Past, Time Future: A Historical Study of Catholic Moral Theology*, New York: Paulist Press.

Génicot, E. and Salsmans, J. (1927) *Instituta Theologiae Moralis*, 2 vols, Bruxelles: A. Dewit.

Hamel, E (1973) 'Scripture, the Soul of Moral Theology?', in C. Curran and R. McCormick (eds) (1984) *Moral Theology No. 4: The Use of Scripture in Moral Theology*, New York: Paulist Press, pp. 105–132.

Häring, B. (1993) 'A Distrust that wounds', *Tablet* 247 (23 October 1993) pp. 1378–1379.

Hauerwas, S, Burrell, D. (1994) 'The Splendor of Truth: A Symposium' *First Things* 39 (January 1994), pp. 21–23.

John Paul II (1995) *Evangelium vitae.*

John Paul II (1993) *Veritatis splendor.*

John Paul II (1981) *Familiaris consortio.*

John Paul II (1997) *The Theology of the Body: Human Love in the Divine Plan*, Boston: Pauline Books & Media (addresses originally given 1979–1984).

John Paul II (1996) *Love and Responsibility* trans. H.T. Willetts, New York: Farrar, Straus, & Giroux (originally published in 1960).

John Paul II (1979) *The Acting Person*, Dordrecht: D. Reidel Publishing Co.

Koch, A. and Preuss, A. (1924) *A Handbook of Moral Theology*, 5 vols, St. Louis: B. Herder Book Co.

Johnson, L.T (2001) 'A Disembodied "Theology of the Body": John Paul II on Love, Sex, and Pleasure', *Commonweal* 128 (26 January 2001) pp. 11–17.

Kurz, W (2007) 'The Scriptural Foundations of The Theology of the Body', in J. M. McDermott and J. Gavin (eds) *John Paul II on the Body: Human, Eucharistic, Ecclesial*, Philadelphia: St Joseph's University Press, pp. 27–46.

MacIntyre, A. (1994) 'How Can We Learn what *Veritatis Splendor* has To Teach?', *The Thomist* 58 (1994) pp. 171–195.

Mahoney, J. (1987) *The Making of Moral Theology*, Oxford: Clarendon Press.

May, W.E. (2004) 'Pope John Paul II's Encyclical *Veritatis Splendor* and Bioethics', in C. Olafsen, *Pope John Paul II and Bioethics*, Dordrecht: Kluwer Academic Publishers (Philosophy and Medicine Series), pp. 35–50.

May, W.E. (2005) 'Charles E. Curran's Grossly Inaccurate Attack on the Moral Theology of John Paul II' http://www.christendom-awake.org/pages/may/curran.htm, 25 March 2008.

McBrien, R. (1993) 'Teaching the truth; John Paul II on Moral Theology' *Christian Century* 20 October 1993, pp. 1004–1006.

McCormick, R. (1981) 'Scripture, Liturgy, Character, and Morality', reprinted in C. Curran and R. McCormick (eds) (1984) *Moral Theology, The Use of Scripture in Moral theology*, New York: Paulist Press, pp. 289–302.

McCormick, R. (1994) 'Some early Reactions to *Veritatis Splendor*', *Moral Theology No. 4 Theological Studies* 55 (1994) pp. 481–506.

McCormick, R. (1999) 'Moral Theology 1940–1989: An Overview', in C. Curran and R. McCormick (eds) (1999) *The Historical Development of Fundamental Moral Theology in the United States*, New York: Paulist Press, pp. 46–73.

McHugh, J. A. and Callan, C. J. (1929) *Moral Theology: a complete course based on St. Thomas Aquinas and the best modern authorities* 2 vols, New York: Joseph F. Wagner, Inc.

McKeever, P. E. (1999) 'Seventy-Five Years of Moral Theology in America', in C. Curran and R. McCormick (eds) (1999) *The Historical Development of Fundamental Moral Theology in the United States*, New York: Paulist Press, pp. 5–21.

Meilaender, G. (1995) '*Veritatis Splendor*: Reopening Some Questions of the Reformation', *Journal of Religious Ethics* 23 (1995), pp. 225–238.

Merkelbach, B. H. (1946) *Summa Theologia Moralis* 3 vols, 3rd ed. Paris: Desclee de Brouwer et Cie.

Modras, R (1994) 'Some Notes on the Margins of *Veritatis Splendor*', ARCC Light 15/9 (January 1994), pp. 1–2.

Moore, G (1994) 'Some remarks on the use of scripture in *Veritatis Splendor*', in J. Selling and J. Jans (eds) *The Splendor of Accuracy: An Examination of the Assertions made by Veritatis Splendor*, Grand Rapids, Mich.: Eerdmans, pp. 71–97.

Noldin, H. and Schmitt, A. (1927) *Summa Theologia Moralis* 3 vols, Vienna: Fel. Rauch.

O'Donovan, O. (2005) 'Pope John-Paul II' http://www.fulcrum-anglican.org.uk/news/2005/20050418odonovan.cfm?doc=26, 25 March 2008.

O'Donovan, O. (1996) 'Review of *Evangelium Vitae*', *Studies in Christian Ethics* 9 (1996) p. 94.

Paul VI (1968) *Humanae vitae.*

Pinckaers, S. (1995a) *The Sources of Christian Ethics* trans. M.T. Noble, Washington: Catholic University of America Press.

Pinckaers, S. (1995b) 'The Use of Scripture and the Renewal of Moral Theology: The *Catechism* and *Veritatis Splendor*', *The Thomist* 59 (1995) pp. 1–19.

Pius IX (1930) *Casti connubii.*

Pius XII, *Allocution to Midwives,* 29 October 1951.

Prümmer, M. (1928) *Manuale Theologiae Moralis,* 3 vols, Freiburg: Herder.

Sabetti, A. and Barrett, T. (1924) *Compendium Theologiae Moralis*, 30ᵗʰ ed. New York: Frederick Pustet.

Slater, T. (1908) *A Manual of Moral Theology for English-Speaking Catholics*, New York: Benziger Bros.

Slater, T. (1925) *Back to Morality*, London: Burns Oates & Washbourne.

Stegman, T. (2007) 'Actualisation: How John Paul II Utilizes Scripture in *The Theology of the Body*: A Response to William S. Kurz', in J. McDermott and J. Gavin (eds) *John Paul II on the Body: Human, Eucharistic, Ecclesial*, Philadelphia: St Joseph's University Press, pp. 47–64.

Schüssler Fiorenza, E. (1983) *In Memory of Her: a Feminist Theological Reconstruction of Christian Origins*, London: SCM Press.

Tanner, N. ed. (1990) *Decrees of the Ecumenical Councils*, London: Sheed and Ward.

Vann, G. (1937) *Morals Makyth Man*, London: Longmans, Green and co.

Yeago, D. (1998) 'Martin Luther On Grace, Law, And Moral Life: Prolegomena to an Ecumenical Discussion of *Veritatis Splendor*', *The Thomist* 62 (1998) pp. 163–191.

Zalba, M. (1958) *Theologiae Moralis Compendium*, 2 vols, Madrid: Biblioteca De Autores Cristianos.

Chapter 6

The Legacy of Pope John Paul II: Ecumenical Dialogue

Archbishop Kevin J. P. McDonald

Pope John Paul II's pontificate (1978–2005) was one of the longest in history. It was also extraordinarily prolific in all sorts of ways and, of course, in ways that simply would not have been possible in previous generations. But when people think about Pope John Paul II, about his message, his priorities, his legacy, they might not think immediately of the areas of ecumenism and interreligious dialogue. Media attention, certainly in this country, tended to be focused elsewhere. From 1985 to 1993 I worked for the Pope in ecumenism in the Secretariat for Christian Unity which in 1988 became the Pontifical Council for Promoting Christian Unity. It was frequently a disappointment for me that the British media did not seem either interested in, or able to grasp, the huge significance of some of the ecumenical and interreligious events that took place during those years. Let me give just one example. In 1986, the Pope called together Christian leaders and other religious leaders from all over the world to pray for peace in Assisi. It was a historic gesture of huge significance and was virtually ignored by the British press. One person who did understand its significance was Robert Runcie, the then Archbishop of Canterbury, who also realized that only the Pope could have done this. He said, 'In Assisi we saw that the Bishop of Rome could gather the Christian Churches together. We would pray together, speak together and act together for the peace and well-being of humankind, and the stewardship of our precious earth.' He went on to ask: 'Could not all Christians come to reconsider the kind of primacy that the Bishop of Rome exercised within the early

Church, a 'presiding in love' for the sake of the unity of the Churches in the diversity of their mission?.'

Pope John Paul II's contribution to the ecumenical movement was simply colossal. His countless pastoral visits around the world very often included a significant ecumenical component. He met with most other Christian leaders, made many joint statements that were sometimes a real breakthrough, and presided over many ecumenical dialogues that were undertaken and pursued on his behalf by the Pontifical Council for Promoting Christian Unity. My own particular brief included relations with the Anglicans and Methodists, but our office was also engaged in dialogue with the Oriental Orthodox Churches, the Byzantine Orthodox, Lutherans, the World Alliance of Reformed Churches, the Disciples of Christ, Baptists, Pentecostals and Evangelical groups. Again, I would point to two things that were not well understood in England. One was the immense significance of relations with the Churches of the East, both Orthodox and Oriental Orthodox. It was Pope John Paul who initiated the Catholic–Orthodox dialogue when he visited Constantinople in 1979, and it is my view that the early reports of that dialogue are among the most profound ecclesiological writings of modern times. Of course, huge problems arose with the fall of Communism and the revival of the Eastern-rite Catholic Churches. This created a very difficult and hugely complex situation which the Pope negotiated very diplomatically. Another point not well understood was the seriousness with which the Pope took relations with Protestant Ecclesial Communities that were far removed in theology and ecclesiology from the Catholic Church. Sometimes Anglicans or Catholics would say to me that if the Church of England went ahead with the ordination of women that would be the end of ecumenical relations between Catholics and Anglicans. I had to remind them that the Catholic Church held extremely fruitful dialogues with Ecclesial Communities that were much more distant historically and theologically from the Catholic Church than were the Anglicans.

The Pope had an open heart and an ecumenical heart. The fact that he was very firm and clear on matters of doctrinal and moral orthodoxy was seen by some as a sign that he was not fully ecumenical, though how one could arrive at that conclusion from those premises is quite unclear to me. Ecumenism was integral to his whole understanding of his ministry.

Some key developments

Before looking in more detail at Pope John Paul II's contribution to ecumenism and at the progress that took place during his papacy, it is good to remind ourselves of some key developments in the twentieth century that brought the modern ecumenical movement into being. It is generally agreed that the modern ecumenical movement began with the World Missionary Conference in Edinburgh in 1910. This was a gathering of Protestant missionaries. It was at this meeting that it became clear that there was a fundamental problem in their missionary endeavours, namely that the one Gospel of Jesus Christ was being preached from competing and, indeed, conflicting pulpits. The need was clearly seen for collaboration and for common witness. Out of this meeting grew two movements which were designed to address these problems and which went on to shape ecumenism throughout the century; they were Life and Work, and Faith and Order. Life and Work was concerned with the challenge to Christians to work and witness together practically as much as possible. Faith and Order was concerned with the need to work for agreement of faith since Christians can only preach and worship together to the extent that they share a common faith. Out of these movements grew the World Council of Churches (WCC), which came into being in Amsterdam in 1948 and became a key institution in modern ecumenism. The Orthodox Churches joined the WCC, but the Catholic Church never has for both practical and theological reasons. But the Catholic Church works closely with the WCC. The Faith and Order Movement became the Faith and Order Commission of the WCC and the Catholic Church is a full member of that body. The most important fruit of that Commission was the so-called Lima document on Baptism, Eucharist and Ministry (BEM). This text, published in 1984, was the result of 50 years of multilateral dialogue involving the whole spectrum of Christianity. It addressed three key divisive issues on which agreement would be vital for Christian unity. The document is not a statement of agreement but it articulated the nature and degree of agreement that existed at the time and detailed the outstanding areas of disagreement. The Catholic Church is also involved with the WCC through a body called the Joint Working Group which draws together representatives of the Catholic Church and the WCC.

Lumen gentium

The Catholic Church entered the ecumenical movement at Vatican II and its involvement with the WCC dates from then. Obviously I can't deal in detail with the Catholic Church's engagement with the ecumenical movement but I want to mention some key developments which shaped the ecumenical scene which John Paul II inherited. Crucial was the Dogmatic Constitution on the Church, *Lumen gentium*, which formally adopted an inclusive attitude to other Christians by affirming the importance of our common baptism. This was followed by the Decree on Ecumenism, *Unitatis redintegratio* which said: 'Those people who believe in Christ and have been properly baptised are put in some though imperfect, communion with the Catholic Church' (no.3) That word communion was and has remained fundamental, and I will come back to it. The Catholic Church believes that all the gifts that Christ wishes to bestow on his Church for its life and witness are fully present in the Catholic Church. Other Churches and Ecclesial Communities share these gifts in varying degrees. As regards the Eastern Orthodox Church we recognize that they share the same ministry and sacraments. Pope Paul VI spoke of an 'almost complete communion' between the Catholic and the Eastern Orthodox. With the Protestant Ecclesial Communities, we do not have that degree of communion but crucially we have a common baptism, common scriptures and many other common gifts as well.

Pope John XXIII set up the Secretariat for Christian Unity prior to Vatican II, and after the Council, Pope Paul II made it an integral department of the Roman Curia tasked with taking forward the ecumenical agenda that emerged from the Council. That agenda was to enter into dialogue with our fellow Christians in other Churches and Ecclesial Communities with a view to moving from a situation of imperfect communion to one of full communion of faith and sacramental life. The work was already well in hand when Pope John Paul II was elected in 1978.

John Paul II after His Election

It was clear that Pope John Paul II understood the challenge of the ecumenical movement from the outset and saw it as a key dimension of his papacy. He initiated new dialogues, encouraged those already in progress and was unrelenting in pursuing the cause of Christian Unity. One particular feature of his understanding of the ecumenical task and of ecumenical dialogue was that of seeing it as the reclaiming of a common heritage. He visited the World Council of Churches at their offices in Geneva in 1984, and said that the Catholic Church and the WCC member churches 'have never ceased to have in common many elements and endowments which together build up and give life to the Church'. Obviously he was referring in particular to our common baptism and Scriptures. And he also said: 'The teaching of the First Council of Constantinople is still the expression of the one faith of the whole of the Christian Community.'

And these kinds of convictions found their way into his more general teaching. His first encyclical was *Redemptor hominis* (1979) in which he clearly saw all Christians as sharing in and witnessing to the redemption and called Christian unity 'the will of Jesus Christ himself' (no. 6). The Pope designated 1983–1984 as a special Holy Year marking the 1950th anniversary of the death and resurrection of Jesus. Speaking of its ecumenical significance, he said: 'Celebrating the redemption, we go beyond historical misunderstanding and contingent controversies, in order to meet each other in the common ground of our being Christian, that is redeemed. The Redemption unites all of us in the one love of Christ, crucified and risen'.

He also saw the saints as constituting our common heritage of holiness and expressed this very clearly at the time of the millennium, the Great Jubilee of 2000. In the document *Tertio millennio adveniente* (1994) he wrote: 'Perhaps the most convincing form of ecumenism is the ecumenism of the saints and martyrs. The *communio sanctorum* speaks louder than the things which divide us' (no., 37). His great encyclical on ecumenism, *Ut unum sint* (1995), takes this further. He says the incomplete communion among Christians

is truly and solidly grounded in the full communion of the Saints – those who at the end of a life faithful to grace are in communion with Christ in glory. These saints come from the Churches and Ecclesial Communities which gave them entrance into the communion of salvation. (no. 84)

So he is speaking of Orthodox, Anglican and Protestant saints and martyrs as well as Catholic and saying that we must take our bearings for the modern ecumenical movement from them.

Reclaiming our shared heritage, and looking at our history together then was a key theme in Pope John Paul II's thinking on ecumenism and that shaped his view and his assessment of ecumenical dialogue in various ways. So let's look more closely at the actual dialogues that were taking place during his pontificate. Some, as I said, began before he became Pope. Others he initiated. Pope John Paul II fully endorsed the conviction that unity of faith is the prerequisite for full communion of faith and sacramental life, and saw dialogue as the path – albeit long and arduous – to realizing this goal. I well remember at a joint meeting of the Congregation of the Doctrine of Faith and the Pontifical Council for Promoting Christian Unity when he gave an address at the end of which he put down his text and said very simply that you cannot repair in a short period of time things that have been undone over a very long period of time. That I think is very important and I have always felt it unrealistic to expect ecumenical dialogue to yield results quickly. When divisions take place, differences are quickly compounded and it's important to remember that many of the most acute differences are of recent origin: I think, for example, of differences on issues of marriage and sexuality. They are differences that didn't really arise at the time of the historic divisions.

Dialogues

I think it's useful to distinguish between different kinds of ecumenical dialogue. I have mentioned the dialogue sponsored by the Faith and Order Commission of the WCC. That is a multilateral dialogue involving a wide spectrum of Christian Churches and Ecclesial Communities. Most dialogue is bilateral, however, and when I was working in Rome the Catholic Church was involved in 11 bilateral conversations. I referred to them earlier. I think an important distinction has to be drawn between dialogues with Churches or Ecclesial Communities with whom the Catholic Church has had a historic break – the Orthodox, Lutheran, the Reformed and the Anglicans – and those communities that have come into being since the Reformation – Methodists and Pentecostals. The dynamic is quite different. With those Churches and Ecclesial Communities with which the Catholic Church has broken in the past, ecumenical dialogue has tended to focus on the specific issues that caused or compounded the break in communion. With the others, it has been a question of discerning the most promising topics for finding rapprochement.

But what is dialogue and how does it work? This is something that is often not well understood. Pope Paul VI's encyclical *Ecclesiam suam* (1964) was a foundational text for dialogue and, indeed, for contemporary Catholicism. He spoke of Christianity as being essentially dialogical in nature. He said: 'This relationship, this dialogue, which God the Father initiated and established with us through Christ in the Holy Spirit, is a very real one, even though it is difficult to express in words' (no. 71). And he went into a very profound reflection on what dialogue is. Pope John Paul II in his encyclical *Ut unum sint* gave his own distinctive understanding of the importance of dialogue and since this touches on the heart of my topic today, I'll quote it more extensively. He wrote:

> If prayer is the 'soul' of ecumenical renewal and of yearning for unity, it is the basis and support for *everything the Council defines as 'dialogue'* . . . This definition is certainly not unrelated to today's *personalist way of thinking*. The capacity for 'dialogue' is rooted in the nature of the person and his dignity. As seen by philosophy this approach is linked to the Christian truth concerning man as expressed by the Council: man is in fact 'the only creature on earth which God willed for itself'. Dialogue is an indispensable step along the path *towards human self-realisation*, the self -realisation both of *each individual and of every human community*. Although the concept of 'dialogue' might appear to give priority to the cognitive dimension *(dia-logos)*, all dialogue implies a global, existential dimension. It involves the human subject in his or her entirety; dialogue between communities involves in a particular way the subjectivity of each. (no. 28)

Several points about this profound articulation of the meaning of dialogue merit mention here. Just as Paul VI showed that dialogue is integral to Christianity, Pope John Paul II saw it as integral to being a person. It is something that profoundly engages the human subject and not just at the intellectual level. It also engages communities as well as individuals. It is part of life.

Crucially, dialogue is part of the life of the Church today as the Pope goes on to affirm:

> Dialogue is also a natural instrument for comparing different points of views and, above all, for examining those disagreements which hinder full communion between Christians . . . There must be charity towards one's partner in dialogue, and humility with regard to the faith which comes to light and which might require a review of assertions and attitudes. (no. 36)

In these words, Pope John Paul II is making the culture of dialogue his own and making his own contribution to Church teaching about dialogue. His profound understanding of dialogue is evident not only from what he said about it but from the fact that so many dialogues were prolifically fruitful during his pontificate. Before going on to consider particular dialogues that flourished during his pontificate, it is important to note some key points about dialogue which he endorsed both in principle and in practice.

One is about the method of dialogue which depends on a crucial distinction that was famously articulated by Pope John XXIII at the beginning of the Council. He said:

> This certain and unchangeable doctrine, to which faithful obedience is due, has to be explored and presented in a way that is demanded by our times. The deposit of faith which consists of the truth contained in sacred doctrine, is one thing, the manner of presentation, always however with the same meaning and signification, is always something else.

This statement was made in relation to the overall theological renewal which the Council sought to bring about but it has frequently been invoked to explain the method of ecumenical dialogue: to find language that expresses fully the faith of both parties but which avoids concepts and terminologies that were divisive in the past. We shall see how Pope

John Paul II himself adopted this method very significantly in his joint statements with leaders of the ancient Oriental Churches. But he expressed it himself in an address to members of the Anglican–Roman Catholic International Commission (ARCIC) in 1980:

> Your method has been to go behind the habit of thought and expression born and nourished in enmity and controversy to scrutinize together the great common treasure, to clothe it in a language at once traditional and expressive of the insights of an age which no longer glorifies in strife, but seeks to come together in listening to the quiet voice of the Spirit.

I want to mention two other methodological principles that were central to the progress and development of ecumenical dialogue during Pope John Paul II's long pontificate. One was what I would call the principle of gradualism – beginning by articulating together those things that the two parties are agreed on and building on that in order to eventually address and articulate together the issues that have been historically divisive.

The other is the use of the theological concept of *koinonia* (communion) as an agreed theological framework within which to explore together issues that have been historically divisive. We have already referred to its significance for explaining ecumenism in the Conciliar texts *Lumen gentium* and *Unitatis redintegratio.* Ecumenical dialogue is possible to the extent that the partners in dialogue recognize one another as fellow sharers in the gifts of the Holy Spirit. As we said earlier, from the Catholic point of view, the strongest recognition is of the Eastern Churches whose sacraments and ordination we recognize. Shared baptism is the basis of dialogue with the Churches and Ecclesial Communities of the West, and this should not be underestimated since it is absolutely fundamental.

Dialogues under John Paul II

So let us turn, then, to some of the dialogues that were initiated or taken forward during the pontificate of Pope John Paul II. It is not possible to go into them in detail or to look at all of them. I will speak presently of the Anglican–Roman Catholic dialogue, but I will begin by talking about the dialogue with the Eastern Churches. As I have said, Pope John Paul II saw *all* ecumenical dialogue as important and as being a serious personal responsibility. Inevitably, though, both for theological reasons and because of his own background as an Eastern European, this dialogue assumed a particular significance. It was Pope John Paul II's view that reconciliation between Eastern and Western Christianity would benefit the whole of the ecumenical movement because – as he said on numerous occasions – it would enable the Church to breathe with both lungs.

Addressing the Secretariat for Christian Unity in 1980, he said:

I am convinced that a re-articulation of the ancient Eastern and Western traditions and the balancing exchange that will result when full communion is found again, may be of great importance to heal the divisions that came about in the West in the 16ᵗʰ Century.

The Eastern Churches, of course, fall into two distinct categories. There are Oriental Orthodox Churches (also known as the Ancient Oriental Churches) and the Byzantine Churches: the 14 autocephalous (independent) Eastern Churches that are in communion with the Ecumenical Patriarch in Constantinople. These are usually referred to simply as the Orthodox Church.

The oldest division in Christianity was with the Oriental Orthodox Churches – those which rejected the dogmatic formulations of the Council of Ephesus (431) and the Council of Chalcedon (451). What they rejected was the *language* of the teaching that Christ was a divine person with two natures, one human and one divine. These were the great Christological controversies which were central to the first serious rupture within Christianity. As always happens when communion is broken, differences are compounded and different theological, liturgical and cultural traditions develop. The gifts bestowed on one communion are not able to be at the service of the whole Church as they would be if there was full communion of faith and sacramental life. The dialogues with these Churches therefore – separated from the West for 1600 years – was an ambitious venture. Already in 1973, Pope Paul VI had made a Common Declaration with Pope Shenouda III, Pope of Alexandria and Head of the Coptic Church in Egypt, in which they

expressed together their faith in Christ but without using the historically divisive language of 'person' and 'nature'. They also set up a joint
commission between the Catholic Church and the Coptic Church to
address outstanding differences. That dialogue was ongoing during my
time in Rome.

Pope John Paul II picked up on the dialogue with the Oriental
Orthodox Churches, and in 1984 made a Common Declaration with
Mar Ignatius Zakka 'I was, the Head of the Syrian Orthodox Church,
another of this group of Churches. Pope Paul VI had already made an
agreed statement of Christological faith with the previous head of the
Syrian Orthodox Church in 1971. Pope John Paul II ratified this
agreement and built on it. A few quotations give a flavour of the 1984
Common Declaration.

> We wish to reaffirm solemnly our profession of common faith in the
> incarnation of Our Lord Jesus Christ, as Pope Paul VI and Patriarch
> Moran Mor Ignatius Jacoub III did in 1971. They denied there was
> any difference in the faith they confessed in the mystery of the Word
> of God made flesh and become truly man. In our turn, we confess
> that He became incarnate for us, taking to himself a real body with a
> rational soul. He shared our humanity in all things except sin. We
> confess that our Lord and our God, our Saviour and the King of all,
> Jesus Christ, is perfect God as to his divinity and perfect man as to
> His humanity.

The Declaration goes on to affirm that the Catholic Church and the
Syrian Orthodox Church share the same sacraments 'in one and the
same succession of Apostolic Ministry'. The Declaration also has practical implications. While it recognizes that the two Churches are not at
the point where they can concelebrate the Eucharist, permission is given
in the case of real pastoral need for members of one Church to seek the
sacraments from priests of the other Church.

Needless to say, much work is needed and still needs to be done in
developing this dialogue and in 'receiving' these agreements at grass
roots level. But Pope John Paul II gave a significant lead and during his
pontificate four other Churches from this group entered into this process of reconciliation. In 1999, Cardinal Cassidy, then President of the

Pontifical Council for Promoting Christian Unity, affirmed that the ancient Christological controversies are now virtually resolved.

The other group of Eastern Churches, as I have said, are referred to simply as the Orthodox Church. The split with these Churches is usually dated as beginning with the mutual anathemas of 1054. Both Eastern and Western Christianity had been growing apart throughout the first millennium. The final blow came at the time of the Fourth Crusade when Latin Christians from the West turned on Eastern Christians in Constantinople (1204). That sealed the separation and break in communion, and in the intervening centuries there has been little contact between Eastern and Western Christianity. The West lived through the great Christian Middle Ages, the Reformation, the Catholic Reformation, the Enlightenment and in the Catholic Church the great renewal of Vatican II. So when during, and after, Vatican II the Catholic Church reached out to the Orthodox Church, it was two very different kinds of churches that were looking at each other.

The cultural differences are enormous but the principal theological issue between the two is the question of the Bishop of Rome: the Papacy. For many Orthodox, it is the symbol and sign of the difference between Eastern Christianity and Western Christianity. And the first significant contact between the two Churches was the personal contact between Pope Paul VI and the Ecumenical Patriarch. The Ecumenical Patriarch, Patriarch of Constantinople, has a primacy of honour among the Patriarchs of the 14 Orthodox Churches. Pope Paul VI built up a very close relationship with the Ecumenical Patriarch Athenagoras who he met in the Holy Land and their correspondence is a remarkable testament to ecumenical love and fraternity. It was published under the title of the *Tomos Agapis*. This was the groundwork that had been done when Pope John Paul II became Pope, and he built on it systematically and enthusiastically. Pope Paul and Patriarch Athenagoras had already spoken about their Churches as 'Sister Churches' and Pope John Paul II, speaking of the ecumenical journey, said 'the traditional designation of "Sister Churches" should ever accompany us along this path.'

The official dialogue between the Catholic Church and the Orthodox Church began with Pope John Paul II's visit to Constantinople in 1979. The dialogue that grew out of that visit was at a very high level in that on both sides there were members whose ecclesiastical position meant that they could speak officially for their Churches. On the Orthodox side, there were 14 Metropolitan Archbishops from each of the 14 Autocephalous Orthodox Churches together with 14 theologians. On the Catholic side, there were 14 Cardinals and Bishops plus 14 theologians. So the 'Sister Churches' came together, engaged in articulating what they had in common and seeking to focus accurately what divided them. Their first report published in July 1982 was entitled *The Mystery of the Church and of the Eucharist in the Light of the Mystery of the Holy Trinity*. They explicitly acknowledged that in the theology of *koinonia*, the Commission found the possibility of articulating and substantiating their agreement.

Dialogue reports were subsequently published in 1987 and 1988 and the approach was gradualist. The concept of *koinonia* enabled the participants to express a shared and agreed understanding of the Church, of sacraments, and of the ordained ministry. In his encyclical *Ut unum sint*, Pope John Paul II acknowledged and affirmed the achievements of this dialogue. He recognized that Catholics and the Orthodox were able to express a shared and agreed understanding of the Church and said 'in our Churches apostolic succession is fundamental for the sanctification and unity of the people of God.' He wrote, 'these affirmations are important points of reference for the continuation of the dialogue' and that they 'represent the basis for Catholics and Orthodox to be able from now on to bear a faithful and united common witness in our time, that the name of the Lord may be proclaimed and glorified' (UUS,59).

But the dialogue, so rich and so promising ran into serious difficulties with the fall of European Communism in 1989. This event brought with it the re-emergence and revival of the Eastern-Rite Catholic Churches. These were churches which celebrated the liturgy according to the Orthodox rites but which at different stages in previous centuries had entered into communion with Rome and so became Catholics of the Eastern-rite. These Churches, referred to disparagingly as 'Uniate' Churches, were driven underground by the communist governments of the Warsaw Pact. They had always been a bone of contention with the Orthodox Churches who saw them at the fruit of Catholic proselytizing on Orthodox territory. Their revival saw bitter disputes between Orthodox and Eastern Rite Catholics about ownership of Church buildings, specially in the Western Ukraine. These developments created huge strains for the dialogue and effectively put it on hold. Pope John Paul II had the delicate task of combining pastoral care for the reviving Eastern Rite Catholic Churches with maintaining the dialogue with the Orthodox.

So it was that instead of moving towards discussion of the key issue of papal primacy on the basis of agreement in ministry and apostolic succession, the Orthodox insisted that the dialogue address the question of Uniatism. In 1993, a joint statement was published significantly entitled *Uniatism, Method of Union of the Past, and the Present Search for Full Communion*. Pope John Paul II in his public utterances urged dialogue to resolve practical property issues, but was quite clear that the Orthodox Churches are 'Sister Churches' and that Catholics should not proselytize in Orthodox territories. Tensions still exist to this day especially with the Russian Orthodox, but the dialogue is now up back on track and is building on the earlier statements as a framework for exploring together, historically and theologically, the question of the universal primacy of the Bishop of Rome.

Turning to the Churches and Ecclesial Communities of the West, I cannot go into all dialogues in detail. I repeat what I said earlier that Pope John Paul II had a deep sense of responsibility for all these dialogues, and my observation was that the dialogue with the Lutherans was particularly dear to his heart. His visits to the Scandinavian Lutheran Churches were especially significant as was their return visits to Rome. One of the most dramatic ecumenical events of the 1990s was the development and official acceptance by the Lutheran World Federation and the Catholic Church of the *Joint Declaration on the Doctrine of Justification*. In 1998, Cardinal Cassidy, then President of the Pontifical Council for Promoting Christian Unity, said 'it virtually resolves a long disputed question at the close of the twentieth century', even though the agreement itself acknowledged issues that required further work and clarification between the two sides. I would also want to mention the dialogue between the Catholic Church and the World Methodist Council. This dialogue has produced numerous joint statements of great theological depth exploring the fundamental questions that must be addressed in all ecumenical dialogue – Scripture, Tradition, Church and Sacraments. The reports constitute a great resource of serious ecumenical theology that can serve the ecumenical movement as a whole.

I want to move on, however, to the dialogue with the Anglican Communion. Like the Catholic–Methodist one, this is a dialogue I know
about at first hand and which for various reasons attracts a great deal
of interest and attention. Unlike the dialogue with the Orthodox, the
Anglican–Roman Catholic dialogue was well under way when Pope
John Paul II began his ministry in 1978. It began with the Common
Declaration signed in 1966 by Pope Paul and the then Archbishop of
Canterbury, Dr Michael Ramsey. The Anglicans had been among the
most enthusiastic in their response to the ecumenical initiative of
Vatican II, and Archbishop Ramsey was very quick to visit Rome after
the Council. In their joint declaration they said:

> In willing obedience to the command of Christ who bade his disci-
> ples to love one another, they declare that, with his help, they wish to
> leave in the hands of the God of mercy all that in the past has been
> opposed to this precept of charity, and that they make their own the
> mind of the Apostle which he expressed in these words: 'Forgetting
> those things which are behind, and reaching forth unto those which
> are before, I press towards the mark for the prize of the high calling
> of God in Christ Jesus.' (cf Phil. 3.13–14)

A joint preparatory Commission was set up which produced the
Malta Report (1968) which was important in proposing practical steps
towards rapprochement between Catholics and Anglicans. The first
Anglican–Roman Catholic International Commission (ARCIC) met in
1970 and its work continued into the papacy of John Paul II and concluded in 1981. It produced seven agreed statements on three topics:
Eucharist, Ministry and Ordination, and Authority in the Church. The
choice of topics was determined by the factors that had been in play at
the time of the break between Rome and Canterbury in the sixteenth
century. The Anglican Church came into being because of political
rather than doctrinal factors, and Anglicanism has never been a
'confessional' body in the way that Lutheranism is. However, doctrinal
matters did emerge and placed the Church of England doctrinally
clearly within the Protestant fold. This was certainly the view of *Apostolicae Curae*, the Apostolic Letter of Leo XIII which in 1898 judged
Anglican Ordinations to be invalid. His judgement was that the doctrine

concerning Eucharist and priesthood expressed in and, indeed, controlling the composition of the *Anglican Ordinal* of 1552 was such as to lead to defects both in the sacramental form and in the intention which the rite expressed. Basically, therefore, it was not and could not be a means for conferring Catholic ordinations.

The method adopted by ARCIC was to go back to scriptural and patristic sources to see whether *today* Anglicans and Catholics professed the same faith on the Eucharist and ministry. If it could be confirmed that they did, then although many outstanding issues would remain to be explored, a major blockage would be removed for moving beyond the judgement of *Apostolicae Curae*. At the end of their deliberations, the Commission claimed to have reached 'substantial agreement' on the Eucharist and the ordained ministry and a degree of convergence on authority in the Church.

It is noteworthy that the theme of *koinonia* was key to their agreement. In the introduction to the Final Report they say:

> Union with God in Christ Jesus through the Spirit is the heart of the Christian *koinonia*. Among the various ways in which the term *koinonia* is used in different New Testament contexts, we concentrate on that which signifies a relation between persons resulting from their participation in one and the same reality (cf 1 John 1: 3) . . . This theme of *koinonia* runs through our statements. In them we present the Eucharist as the effectual sign of koinonia, *episcope* envisaged as serving the *koinonia*, and the primacy as a visible link and focus of *koinonia*. (Introduction to Final Report, 5)

There can be no doubt that the Final Report of ARCIC-I (as it came to be called) was an outstanding achievement. Precisely for that reason it elicited reaction and response.

The first came in 1982 with the *Observations* of the Congregation for the Doctrine of the Faith. We are now, of course, well into the papacy of Pope John Paul II and Cardinal Ratzinger, the Prefect of the Congregation for the Doctrine of the Faith, acknowledged ARCIC's achievement. He said: 'This work, achieved in common, is a singular event in the history of relations between the two Communions, and it is at the same time a notable effort towards reconciliation.'

However, the Congregation's conclusion was that:

the Final Report which represents a notable ecumenical endeavour and a useful basis for further stages on the road to reconciliation between the Catholic Church and the Anglican Communion does not yet constitute a substantial and explicit agreement on some essential elements of Catholic faith.

The 1988 Lambeth Conference provided the opportunity for the Anglicans to make their evaluation of the Final Report. The Bishops by a very large majority recognized the ARCIC agreements as 'consonant in substance with the faith of Anglicans'. On authority, the Agreed Statements were welcomed as 'a firm basis' for the future of the dialogue. Later in 1991 there was an official response to ARCIC-I by the Catholic Church which re-echoed in a more developed way the concerns of the 1982 *Observations*. Basically, the Catholic response, while supportive and appreciative of the work of ARCIC-I, thought that in claiming 'substantial agreement' on the Eucharist and Ordination it had claimed too much too soon.

In the meantime, however, another factor emerged which was to considerably compound the problems, namely the ordination of women. There were already women priests in the Anglican Communion when ARCIC-I was at work, but most provinces had not yet gone ahead with this development. It was the 1988 Lambeth Conference that acknowledged the right of individual provinces of the Anglican Communion – all of which are juridically independent – to make up their own minds on this issue. Archbishop Runcie wrote to Pope John Paul II after the Lambeth Conference to report on its decisions. The Pope's reply was significant. He acknowledged 'the signs of openness to fuller communion with the Catholic Church which were evident at several points in the Conference, not least in your opening address and in the resolutions on the final report of ARCIC-I'. But, he went on:

The Lambeth Conference's treatment of the question of women's ordination has revealed a new and perplexing situation for the members of the Second Anglican-Roman Catholic International Commission to whom in 1982 we gave the mandate of studying 'all that hinders the mutual recognition of the ministries of our communions'

. . . it appears to pre-empt this study and effectively block the path to the mutual recognition of ministries.

The year 1982 was, of course, the year of Pope John Paul II's historic visit to England which included the remarkable joint service in Canterbury Cathedral. During that visit, Pope John Paul II and Archbishop Runcie relaunched the Anglican–Roman Catholic International Commission as ARCIC-II to take the task forward. It subsequently has produced a series of important agreed statements. None of these, however, have been officially evaluated in the way that the First Report of ARCIC-I was. It has to be said that the ordination of women changed the atmosphere in Anglican–Catholic relations and affected expectations of what the dialogue could achieve. But the flame of hope is still burning and the continued desire for unity between Catholics and Anglicans is evident in the document *Growing Together in Unity and Mission*, produced by a more recent body called the International Anglican – Roman Catholic – Commission for Unity and Mission (IARCCUM).

The Anglican–Roman Catholic dialogue could be seen as focusing and illuminating Pope John Paul II's attitude towards ecumenism. He was an avid and committed promoter of ecumenical dialogue and saw himself as a key protagonist of it. He felt a keen sense of ecumenical responsibility and even spoke of himself as having primacy in the search for Christian unity. But his commitment to Christian unity went hand-in-hand with an unswerving commitment to the upholding of doctrinal truth. As I have already intimated, it would be false to see these two things as being in conflict. On the contrary, this creative tension was central to his contribution to Christian culture in the closing decades of the twentieth century. It was, perhaps, focused most of all in what he had to say about his own ministry. One could say that both with Eastern Christianity and Protestant Christianity his own ministry was seen by dialogue partners as both a source of hope and as the major stumbling block to Christian unity. He himself was acutely aware of this and longed for some way in which his own ministry of universal primacy could be at the service of all Christians. He expressed this on several occasions most notably in the encyclical *Ut unum sint:*

As Bishop of Rome I am fully aware, as I have reaffirmed in the present Encyclical Letter, that Christ ardently desires the full and visible communion of all those Communities in which, by virtue of God's faithfulness, his Spirit dwells. I am convinced that I have a particular responsibility in this regard, above all in acknowledging the ecumenical aspirations of the majority of Christian Communities and in heeding the request made of me to find a way of exercising the primacy which, while in no way renouncing what is essential to its mission, is nonetheless open to a new situation. (no. 95)

Pope John Paul II, as I have said, undoubtedly had a deep longing for Christian unity and saw it as integral to his mission. The time and energy he devoted to this cause was eloquent witness to that. Throughout his pontificate, ecumenical dialogue was pursued with enthusiastic commitment.

As I said earlier, once Communions are separated, differences are compounded. But there can be no going back in the Catholic Church's commitment to Christian unity. Vatican II made that clear and Pope John Paul II tirelessly implemented the teaching of the Council. His positive legacy is unquestionable, both in taking the enterprise forward and in honestly exposing the scale and complexity of the challenge.

Response to Chapter 6 Archbishop Kevin McDonald

The Legacy of Pope John Paul II: Ecumenical Dialogue

Rt Revd Christopher John Hill

This is not the first time Archbishop Kevin and I have done a double act: I hope it illustrates positively what Archbishop Kevin says about dialogue being at the heart of ecumenical method – and indeed 'being human': following Pope John Paul II's own understanding of humanity and being 'a person'. My response will be in two parts: first, some comments on the previous chapter and second, something more general of my own in assessing the ecumenical significance of Pope John Paul II and his pontificate.

I

My comments on Archbishop Kevin's text will be somewhat condensed and I hope you will forgive some shorthand. As Archbishop Kevin himself notes in his chapter, there cannot be space for fuller or an intensively detailed panorama of so large a subject.

a. I worked in the ecumenical bureau at Lambeth from 1974–1989. Like Archbishop Kevin (we were co-secretaries of ARCIC for a number of years) I had particular responsibilities but also saw the wider ecumenical picture. I agree that it was always disappointing – in the extreme – how little the British media – or others – understood of the significance of John Paul II's ecumenical initiatives. I think this lack of interest by the public and the media reflects something of the cultural and political 'isolationism' of Britain in respect to Europe. While the Pope's ministry is global, historically England (and I think I am right in saying England rather than the United Kingdom at this point) has regarded 'the Papacy' as another 'European Power' – as at the Congress of Vienna. This is a legacy of our 'unhappy divisions' (to quote the *Book of Common Prayer*) and the Henrician and Elizabethan invention – with the help of the common lawyers – of England as an 'Empire Sole'. So – to agree with John Paul II as quoted by Archbishop Kevin in addressing the Congregation for the Doctrine of the Faith (CDF) and the Pontifical Council for Promoting Christian Unity (PCCU) – 400 years of separation cannot be undone in even 40 years. I fear that over enthusiastic estimates – in the early days of ARCIC for example – of how quickly some degree of communion could be restored have led to a sense of disappointment that 'nothing happened' (I put this in quotes) following the work of ARCIC-I. So John Paul II was blamed as a 'conservative' (again in quotes). There remains further a certain pent up resentment among Anglicans over *Apostolicae Curae* which blocks recognition of other ecumenical achievement.

b. Archbishop Kevin cites *Lumen gentium* and *Unitatis redintegratio* as foundational. To these I would add the Decrees on the Liturgy and on Religious Freedom, and, particularly, *Dei verbum* as Vatican II documents which were explicitly referred to by Archbishop Michael Ramsey in discussion with fellow Anglican Primates prior to going to visit Paul VI in 1966 as evidence why dialogue would be right at that time. In passing, I note that Cardinal Augustin Bea, President of the Secretariat for Christian Unity (SCU), had a significant hand in *all* these foundational documents. They all had profound ecumenical significance.

c. I was struck by Archbishop Kevin's stress – as cited in *Ut unum sint* – on the importance of the communion of saints for John Paul II: including the saints of other churches and ecclesial communities. In my study I have a photo of Archbishop Robert Runcie and Pope John Paul II praying together at the Shrine of St Thomas of Canterbury: a shrine now restored in Canterbury Cathedral, but destroyed, of course, by Henry VIII's Commissioners. Later in the Ecumenical

Service in Canterbury Cathedral Pope John Paul II and Christian leaders from all the churches in England lit candles in memory of seven twentieth-century martyrs: Maximilian Kolbe, Dietrich Bonhoeffer, Janani Luwum (the Anglican Archbishop of Uganda not long before tortured and shot by Idi Amin), Maria Skobtsova (the Russian Orthodox nun), Martin Luther King, Oscar Romero and the unknown and unnamed martyrs of our time. This may well have been remembered when John Paul II penned *Ut unum sint*.

d. I am sure Archbishop Kevin is right to stress Karol Wojtyla's personalist philosophy. In the early days of his pontificate I recall a series of General Audiences on Genesis and what it was to be human. I think they revealed his philosophy as much as a theology of Genesis: I suspect they included material from his time as a theological teacher! This side of the Pope will not easily have been appreciated in Britain or the English-speaking world, with our very different dominant schools of philosophy, the logical positivism of the late second part of the twentieth century in particular. But I must not be too critical of an astringent philosophical continence. I have Ockham in my diocese.

e. I believe in Archbishop Kevin's stress on John XXIII's distinction between the deposit of faith and its particular expression to be fundamental. John XXIII's exposition of this on the eve of Vatican II was added by him in Italian at the last minute. When I quoted this some years ago in a piece in *The Tablet*, an acrimonious correspondence followed from a somewhat right-wing Catholic layman arguing that this was not an authoritative part of the text. So the matter is not wholly uncontroversial. John Paul II's endorsement of the method of ARCIC – embodying the same principle – was drafted, as its beautiful English might suggest by Archbishop's Kevin's predecessor but one in the PCCU, Mgr. Bill Purdy. But Pope John Paul II iterated it with conviction. I have a nagging worry that the last two documents of ARCIC II have sometimes appeared to have forgotten this principle. *Mary, Grace and Hope in Christ* is a wonderful exposition of Christology and Mariological tradition, but it remains unclear to me where the truths behind the two Roman Catholic definitions are expressed in common and whether nevertheless Anglicans are being invited to accept the definitions themselves.

f. But this method – going behind even formal definitions and claiming common ground – is embodied perfectly in Archbishop Kevin's important reference to the Oriental Orthodox Churches. And the definition is that of the Council of Chalcedon *itself*. Anglicans too have had long engagement with the Oriental Orthodox. Inspite of huge cultural and theological differences there is an ecclesiological similarity in terms of autonomous communions of churches. Happily, the Christological agreements between the Popes and the Syrian Orthodox and Coptic Orthodox Churches have *also* been assimilated into Anglican – Oriental Orthodox agreement. But both Rome and Canterbury bump into the sternest opposition from the Coptic Church because we have *also* developed increasingly good relations with the East Syrian (i.e. so-called Nestorian) churches: the Assyrian Church and the Chaldean Catholic Church. We mourn the Chaldean Archbishop at the present moment. There is an important point here about anthropology. Aloys Grillmeier S.J. has demonstrated in his monumental christological studies that the key differences between Antioch and Alexandria were anthropological. These unrecognized and undiscussed differences in anthropology then erupted into different christologies, anathemas and schism. I suspect that differences in our understanding of sexuality and being human today are the underlying fissures which divided Christians – within and between churches – on ethical questions of sexual orientation and practice.

g. Archbishop Kevin strongly emphasises the underlying concept of *koinonia* in all ecumenical dialogue. I fully concur, though we need to balance the tendency of a *koinonia* ecclesiology to ignore the reality of conflict in the Church. *Koinonia* needs to be understood in a realistic rather than idealized way. This is where the language – canonized by Paul VI and John Paul II – of imperfect communion is so helpful. Archbishop Kevin notes the different degrees of communion between the Roman Catholic Church and the Orthodox Churches and the separated churches and ecclesial communities of the West. There is, I think, a continuing question here which needs further ecumenical elucidation. I would express it as follows: if we can recognize another Christian body as in some real sense a church or ecclesial community (what is the precise difference between the two, by the way?), does not this recognized ecclesiology imply sufficient (if not full) structures of ecclesiality such as the *episcopé* of an ordained ministry and at least minimum expressions of sacramentality, whether sacraments as such or *ecclesiality itself* as sacramental?

Anglicans need to wrestle with this question in relation to our dialogue with the Free Churches and with Continental Protestant Churches, as do Roman Catholics with all the 'separated' churches of the West, if we are eventually to find a way forward to the reconciliation of churches and ministries. I put it in that order deliberately, churches and ministries.

h. I am certain that Archbishop Kevin is right in saying that the Catholic–Orthodox dialogue had a certain historical and ecclesial priority for Pope John Paul II. I am equally certain the Agreed Statements of the Catholic–Orthodox dialogue are extremely important texts. In the past Anglican–Orthodox Agreed Statements contained implicit criticism of the Roman Primacy, and champion autocephalous churches with a purely honorary, non-jurisdictional primacy *inter pares*. I am glad to say that this is no longer the case. Not only has the work of ARCIC affected the Anglican–Orthodox dialogue but the title alone of the recently published Anglican–Orthodox Agreed Statement is suggestive. *The Mystery of the Church and the Eucharist in the Light of the Holy Trinity* can be compared with the Anglican–Orthodox title: *The Church of the Triune God*. And the omission of the word eucharist in the Anglican title is not significant, as there is an extended section on eucharistic communion in the Anglican–Orthodox document. The two texts are *very* compatible, though there is more on diversity in the Anglican–Orthodox text. Metropolitan John Zizioulas is a significant, 'higher common factor' in the two dialogues! The tensions over the Catholic Eastern Rite Churches are well flagged by Archbishop Kevin. Ultimately, having two Roman dicasteries, with perhaps different emphases may not help. The Congregation for Eastern Churches opposed the establishment of Cardinal Bea's Secretariat if it was to deal with the Orthodox Churches. Frankly, I am *ecclesiologically* on the side of the Orthodox here. The Greek and Slavic Churches have never been subject to 'ordinary' jurisdiction from Rome, even in times of full communion up to 1054. Is there confusion here between what pertains to Universal Primacy and what pertains to the 'Western Patriarchate'? But my *heart* tells another story, relating to the terrible persecutions of the Catholic Eastern Churches under Marxism. In the Bucharest Patriarchate there is an extraordinary fresco of the 'happy' coming together of Christian brothers when the churches were united in

1945. It was painted while Catholic Eastern Rite bishops and priests were being thrown into prison and tortured.

i. My final comment in direct response to Archbishop Kevin is on ARCIC. I agree that the ordination of women has changed the atmosphere and no doubt the time lines of Anglican–Catholic dialogue. But I also believe that the hesitancy of the CDF, to be more wholehearted about ARCIC-I on eucharist and ministry, also contributed materially to this change. The sincere brotherly requests to reconsider advance to the ordination of women to priesthood and episcopacy would have carried so much more weight if there had been some visible prospect of the reconciliation of ministries. The delay in official response from the Vatican to ARCIC-I, in part because of the different approaches of the two relevant dicasteries, fuelled Anglican suspicion that nothing would ever change. There was therefore no point in ecumenical delay.

II

I now move to a more personal assessment of John Paul II's ecumenical significance, though some of the themes I have already mentioned will recur.

a. I will begin an Anglican assessment of the pontificate of Karol Wojtyla with some anecdotage. His election coincided with the birth of our eldest son. My wife, Hilary, was in St Thomas' Hospital at the time of the conclave. We heard the news on the radio at her bedside: a somewhat uncertain announcement – not the ritual proclamation to rejoice, we have a Pope, but an Italian struggle with a Polish surname which left me in the dark. I needed to do a brief for the Archbishop of Canterbury that evening and messages of congratulations would also be sent. An exasperated wife said: 'Christopher, go home and look up the *Annuario Pontificio* so you can brief the Archbishop!' My point is the then novelty of a non-Italian Pope, even a Polish Pope. Suddenly the Roman Primacy had become *visibly* international. The first non-Italian for centuries. This was almost everywhere regarded as 'a good thing' ecumenically. ARCIC language about a universal primacy began to have personal meaning. I said, almost.

I recall one astute Anglican theological critic. This was Professor Geoffrey Lampe, a liberal evangelical, a biblical and patristic scholar of some distinction. He said there is nothing wrong with the bishop of Rome *being an Italian*. He saw the argument for a universal primacy as not deriving from a universal bishop, rather from the primacy of a particular local church, a primacy not to be detached from the oversight of a particular diocese of the universal church. So with all the *plusses* of the new Pope's international credentials there remains the question of whether the primacy is to be seen in the context of the *koinonia* of the local churches or as the universal bishop of the global Church. Clearly, *official* ecclesiology always carefully avoided the latter but as Pope John Paul II began his extraordinary ministry as a world evangelist (like John Wesley, the world seemed to be his parish) and as some aspects of the working of the Roman dicastaries continued (continue!) to presuppose direct oversight and daily intervention in the life of the dioceses, there remains something of a tension which is a matter for debate with the communion of churches in communion with Rome (I think of Archbishop Quinn's book and other criticisms) and with ecumenical partners.

b. Leading on from this is another tension. Thousands, millions of Catholics – and other Christians too – were inspired by Pope John Paul II's visits around the world: the Petrine ministry of 'strengthening the brethren'. But while the Pope was away from Rome he was not at home. Were there important issues such as the balance between the Vatican and the Episcopal Conferences of the worldwide church which would have benefited from scrutiny? Paul VI began such reforms, notably the creation of the Synod of Bishops. But it seems to me that that Synod of Bishops – and all it represents in terms of catholic communion – will never come to its true potential unless its relation to the Curia and to the papal office itself is examined. But that was not, I think, Pope John Paul II's particular gift. Perhaps it will take an Italian Pope to know how to grasp this particular nettle; it will certainly need someone to distinguish what of *romanitas* is of *imperium* and what is of Catholicism.

c. My *third* observation relates to something Archbishop Kevin has alluded to: Pope John Paul II's passionate concern for the 'two lungs' of Europe. (I ought to flag the question as to whether the earth has more than two lungs: was Pope John Paul II too euro-centric? What of South American or Asian culture?) But his passion for Europe is something English Christians *do* need to hear: not for nothing were Britain and Ireland referred to as the 'ultimate edge of the world'. But open an atlas of Europe, and without looking at the countries or cities place a pin in the centre. You will be closer to Warsaw than anywhere else. Current British xenophobia – for example the *Daily Mail* campaign against the Polish community in Britain – is un-catholic and un-Christian. But one's strength is also one's weakness. Pope John Paul II's deep loyalty and nationalism as a Pole may also have had drawbacks. His cultural identity with his homeland – invaded in his lifetime by Germany and the USSR – also made for a very strong sense of patriotism. I think of his moving gesture of kissing the soil of every country he visited. Yet the tarmac of Gatwick airport is not to my mind quite so sacred as all that. Are not nationalisms one of the biggest current threats to world peace? It is to John Paul II's huge credit that he really was so committed to the ecumenical imperative. To a patriotic Polish Catholic the two major wounds to the unity of the church, the Schism of 1054 and the Reformation, will also have corresponded with the two nations which had most endangered Polish national integrity – Germany and Russia. As an aside, this will have made Anglicanism difficult to understand because of the lack of any direct experience. Sometimes Anglicans read as a Catholic schism, sometimes as a kind of 'western version of Orthodox autocephaly', sometimes as plain Protestant. Here is the importance of Pope John Paul II's visit to England and Wales, and especially his visit to Canterbury Cathedral. Worship is at the heart of Anglicanism. Interestingly, one area that the Reformation historians Eamon Duffy and Diarmaid MacCulloch fully agree on is that in the second phase of the English Reformation (after the first, legal phase under Henry VIII) the Church of England was undoubtedly doctrinally Protestant. But they also agree that England differed from Continental Protestantism in two significant ways: it retained episcopacy and it retained cathedrals. So the significance of the Canterbury visit with the Archbishop of Canterbury cannot be underestimated: especially when we add the 'power' of the communion of saints I have already referred to. When Archbishop Robert Runcie first visited Rome,

John Paul II, after the *formal* discussions and an *informal* lunch together, said farewell with the fascinating but enigmatic words: '*affective* collegiality must become *effective* collegiality'. I translate that as an (imperfect) communion of love must become a fuller unity of visible communion. I don't think Pope John Paul II would have spoken of collegiality in quite that way had he not entered Canterbury Cathedral with the Archbishop of Canterbury and had they not prayed together in a real but imperfect communion of common worship. As Clifford Longley, looking back on the old antagonism and rivalry between the two churches in England over four centuries, and while being realistic about the unlikelihood of immediate unity, said of the new ecumenical atmosphere: 'the way *back* has been blocked for ever.'

d. My penultimate observation is going to be phased delicately: and I owe its substance to a conversation many years ago with the Polish Jesuit Wenceslas Hryniewicz, who then taught ecclesiology at the Catholic University of Lublin. He was speaking to me of the Polish bishops in general, and this conversation was well before the election of Karol Wojtyla to the Papacy. His observation was this. During the Nazi period and then that of the Soviet domination, the Polish Church had neither the time nor the luxury of debating some of the issues which came to the fore at Vatican II but which were being discussed in Germany, France and Belgium (in particular) for decades before. What was required in Poland was a tightly disciplined Church, facing the persecution or harassment of an atheistic government. Questions of *Western* materialism did not arise. This is a more subtle corrosion of faith and Christian cohesion than the overt opposition of Marxism. I cannot help thinking that, because in his formative teaching and pastoral years Karol Wojtyla never had to face some of the questions such as were already facing the Churches in the USA and especially Western Europe, he may have found it difficult to find empathy with Catholics and other Christians who were wrestling with Western or even developing world cultural questions: for example, a married priesthood or the ordination of women. In retrospect I think the latter two questions, which are interrelated at a deep psychological level, were particularly difficult for a Polish Pope. At the beginning of the last century the Mariarvite schism in

Poland contained married priests, free love and the ordination of women, as well as an iconography of Mary which included depicting her in priestly vesture!

e. All the above in no way at all to diminish the huge ecumenical achievement of Pope John Paul II. In the end the questions he raises about his own office in *Ut unum sint* set the ecumenical agenda for the future and establish him as having moved the ecumenical agenda substantially forward. Without asking the right questions, without sifting the real agenda there will be no movement. In his great ecumenical encyclical John Paul II does really move matters forward. We cannot blame him for being what he was. His strengths were huge and that they should have their downside is inevitable. The rejoicings at the election of John Paul II – ecumenical as well as catholic rejoicing were not misplaced, even if Geoffrey Lampe *may* have had a theological point!

Chapter 7

Pope John Paul II and Lutherans: Actions and Reactions

Jared Wicks, S.J.

0.1 General Introduction

This contribution takes up one section of ecumenical developments during the pontificate of Pope John Paul II. It will analyses in Section I his interactions with Lutheran Christians and their churches. From this basis, Section II will present how Lutherans in their variety perceived John Paul II and reacted to his actions, especially those in their regard.

The added Appendix 1 gives a chronicle of John Paul II's meetings with and actions of outreach to Lutherans and their churches. Section I of this chapter will describe in moderate detail the main contents of these encounters with an eye to the doctrinal and theological themes that the Pope consistently raised in these settings.

Appendix 2 lists documents that accompanied John Paul II's interactions with Lutherans, namely, texts produced by official Lutheran–Catholic dialogues during his pontificate. These documents culminated in the *Joint Declaration on the Doctrine of Justification* signed in Augsburg on 31 October 1999, by high officials of the Catholic Church and of the Lutheran World Federation. This ecumenical milestone was the outcome of several prior Lutheran–Catholic dialogues, both on the world level and in the local contexts of the USA and Germany. After its signing, the *Joint Declaration* quickly became an essential point of reference in John Paul II's relations with Lutherans and in Lutheran–Catholic dialogues continuing to this day.

0.2 Vatican II beginnings and the early Lutheran–Catholic dialogues

The starting point of the ecumenical dialogues with Catholic participation was the presence and activity of delegated observers at Vatican Council II. These individuals attended the Council by mandate of different umbrella organizations of the separated churches and denominations. The Lutheran World Federation (LWF) sent a total of ten observers, with two of them, Professors Kristen Skydsgaard (Copenhagen) and Vilmos Vajta (LWF Ecumenical Research Institute, Strasbourg), attending all four sessions, of Vatican II. Prof. Edmund Schlink (Heidelberg) also observed the whole Council as delegate of the Evangelical Church in Germany and at different times during Vatican II representatives of the Lutheran Church – Missouri Synod were among the Council guests of the Vatican Secretariat for Promoting Christian Unity (SPCU).[1]

At the SPCU the Lutheran observer Prof. George Lindbeck (Yale) floated in early 1964 the idea of a joint dialogue commission of Catholics and Lutherans to continue the exchanges then going on during Vatican II, a practice which seemed to be foreseen by the emerging schema *De oecumenismo* which was promulgated as the Decree *Unitatis redintegratio* in November 1964. This proposal gained the required approvals, including that of Pope Paul VI, and a world-level planning Commission, formed by the SPCU and the LWF, met in August 1965 and April 1966 to sketch topics and methods for bilateral dialogue. The dialogue began in a joint commission that met annually from 1967 to 1971, leading to the 'Malta Report', *The Gospel and the Church*, issued in 1972.[2]

A second, remarkably productive, phase of Lutheran–Catholic dialogue on the world level began in 1973 and continued until 1984, completing as its first text the widely studied consensus document, *The Eucharist*, in 1977.[3] This, then, was the background of dialogue between the Catholic Church and Lutherans as Pope John Paul II began his pontificate in October 1978.

Section I – Pope John Paul II in action regarding Lutheran Christians and with them

1. As he began his pontificate, Pope John Paul II received reports on the bilateral dialogues then underway under the auspices of the SPCU from its President, Cardinal Jan Willebrands. A first occasion for the Pope to refer publicly to Lutherans came in 1980 with the 450th anniversary of the submission of the *Augsburg Confession* at the German Imperial Diet on 25 June 1530.

1.1 The stage for John Paul II's words had been set by the Lutheran–Catholic dialogue commission, which worked out a concise but appreciative statement on the *Confession* in *All under One Christ*, approved on 23 February 1980.[4] The aim of the *Confession* of 1530 was, according to the Commission statement, to bear witness to the faith of the one, holy, catholic, and apostolic church. Its concern is not with peculiar doctrines nor indeed with the establishment of a new church, but with the preservation and renewal of the Christian faith in its purity (no. 10). On the basis of research on the *Confession*, the Commission states that the text of 1530, especially its initial articles, shows that Lutherans and Catholics are one in confessing faith in the Triune God and the saving work of God through Jesus Christ and the Holy Spirit. 'Lutheran and Catholic Christians [have] remained one in this central and most important truth of the Christian faith' (no. 13).[5]

1.2 On the day of the anniversary, 25 June 1980, the Pope gave a short address of six paragraphs on the *Augsburg Confession*. The aim in 1530 had been to resolve differences between the Catholic Church and the emerging Lutheran territorial churches of the German Empire. But this attempt at bridge-building failed. Still, we have come to see today 'that if there was no success in building a bridge, the storms of that age spared important piers of that bridge.' The dialogue since the Council has enabled Lutherans and Catholics 'to discover how great and solid are the common foundations of our Christian faith'.

Looking to the future of the churches, John Paul II insisted on fidelity to Christ and to our common Church Fathers and early councils, so that 'we may seek all there is in the apostolic heritage that unites us with our brothers and sisters, in order that we may discover anew the treasure of one common creed.'[6] Thus, whatever may have been under dispute in 1530, we know today that the central binding statement of the Lutheran Reformation articulates core truths of the perennial faith of Christians.

John Paul II's words focus on God and Christ while making no mention of the all-important Article IV of the *Augsburg Confession* on justification 'out of grace for Christ's sake through faith,' which the Joint Commission had affirmed in its statement earlier in 1980.[7]

2. Later in 1980 John Paul II had a face-to-face meeting with the leadership of the Evangelical Church in Germany (EKD), at Mainz, during the first of his three pastoral visits (1980, 1987, 1996) to Germany.[8] The Pope spoke of his interlocutors as 'spiritual heirs of Martin Luther' with whom he has come to 'set . . . a sign of union in the central mystery of our faith'. From St Paul's letter to the Romans, we have to admit our sin (Rom. 3.23), but also that 'God does not cease to 'have mercy upon all' (11.32). He gives his Son, he gives himself, he gives forgiveness, justification, grace, eternal life. We can recognize this together.' Our agreement on fundamental and central truths is clearer after the attention given to the Lutheran *Augsburg Confession*, but this calls us to strive further toward full unity in faith.

> According to the conviction of Catholics disagreement revolves around 'what is Christ's' . . . around his Church and its mission, her message, her sacraments and the ministries placed in the service of Word and Sacrament. The dialogue established since the Council has brought us a good way further in this respect. Precisely in Germany many important steps have been taken. That can inspire us with confidence with regard to problems not yet solved.[9]

In the Mainz exchange, Regional Bishop Eduard Lohse, President of the EKD's governing Council, raised with Pope John Paul II three issues on which German Protestants were hoping for improved cooperation with the Catholic Church: (1) permitting Catholics to fulfil their Sunday and feast day obligation of worship, on occasion, by attendance at an evangelical liturgy or ecumenical service of the word, (2) opening more possibilities of joint pastoral care of those in mixed marriages and (3) granting some possibilities for mutual Eucharistic hospitality, especially for spouses in mixed marriages at liturgies of the other church to which one spouse belonged.[10]

The action resulting from the Mainz meeting was the formation of a Joint Ecumenical Commission, headed by Bishop Lohse and Cardinal

Joseph Ratzinger (then, Archbishop of Munich). At the Commission's first meeting, in May 1981, the question arose of the sixteenth-century anathemas, both those levelled by Lutherans against Catholics and by the Catholic Church at the Council of Trent against Lutherans. These condemnations, especially on grace and justification, sacraments and Eucharist, and the ordained ministry, were part of the confessional heritage on both sides, but many individuals were questioning their ongoing validity, because now each side has a better grasp of the true intent and content of the other side's teaching. Could the churches come to formally adopt what many sensed? Such a step would remove a significant obstacle now impeding both common witness by Lutherans and Catholics and the pastoral adaptations requested by Bishop Lohse. This topic will return in sections 4 and 8 where I will recount the steps leading to the *Joint Declaration on the Doctrine of Justification* of 1999.

3. The year 1983 brought the 5th centenary of Martin Luther's birth on 10 November 1483, and led to two significant actions by Pope John Paul II, with his letter of 31 October 1983, to Cardinal Willebrands on Luther and then his personal visit on December 11, 1983, to the Lutheran Christuskirche of Rome for an evening vespers service.

3.1 As in 1980 with the *Augsburg Confession*, also in 1983 the Lutheran–Catholic Joint Commission issued an enlightening statement, *Martin Luther – Witness to Jesus Christ*, brought out on 6 May, which singled out Luther's intense study of Scripture and his discovery of God's mercy as central to what Rom. 1.17 calls 'the righteousness of God'. Luther then became a tireless witness to this message and consoling word all through his theology and further interpretation of the Bible. In later generations too many have seen Luther as the founder of a new church – an idea however that was far from his mind and strongly rejected by him. 'It was not Luther's understanding of the gospel considered by itself which brought about conflict and schism in the church, but rather the ecclesial and political concomitants of the Reformation movement.'[11]

3.2 Pope John Paul II's letter concerning Luther notes that for the Catholic Church the memory of the Reformation is a sad one, because it led to deep ecclesial divisions.[12] But he is appreciative that Lutheran leaders want the commemorations of 1983 to also engage Catholics and contribute to 'a deepened and more complete vision of the historical events and at a critical assessment of Luther's manifold legacy'.

Scholarly study of Luther is bearing valuable insights into Luther's person and the complexities of social and church historical realities of his age.

Central among the results of research, 'there is clearly outlined the deep religious feeling of Luther, who was driven with burning passion by the question of eternal salvation.'

But the Pope is also cautious about oversimplifications in explaining how Luther's efforts relate to the breach of Church unity during the Reformation era. The tragic outcome cannot be simply laid at the door of Catholic authorities for not understanding Luther, nor was it solely due to Luther not knowing well the true Catholic heritage. Such factors played their part, but one must go deeper into fundamental doctrinal principles.

The decisions taken had much deeper roots. In the dispute about the relationship between Faith and Tradition, there were at stake fundamental questions on the correct interpretation and the reception of the Christian faith which had within them a potential for ecclesial division which cannot be explained by purely historical reasons.

For the task at hand concerning Luther and Christian unity, Pope John Paul II drew two conclusions. First, a disciplined and intense historical effort is needed, one unclouded by prejudice and with the pure intention of understanding what happened. Historians must become not judges of history but messengers of truth.

Second, the Unity Secretariat headed by Card. Willebrands has to pursue 'the dialogue of faith' which is already underway, greatly aided by the Lutheran confessional documents, which give the solid basis of 'what unites us even after the separation, namely, in the word of Scripture, in the confessions of faith, and in the Councils of the ancient church.'

3.3 In contrast with the letter's emphasis on history and fundamental theology, Pope John Paul II's visit to the Lutheran church in Rome radiated spiritual warmth. The question of such a visit was raised in January 1982, in the church hall of the neighbouring Catholic parish of St Teresa of Avila. A group of Lutherans were at an informal reception after the Pope celebrated Sunday mass at St Teresa's and one Lutheran parish council member asked John Paul II if he would be open to an invitation to their church. To this, the Pope answered immediately that, yes, he wanted to visit their church before too long.

The event occurred in the evening of the Third Sunday of Advent 1983. John Paul II entered the Lutheran church deep in thought, took his seat in the sanctuary beside the Pastor, Rev. Christoph Meyer, and after hymns and readings gave his homily, not from the chair but from the pulpit just like any other preacher.

In Advent, John Paul II said, we recall our common origin, the gift of redemption, and the goal of our pilgrim life. 'We are all under the grace of our Lord Jesus Christ. He is the centre, the hinge, in which the whole existence, meaning, and salvation of this world are contained.'[13] Advent and the figure of John the Baptist make us alert to God's gift in Christ: 'Jesus came to meet the anguished question of his precursor and brought his faith to certainty: the time of salvation.'

Sharing the service with the Lutherans is a gift that is deeply moving for the Pope, especially with it occurring during Advent. 'I have come to commemorate with you, in prayer and meditation, the mystery of faith of Advent which we share, its deep and many-sided richness. Advent solidarity unites us, even amidst the divisions that persist. It is important not to be discouraged by difficulties along our way. We can look ahead, from Luther's fifth centenary, to a dawn now arising of restored unity and community, arising from daily renewal in the light of God's eternal word.'

Adapting himself to the setting, John Paul II did not close his homily with words of blessing but with the heartfelt wish that all present might have a truly blessed Christmas.

4. The year 1985 brought with it two important encounters between Pope John Paul II and leaders of particular but tone-setting Lutheran churches of the world.

4.1 On 22 May 1985, in an unprecedented action, James R. Crumley, 'Bishop of the church' of the Lutheran Church in America (LCA), wrote a personal letter to the Pope describing the encouraging development of mutual understanding and of agreements, termed 'theological convergence', through dialogues between Catholics and Lutherans in the USA.[14] Bishop Crumley recalled what John Paul II had said to him at a previous personal meeting, 'We must remember that there is far more that unites us than divides us.' For the American bishop that is a source of joy but also of the painful realization 'that the unity given and intended by God is tragically broken.'

A central point of Bishop Crumley's letter is the desire that both he and the Pope give encouragement to each other and to their churches to persevere in the difficult task of work for unity. The dialogues to date make it possible that 'Lutherans and Catholics can acknowledge substantial convergences in the areas of justification, baptism, Eucharist, and ministry. These convergences make us increasingly aware of how close we are to each other in the "heart of the Gospel", in proclaiming Jesus Christ as Savior of the world'.[15] Bishop Crumley recalled the Pope's own words of 25 June 1980, that 'important piers' of a bridge joining Lutherans and Catholics were not destroyed by the Reformation era conflicts. Therefore, there is good reason for both a Lutheran church leader and the Pope to urge study of the dialogue results as a way to deepen in their faithful the sense of the unity even now existing.

Pope John Paul II responded in a letter to Bishop Crumley on 22 July 1985, in which he reaffirmed his own concern for Christian unity, since the See of Peter 'by its very nature exists to serve the unity of Christ's Church.' For the Pope, the Lutheran–Catholic dialogue must draw on the Gospels, since, as the international dialogue document, the Malta Report (*The Gospel and the Church*, 1972) says, 'The unity of the Church can be a unity only in the truth of the Gospel,' and the issue of how to rightly understand the Gospel was at the origin of the Lutheran–Catholic separation. Fortunately, the same Malta report states as agreed between Catholic and Lutherans what the centre of the Gospel is, namely, 'the eschatological saving act of God in Jesus' Cross and Resurrection'.

The division is felt at the local level where Catholics and Lutherans are neighbours but are pained by disunity, 'since they do yet confess in the fullness of unity the same faith and therefore cannot take part in the fullness of Church life together.' The Pope makes clear that here he is referring to division at the altar and in Holy Communion, by citing his own words in Mainz to the Council of the Evangelical Church in Germany, in 1980, on full unity in faith being needed by those who gather at the Lord's one table.

So, the dialogue has to continue and John Paul II acknowledges the series of US Lutheran–Catholic convergence texts which now includes the recent joint statement, which he mentions by name, *Justification by Faith*. Such contributions are important on the way to 'that unity in faith which is our goal'. At the end, the Pope notes that the LCA headed by Bishop Crumley will soon enter into the formation of a new church, The Evangelical Lutheran Church in America (ELCA). This is a development which the Pope keeps in his prayers and which he sees as important in preparing a large number of American Lutherans to enter the stage of history that will come with the twenty-first century.[16]

The letters exchanged by Bishop Crumley and Pope John Paul II were published on 27 September 1985, on the occasion of the visit to Rome and audience with the Pope of a LCA group that included nine bishops. At the audience, the Pope spoke again of the sharing by Lutherans and Catholics in basic tenets of faith, about which the Lutheran–Catholic dialogue of the past 20 years has made us aware. Yet, 'there are important issues which still divide us in the profession of faith, preventing us from celebrating the Eucharist together.'[17]

Even though John Paul II did not take up Bishop Crumley's point about substantial doctrinal convergences on justification, baptism, Eucharist and ministry, the exchange did bring new themes into the Pope's relations with Lutherans, for instance, that he went beyond general references to the dialogue of recent years to speak of and even cite particular documents produced by Lutheran–Catholic commissions for theological dialogue. Also, the Pope indicated repeatedly the challenging Catholic principle in the ecumenical engagement, namely, that 'full unity in faith' is essential to unity in the Church and to sharing in the Eucharistic high point of sacramental life.

4.2 Also in 1985, on 13 June Pope John Paul II received in private audience Bishop Eduard Lohse of the Evangelical Church in Germany, who came as co-chairman of the Joint Ecumenical Commission formed in Germany after the papal visit of 1980.[18] Bishop Lohse came to report on the common projects undertaken, such as a 1981 declaration on the Creed of Nicea–Constantinople, statements on marriage and observance of Sunday and common guidelines for pastoral ministry to those in mixed marriages.

Most importantly, he brought information about the Commission's action regarding the sixteenth-century doctrinal condemnations. The Commission had in 1981 mandated the long-established Ecumenical Working Group of Catholic and Evangelical Theologians to undertake a scholarly investigation of Lutheran and Catholic confessional texts in order to ascertain whether the general opinion was correct: that the condemnations were so historically conditioned that they no longer touched the doctrine of the partner church of the present day.

In mid-1985 it was clear that the Working Group, led by Prof. Wolfhart Pannenberg and Bishop Karl Lehmann, was close to delivering an ecumenically significant report that would remove major obstacles not only to Lutheran–Catholic agreement especially on justification, but also on points concerning the Eucharist and ordained ministry as well. Bishop Lohse saw clearly that the insights of the German theologians would become officially binding only if they were confirmed by the magisterium of the Catholic Church, and so the Pope had to be informed.

In section no. 8 of this Part, we will follow the trail from the German study of the condemnations to the *Joint Declaration on the Doctrine of Justification*. Here, I cite Bishop Lohse's appreciation of how Pope John Paul II received him on 13 July 1985 and entered into the topics on their agenda.

Pope John Paul II knows how to meet a discussion partner seriously, attractively and warmheartedly. He makes it clear that he takes his office as Bishop of Rome as a ministry for all Christians and not only for the Roman Catholic Church. One senses the burden he bears of a responsibility quite consciously felt, but at the same time there is his joy of giving witness to the Gospel in the whole world. A personal meeting with him is an experience of brotherly community far outweighing the differences between our traditions and understandings of ministry, along with the doctrinal issues connected with these differences. The Pope takes very much to heart the promotion of ecumenical dialogue, but he, like us, also has reservations about simply erasing differences in moments of exalted enthusiasm by actions taken rashly.[19]

5. A highpoint of Pope John Paul II's personal contacts with Lutherans came in 1989 during his pastoral visit to the five Nordic countries of Norway, Iceland, Finland, Denmark, and Sweden, 1–10 June. A certain preparation occurred 1980–1988 in the Pope's encounters with ambassadors to the Holy See representing these countries, which gave him opportunities to speak of the majority presence of Lutherans in their lands, in whom 'the Catholic Church loves to see brothers, seeking along with us the unity willed by our common Lord.'[20]

Among Pope John Paul II's journeys, the 1989 visit to Scandinavia was singular in including seven prayer services celebrated with Lutherans in their churches or shrines. The Pope's addresses on these occasions were significant for the ecumenical themes he took up and developed. We can note eight such topics:

- The baptism common to Lutherans and Catholics, through which 'we are all incorporated into the crucified and risen Christ.' This ensures a true but imperfect communion, because baptism is 'a sacramental bond among all who have been reborn'.[21]
- Lutherans and Catholics share common elements of the apostolic heritage, especially the Holy Scriptures.[22]
- Deep regard for the patron saints of these countries links Lutherans and Catholics, for example, St. Olav in Norway and Sts. Erik and Birgitta in Sweden.[23]
- Citation of Pope Hadrian VI's declaration of guilt for divisions, read before the Nürnberg Diet of 1523, and of Vatican II's urging to seek pardon for sins against unity (UR 7).[24]
- A clarification that Luther's excommunication ceased with his death in 1546.[25]
- Still, Eucharistic sharing must wait until it can seal the restoration of full communion in faith in the Eucharist and the Church between the churches.[26]
- Appreciative words on the Lutheran–Catholic bilateral dialogues to date, with specification that now is the time for the churches to study and formally receive their conclusions.[27]
- Citation of Vatican II that the separated churches and communities 'have been by no means deprived of significance and importance in the mystery of salvation. For the Spirit of Christ has not refrained from using them as means of salvation which derive their efficacy from the very fullness of grace and truth entrusted to the Catholic Church' (UR 3).[28]
- Pope John Paul II's visit to the Nordic lands brought a concentration on the doctrinal foundations and goals of the Catholic commitment to ecumenical work, along with remarkable statements sketching the Pope's understanding of his own primatial and Petrine ministry.[29] Upon his return to Rome, he spoke of having prayed for Christian

unity in cathedrals dating back to the era of those lands' full communion with the Church of Rome. 'The welcome I received everywhere often took the form of a joyous meeting of brothers who find
one another again. The renewed and intensified charity, expressed in
common prayer, strengthened the hope that inspires the ecumenical
movement.'[30]

In his traditional pre-Christmas gathering with the staff members of
the Roman Curia, on 22 December 1989, John Paul II spoke of his visit
to the Nordic lands as a significant moment in the year then ending.

I undertook last June a pilgrimage of faith to the Christians of the
Nordic countries. I paid homage to the Christian tradition of these
peoples. Together with my Catholic and Lutheran brothers, I was able
to experience intense and significant moments of spiritual ecumenism in prayer and reflection on the common mission of Christians in
Europe and in the world. My pastoral journey, which up to a short
time ago would have been unimaginable, has undoubtedly constituted at the local level and in the long term an important stage along
the way of ecumenism. As Bishop of Rome, to whom the ministry of
unity has been entrusted in a very special way, I have thus been able
to make a special contribution to the ecumenism that is asserting
itself in the Nordic lands just as in every part of the world, and not as
the fruit of our solely human efforts, but as a gift of divine grace. [31]

In 1995, in *Ut unum sint*, Pope John Paul II also recalled his 1989
visit to the Nordic countries, with mention of one aspect of his public
celebrations of mass in Sweden and Finland.

At Communion time, the Lutheran Bishops approached the cele-
brant. They wished, by means of an agreed gesture, to demonstrate
their desire for that time when we Catholics and Lutherans will be
able to share the same Eucharist, and they wished to receive the cele-
brant's blessing. With love I blessed them. (*Ut unum sint*, no. 72)

For the Pope this act of 'spiritual communion' demonstrated both
fraternal charity and the central ecumenical aspiration. It made a
profound impression on Pope John Paul II.

6. The previous section began with reference to Pope John Paul II's audiences in Rome with diplomatic representatives of the Nordic countries. The years of his pontificate were also notable for the stream of Lutheran leaders whom he received in private audiences during their visits to Rome.

6.1 Successive Presidents of the Lutheran World Federation came to Rome, accompanied by the Federation's General Secretary, and had audiences with Pope John Paul II in 1985, 1988, 1993 and 2003.[32] In addressing LWF President Dr. Gottfried Brakemeier at their 23 April 1993 audience, the Pope noted that the world-level dialogue had gone on now for 25 years, for which both sides should be grateful.

> Through the examination of such vitally important questions as justification and the nature and mission of the Church, I am confident that this dialogue will make a lasting contribution to our progress toward unity in the apostolic faith. Since the two issues I have mentioned are so closely linked to the authentic proclamation of the Gospel, and since disagreements about them at the time of the Reformation were decisive in bringing about the sad division which still exist, it is all the more essential that they should be studied patiently and in a spirit of fidelity to the Word which the Father has spoken to us 'in these last days'. (Heb. 1.2)
>
> In this regard, I would express my conviction that ecumenical dialogue must strive for an ever deeper understanding of the mystery of our salvation, accomplished through the Incarnation, Death, and Resurrection of Jesus Christ. Within this perspective, theological dialogue will become a source of mutual enrichment and will certainly lead to that growth in truth which the Lord promised as the work of the Holy Spirit (cf Jn 16.13).[33]

Pope John Paul II mentioned in his Sunday Angelus talk on 22 July 1984, that the LWF General Assembly was meeting at that time in Budapest and he invited his hearers to pray to the Holy Spirit for the Assembly. In 1987, the Pope wrote to the General Secretary of the LWF when the Federation celebrated its fortieth anniversary at Lund, Sweden, saying that the Catholic Church values its many contacts with the Federation, especially the theological dialogue aiming at seeking unity in faith. In January 1990, Pope John Paul II sent greetings to those participating in the LWF Eighth General Assembly in Curitiba, Brazil, echoing the Assembly theme ('I have heard the cry of my people' Exod. 3.7–10) as a reason why 'Catholics and Lutherans have a shared confidence that our striving for unity will one day come to fruition.'[34]

6.2 In section. 4, I related the exchange of letters in 1985 between Presiding Bishop James R. Crumley and Pope John Paul II. The broader setting for this was a series of audiences between the Pope and bishops of the Lutheran Church in America, while the latter were on 'ecumenical pilgrimage' in Europe, in 1981, 1985 and 1986. Such visits, with papal audiences, continued in 1989 and 2003, after the LCA entered in 1988 the new Evangelical Lutheran Church in America (ELCA).[35]

6.3 A particular contact between the Pope and the Lutheran Church of Finland began in January 1985 during the visit of an ecumenical delegation headed by the Lutheran Primate, Archbishop John Vikström, accompanied by the Orthodox Metropolitan and the Catholic Bishop of Helsinki. They established a chapel in the Dominican church *Santa Maria sopra Minerva* where on 19 January each year Finns, both those of the visiting delegation and those residing in Rome, would gather to celebrate their national patron St. Hendrik. Naturally the annual visit includes discussions in the Vatican office for Christian Unity and an audience with the Pope.[36]

6.4 Another saint who brought Lutherans and Catholics together during John Paul II's pontificate was St. Birgitta/Bridget of Sweden. The year 1991 saw the ecumenical celebration in Rome of the 600th anniversary of her canonization, highlighted by the celebration of Vespers in St. Peter's on 5 October, at which Dr. Bertil Werkström, Lutheran Archbishop of Uppsala and Dr. John Vikström, Lutheran Archbishop of Turku, Finland, joined the Pope and the Catholic bishops of Stockholm and Helsinki, in presiding at the service. In his homily, the Pope cited a prayer of St. Bridget and commented on its relevance for present-day ecumenism.

'Lord, show me your way and grant that I may be happy to follow it.' Bridget's prayer can constitute the programme of the Ecumenical Movement. Ecumenism is a journey which is made together, but we are not able to chart its course or its duration beforehand. We do not know whether the journey will be smooth or rough. We only know that it is our duty to continue this journey together.

John Paul II spoke of the bonds uniting Lutherans and Catholics, such as their baptismal rebirth, love of the Sacred Scriptures, confession of the Triune God and incarnation of the Son of God, and the *Apostles' Creed*. He added his assurance that the common heritage would soon expand.

Everyone knows that the Protestant Reformation began from the doctrine of justification and that it destroyed the unity of the Christians of the West. A common understanding of justification – and we think we are very close to this goal – will, we are sure, help us to resolve the other controversies directly or indirectly linked to it.[37]

The question of the meaning of the celebration with the Lutheran Archbishops in St. Peter's was raised by Archbishop Vikström at the Pontifical Council on 7 October.

As we received the Bishop of Rome in our cathedrals [in 1989], so we were received by him. This provokes deep gratitude to God, who through the Holy Spirit has brought us to this point in our history and made it possible to translate dialogues and friendship into joint worship.

But a symbolic act of this density also provokes questions and deserves careful interpretation. As we stood before the altar and before the people, bishops of the church, united in prayer, we asked: in how far is this a full recognition of our episcopal ministry and office within the Church universal? We on our part recognize the orders of the Roman Catholic Church. Our problem is with the universal role of the Pope beyond a symbol of unity. Particularly the claims of infallibility and universal jurisdiction have caused much concern. Our service Saturday makes us ask again: how far and on what conditions is the Roman Catholic Church prepared to recognize the episcopal office of the Lutheran Church in Sweden and Finland?[38]

Thus Pope John Paul II allowed a major ecumenical issue to be posed by his action of joining Lutheran bishops to himself in presiding over an ecumenical service of prayer in St. Peter's Basilica. Furthermore, the successor Lutheran Archbishops carried out the same liturgical roles at similar celebrations in St. Peter's, on 13 November 1999, of St. Bridget being named co-patroness of Europe. Two Lutheran bishops also had co-presiders' roles on 4 October 2002, at the ecumenical vespers in

St. Peter's commemorating the seventh centenary of St. Bridget's birth in 1303.[39]

7. A major ecumenical intervention by Pope John Paul II was his May 1995 encyclical *Ut unum sint*, on the Catholic Church's commitment to the ecumenical search for visible Christian unity, a commitment following from Vatican Council II, especially its decree *Unitatis redintegratio*, of which the encyclical is an actualizing *rélecture*. Lutherans and the Lutheran/Catholic dialogue are not mentioned in the body of this major text, but three points are clearly relevant to this sector of the Catholic ecumenical commitment.

First, no. 11 of *Ut unum sint* speaks to the ecclesiological status of the separated churches and ecclesial communities not in communion with the Catholic Church. She has been preserved in unity, 'with all the means with which God wishes to endow his Church'. But this Catholic fullness is structural, not a fullness of graced vitality and virtue, since her ministers and members display weaknesses, mediocrity and betrayals of their calling. Still, this does not destroy 'what God has bestowed on her as part of his plan of grace'. But because these means or endowments, the 'elements of sanctification and truth', are present as well in the other Christian communities in varying degrees, there is an 'objective basis of the communion, albeit imperfect, which exists between them and the Catholic Church'.

These 'elements', listed in UR 15 and *Ut unum sint*, no. 12, were not invented by the communities after their separation but come from the common heritage. The fact that they are cherished and passed on in the other communities leads John Paul II to this significant conclusion: 'To the extent that these elements are found in other Christian communities, the one Church of Christ is effectively present in them' and the Catholic Church is linked with them 'by a true union in the Holy Spirit' (no. 11). Shortly after, he states this in a denial: 'It is not that beyond the boundaries of the Catholic community there is an ecclesial vacuum' (no. 14).

Second, the encyclical's third part, on the future of ecumenical efforts and dialogue, offers a general appreciation of the work of the joint ecumenical commissions which, based on a certain fundamental unity of doctrine, have gone on to treat baptism, Eucharist, ordained ministry and authority in the Church (no. 78). This leads to John Paul II's carefully crafted list of topics now needing further study in the broader ecumenical striving towards agreement in faith:

1. the relationship between Sacred Scripture, as the highest authority in matters of faith, and Sacred Tradition, as indispensable to the interpretation of the word of God;
2. the Eucharist, as the Sacrament of the Body and Blood of Christ, an offering of praise to the Father, the sacrificial memorial and Real Presence of Christ, and the sanctifying outpouring of the Holy Spirit;
3. Ordination, as a Sacrament, to the threefold ministry of the episcopate, presbyterate and diaconate;
4. the Magisterium of the Church, entrusted to the Pope and the Bishops in communion with him, understood as a responsibility and an authority exercised in the name of Christ for teaching and safeguarding the faith;
5. the Virgin Mary, as Mother of God and Icon of the Church, the spiritual Mother who intercedes for Christ's disciples and for all humanity; (no. 79)

Third, *Ut unum sint* contains Pope John Paul II's account of 'the ministry of unity of the Bishop of Rome' (nos. 88–96), a ministry entrusted to one man among the College of Bishops (no. 94) to ground and ensure the communion of all the churches. The Bishop of Rome is a member of the College, and the Bishops are his brothers in the ministry. Since the primatial bishop has to be concerned about whatever relates to the unity of all Christian communities, John Paul II goes on to draw this remarkable conclusion from which follows an invitation.

I am convinced that I have a particular responsibility in this regard, above all in acknowledging the ecumenical aspirations of the majority of the Christian Communities and in heeding the request made of me to find a way of exercising the primacy which, while in no way renouncing what is essential in its mission, is nonetheless open to a new situation. (no. 94)

This is an immense task, which we cannot refuse and which I cannot carry out by myself. Could not the real but imperfect communion existing between us persuade Church leaders and their theologians to engage with me in a patient and fraternal dialogue in which, leaving useless controversies behind, we could listen to one another, keeping before us only the will of Christ for his Church and allowing ourselves to be deeply moved by his plea 'that they may all be one . . . so that the world may believe that you have sent me' (Jn 17.21)? (no. 96)

Section II of this study will review, in section 13.2, selected responses of Lutheran church leaders and theologians to Pope John Paul II's ecumenism encyclical and especially to his request for a new dialogue concerning the Petrine ministry of unity.

8. In listing dialogue topics in *Ut unum*, no. 79, Pope John Paul II made no mention of sin, grace, justifying faith and personal renewal in the Holy Spirit. He was clearly confident in 1995 that for this doctrinal complex, through the dialogues engaging Lutherans and Catholics, a significant result was near, which came in 1999 with the signing on 31 October in Augsburg of the *Joint Declaration*.[40]

Pope John Paul II spoke in March 1995 of the coming expression of 'a common understanding' of justification, when he received the participants in a conference on Lutheran–Catholic relations. He said that we have to be grateful for thirty years of dialogue, which has dismantled barriers and made clear 'the substantial, constitutive bonds of unity already existing between us.' The conference will examine this.[41]

A very fundamental stage of dialogue was reached when the doctrine of justification became the central issue, and we must look forward with confidence to the document on which Lutherans and Catholics are now hard at work and which aims at expressing a common understanding of this central theme of our faith.[42]

The work about which the Pope spoke can be described in two steps, before we take up his further utterances about the *Joint Declaration*.

8.1 In the proximate preparation of the 1999 declaration, a first step was that of the Lutheran–Catholic dialogue in the USA, which worked from 1978 to 1983 on the consensus and convergence statement *Justification by Faith*. The dialogue attests to agreement on this basic affirmation:

Our entire hope of justification and salvation rests on Christ Jesus and on the gospel whereby the good news of God's merciful action is made known: we do not place our ultimate trust in anything other than God's promise and saving work in Christ.[43]

Beyond this, the US dialogue lists twelve 'material convergences', on topics such as the sheer neediness of fallen humans, justification as God's work, the means (Scripture, proclamation and sacraments) by which God awakens justifying faith, love and good works issuing from faith, the threats buffeting those justified, the firmness of trust in God's leading the justified to salvation, and good works and their reward.[44]

Even before completion of the American document, work had begun in Germany on re-examining the sixteenth-century condemnations that Catholics and Lutherans had levelled against each other's teaching, with a sub-commission of the Ecumenical Working Group of Catholic and Protestant Theologians commissioned to investigate the topic of justification (see section 4.2). The results of the study were published in 1986, in a much discussed volume.[45] But even before its publication, the mandating group, the Joint Ecumenical Commission of Catholic and Lutheran bishops, had received the theologians' study and made public its own report on its conclusions. About the sixteenth-century condemnations, the Commission described the results as follows:

> The investigations bring to light a wide spectrum of differentiated judgments. The general trend of the results is this: a series of condemnatory pronouncements rest on misunderstandings about the opposing position; others no longer apply to the doctrine and praxis of today's partner; in the case of still others, new factual insights have led to a large degree of agreement; but where some of the condemnatory pronouncements are concerned, it cannot be said that there is as yet any agreement at the present day.[46]

The Commission recalls the long history of Lutherans and Catholics opposing each other. This has led to serious differences about church order, the ordained ministry, the sacraments and Holy Scripture. But the theologians' study of justification has put *this* controversial question in a new light, a light which calls in question whether justification is today church-divisive.

> Both churches are concerned to make it clear that toward God human beings can in no way look to their own efforts, but that they are nonetheless penetrated by justification wholly and entirely. The response of faith is brought about by the Holy Spirit through the

Word of promise which comes to men and women. Cooperation cannot be a matter of controversy, if it means that in faith the heart is involved, when the Word touches it and faith is created. On the other hand, the faith of which it is said that it justifies the whole life of human beings brings men and women into a trustful acceptance of the promise of God in Christ. *Because today there is agreement between the churches about this, it must be asked whether the condemnatory pronouncements on justification that were formulated on each side in the sixteenth century, against the doctrine of the other, still have to be maintained today in their church-dividing effect.*[47]

This was a major step toward a common declaration by the churches on justification. But it was followed by the work of the third phase of the international Lutheran–Catholic dialogue, leading to publication of the text *Church and Justification* in 1994. This approach came from another angle, not only to express agreements between Lutherans and Catholics on the foundations of ecclesiology, but to show as well that existing questions and differences between the two sides in understanding the church do not undercut the agreement ascertained on justification.[48]

8.2 The first text having the overall form of the eventual *Joint Declaration* was composed in 1988, early in the work of the third-phase of the international dialogue. This text was called 'Ascertaining the Far-Reaching Consensus on the Doctrine of Justification', and was accepted as the 'platform paper' of the Commission's further work on church and justification.[49]

Beginning in 1988 the staffs of the Pontifical Council and the Lutheran World Federation began developing strategies for the churches' reception of the results of dialogue by their theologians.[50] During this time, positive impulses were coming from Pope John Paul II's trip to Scandinavia and the 1991 celebration of St. Bridget in Rome. The Pontifical Council gathered a group of consulting theologians in 1991–1992, who delivered a positive report on the German conclusions that the Reformation era condemnations on justification were no longer church-dividing. In the newly constituted Evangelical Lutheran Church in America, the question was raised in early 1993 whether the coming 450th anniversary of the Council of Trent's *Decree on Justification* (1547), with its canons censuring putatively Lutheran positions, could not be the occasion for the churches to declare that such older texts no longer apply today. This proposal, however, was quickly taken up by the Lutheran World Federation as being a matter for deliberation and decision by the whole Federation.

Late in 1993 the Pontifical Council was ready to walk with the LWF toward a formal reception of the results on justification, notwithstanding the structural differences between the Catholic Church and the Lutheran Federation. By March 1994 a joint task force produced an initial draft of a declaration on justification, developed from the earlier studies and especially from the 'platform paper' of the international commission from 1988.[51] The draft circulated among experts on both sides and was revised in September 1996, to make it suitable for submission for initial reactions from church bodies in the two communions, which on the Catholic side were the Congregation for the Doctrine of the Faith and some episcopal conferences in lands with large numbers of Lutherans. Among Lutherans, 38 member churches of the LWF gave their comments at this stage.

In June 1996 a fourteen-person drafting committee worked for a week in Würzburg, Germany, to develop the text along lines indicated in the initial reactions, for example, incorporating a more developed account of the 'biblical message of justification'. Work on refining the text had to continue for two days in January 1997 in response to comments on the previous draft from the Congregation for the Doctrine of the Faith and from a Lutheran group assembled by the leadership of the Evangelical Church in Germany. From this process a text was ready as a final proposal for submission to the Holy See and to the member churches of the LWF for their official response.[52]

By June 1998, the Council of the LWF acted on the responses of 86 member churches of the Federation, which were largely favourable to affirming the Lutheran–Catholic consensus set forth in the 1997 text. An even greater number affirmed that the condemnations in the Lutheran confessional doctrines do not apply to Catholic doctrine as contained in the proposed Declaration.[53]

But the same month of June 1998 saw a 'Response of the Catholic Church' to the text, issued by the Congregation for the Doctrine of the Faith and the Pontifical Council, which included references to certain limitations of the proposed Declaration, for example, on 'sin' in a person justified, and on the Lutheran statement of passivity in one's reception of justification. These are 'major difficulties preventing an affirmation of total consensus between the parties on the theme of justification'. To be sure,

> the level of agreement is high, but it does not yet allow us to affirm that all the differences separating Catholics and Lutherans in the doctrine concerning justification are simply a question of emphasis or language. Some of these differences concern aspects of substance and are therefore not all mutually compatible.[54]

Upon receipt of this Catholic Response, the General Secretary of the LWF, Dr. Ismael Noko, declared it had implications which have to be clarified and assessed, since 'reservations are made on essential points, whereby the basis becomes unclear for jointly declaring that the mutual condemnations of the Reformation no longer apply'.[55]

Pope John Paul II did speak on June 28 of the attainment in the Lutheran–Catholic declaration, after a careful evaluation process, of 'a consensus in basic truths of the doctrine of justification,' which is 'an important ecumenical achievement'.[56] But many reactions to the Catholic Response showed that it posed an obstacle that had to be dealt with before the two sides could proceed to formally adopting and signing the *Joint Declaration*.[57] Thus, in early summer 1998, the process had run aground.

In addition to intense exchanges between the Pontifical Council and the LWF, two other figures entered the scene in autumn 1998 and joined in an effort that did help overcome the stalemate of mid-1998 and make possible the adoption of the *Joint Declaration*. They were Cardinal Joseph Ratzinger, then Prefect of the Congregation for the Doctrine of the Faith, and the emeritus Lutheran Bishop of Bavaria, Dr. Johannes Hanselmann. After Pope John Paul II learned of widespread disappointment among both Lutheran and Catholic ecumenists, he appears to have asked Cardinal Ratzinger to try to overcome the malaise occasioned by the Catholic Response of June 1998. The Cardinal and Bishop Hanselmann held a private meeting in Regensburg, Germany, on 4 November 1998, out of which came a draft text of elucidations of issues and questions raised by the Catholic Response of 25 June.[58] After revision in Rome, this text from the Hanselmann–Ratzinger meeting became in the *Joint Declaration* the 'Annex' which served to show to the satisfaction of both sides that the Catholic Response had not raised insuperable difficulties.[59]

At the Augsburg ceremony of the signing of the Lutheran–Catholic *Joint Declaration*, the explanatory 'Annex' receives mention as a 'statement [which] further substantiates the consensus reached' in the Declaration itself. This was part of the 'Official Common Statement' on the Declaration to which the signatories for the Lutheran World Federation and the Catholic Church affixed their names on 31 October 1999.[60]

8.3 Pope John Paul II had not been silent about the *Joint Declaration* during the years leading to its formal signing, for he spoke favourably about it on several occasions, for example, the celebration of St. Bridget of Sweden in St. Peter's in October 1991 (see section 6.4) and in words of March 1995 cited at the beginning of section 8.[61]

During his third pastoral journey to Germany in 1996, the Pope met at Paderborn on 22 June the leadership of the Evangelical Church in Germany and others, and included in his address a reference to the 450th anniversary of the death of Martin Luther in 1546: 'After centuries of painful estrangement and debate, his memory lets us recognize more clearly the great value of his demand for a theology that is closer to Scripture and his desire for the spiritual renewal of the Church.' John Paul II went on to express grateful appreciation of the German study of the sixteenth-century doctrinal condemnations. From that study, important conclusions have followed.

> In the doctrine of justification a broad-reaching rapprochement has been achieved. Whenever one looks at the various consensus statements on the doctrine of justification, there is an ever stronger impression that in the important basic questions of the understanding of the message of justification there is fundamental agreement.[62]

The previous section 8.2 included (at note 56) a reference to the Pope's optimism about developments after the 'Catholic Response' in June 1998. In the following months he received reports on and gave encouragement to the efforts of Cardinals Cassidy and Ratzinger to clarify that Response. By May 1999, Cardinal Cassidy could communicate to Dr. Noko, General Secretary of the LWF, that the Holy See, naturally including Pope John Paul II first of all, approved the 'Annex' and accepted it together with the Declaration as a clear basis for a formal signing of the 'Official Common Statement' affirming the *Joint Declaration.*[63]

On Sunday, 31 October, virtually at the moment of the event at Augsburg, where Cardinal Cassidy and the Pontifical Council's Secretary, Bishop Walter Kasper, affixed their signatures for the Catholic Church, the Pope spoke of the event before reciting the Angelus at noon.

> In Augsburg, Germany, a very important event is taking place at this moment. Representatives of the Catholic Church and the Lutheran World Federation are signing a *Joint Declaration* on one of the principal points which have divided Catholics and Lutherans: the doctrine of justification by faith.
>
> This is a milestone on the difficult path of restoring full unity among Christians, and it is highly significant that it is taking place in the exact city where in 1530 a decisive page in the Lutheran reform was written with the *Augsburg Confession.*
>
> This document represents a sound basis for continuing the ecumenical theological research and for addressing the remaining problems with a better founded hope of resolving them in the future. It is also a valuable contribution to the purification of historical memory and to our common witness.
>
> I would like to thank the Lord for this intermediate goal on our journey, one that is difficult but rich in joy, unity, and communion among Christians.[64]

Thus, Pope John Paul II was a constant ecumenical actor, giving encouragement and his approval, during the complex and at times troubled genesis of the Lutheran–Catholic *Joint Declaration on the Doctrine of Justification.*

9. We turn now to two clarifying, but also controversial, actions of Pope John Paul II, which affected Lutheran–Catholic relations. On 16 June 2000, during an audience with Cardinal Joseph Ratzinger, Prefect of the Congregation for the Doctrine of the Faith, Pope John Paul II ratified and confirmed the Declaration *Dominus Iesus*, which the Congregation released the following 5th September, after which, however, the Pope felt constrained to speak out in a effort to limit the offense

given by the Declaration to Lutheran and other Protestant Christians. Nearly 3 years later, in Holy Week of 2003, Pope John Paul II issued his last encyclical, *Ecclesia de Eucharistia*, which contained, along with much else, passages of ecumenical clarification. These treated, first, the celebration of the Lord's Supper in Protestant ecclesial communities, such as the Lutheran, whose ministers have not been ordained by bishops in apostolic succession. Second, the encyclical of 2003 restated the limitations regarding 'eucharistic hospitality' or intercommunion between Catholics and members of those communities. Section 14 will relate selected Lutheran responses to these two documents of Catholic clarifications in Christology, ecclesiology and Eucharistic doctrine.

9.1 Of the six chapters of *Dominus Iesus* five on the role of Jesus Christ, form the following perspectives: Christ as the Full and Definitive Revelation of God (I, nos 5–8); the Incarnate Word and Holy Spirit in the Work of Salvation (II, nos. 9–12); the Unicity and Universality of the Salvific Mystery of Jesus Christ (III, nos. 13–16); the Church, the Kingdom of God and Kingdom of Christ (V, nos.18–19) and the Church and Other Religions regarding Salvation (VI, nos. 20–22). These chapters, in fact, held a great potential for reception and affirmation by Lutheran Christians, in order to maintain their soteriological concentration on Christ and his redeeming work appropriated in word and sacrament.

But *Dominus Iesus* roiled the waters ecumenically, as Lutherans and other Christians focused their attention on its Chapter IV (nos. 16–17), on the Unicity and Unity of the Church, which addressed the ecclesiological status of churches and communities outside the Catholic communion of churches.

The Church is unique in its salvific mediation of Jesus Christ, which is a truth of the Catholic faith to be firmly believed, and because of the promises of our Lord this unicity and the Church's unity are of the Church's integrity and will never be lacking. In fact, according to Vatican Council II's *Lumen gentium* (no. 8),

> the Church of Christ continues to exist fully only in the Catholic Church, and . . . "outside of her structure many elements can be found of sanctification and truth," that is, in those Churches and ecclesial communities which are not yet in full communion with the Catholic Church. (*Dominus Iesus*, no. 16, citing LG 8).

Since the Orthodox, Ancient Oriental and Old Catholic Churches have bishops in apostolic succession and a valid Eucharist, they are united to the Catholic Church by the closest bonds, so much so that, 'therefore the Church of Christ is present and operative also in these Churches, even though they lack full communion with the Catholic Church.'[65]

But Lutherans read the following paragraph of the Declaration, no. 17, with close attention and many took offense.

On the other hand, the ecclesial communities which have not pre-served the valid Episcopate and the genuine and integral substance of the Eucharistic mystery, are not Churches in the proper sense; however, those who are baptized in these communities are, by Baptism, incorporated in Christ and thus are in a certain commu-nion, albeit imperfect, with the Church. Baptism in fact tends *per se* toward the full development of life in Christ, through the integral profession of faith, the Eucharist, and full communion in the Church.[66]

The following paragraph included a citation of UR 3, on the Holy Spirit using the other communities as means of salvation, which for those who ponder it is a high commendation echoes the self-under-standing of non-Catholic Christians. But the paragraph also spoke to the difference between (1) the fullness of means and elements of the Church of Christ that are configured together in the Catholic Church, and (2) such elements, without this fullness, in the other communities.

9.2 Pope John Paul II was certainly apprised by Cardinal Cassidy about offense taken over *Dominus Iesus*, especially by Protestants, whose communions are declared not to be churches in the proper sense. John Paul II sought on 1 October to clarify the intent of *Dominus Iesus* in his talk before the Angelus at Sunday noon.

The Declaration is above all an invitation to all Christians to renew their fidelity to Christ, for with the Apostle Peter it is so 'that there is salvation in no one else' (Acts 4.12). Salvation is offered to non-Christians, but its ultimate source is Christ in whom man and God are united. The Declaration does not hinder interreligious dialogue, but shows clearly the foundations without which dialogue would be merely verbal and empty.

The Pope continued, regarding Ch. IV of *Dominus Iesus*:

The same also applies to the ecumenical question. If the document, together with the Second Vatican Council, declares that 'the single Church of Christ subsists in the Catholic Church,' it does not intend to express scant regard for the other Churches and Ecclesial Communities. This conviction is accompanied by the awareness that it is not due to human merit, but is a sign of God's fidelity, which is stronger than human weaknesses and sins . . . The Catholic Church – as the Document says – suffers from the fact that true particular Churches and Ecclesial Communities with precious elements of salvation are separated from her.

The document thus expresses once again the same ecumenical passion that is the basis of my Encyclical *Ut unum sint*. I hope that this Declaration, which is close to my heart, can, after so many erroneous interpretations, finally fulfil its function both of clarification and openness.[67]

With this text Pope John Paul II was working at 'damage control' in the hope that the ecclesiological passages of *Dominus Iesus* not become an impediment to Catholic ecumenical efforts and especially that it not undercut the progress represented by the milestone that is the *Joint Declaration on the Doctrine of Justification* signed just 10 months before the release of *Dominus Iesus*.

9.3 Late in his pontificate, Pope John Paul II's encyclical *Ecclesia de Eucharistia* of 17 April 2003, responded to desires and questions which often arise in ecumenical discussions. They had been voiced on behalf of German Lutherans by Bishop Eduard Lohse in Mainz, when he met the Pope during the latter's 1980 pastoral visit to Germany (see section 2).

To the Bishop's first request that Catholics be permitted certain ecumenical substitutes for Sunday Mass, *Ecclesia de Eucharistia* responds in no. 30, first by repeating Vatican II's statement that the ecclesial communities of the Reformation lack the sacrament of Order and therefore have not preserved the genuine and total reality of the Eucharist. Because of this (1) Catholics must refrain from receiving the Communion distributed in the celebrations of these communities, and (2) such celebrations or other ecumenical liturgies with members of those communities may not substitute for Sunday Mass. Thus, Pope John Paul II felt constrained to draw a clear line of delimitation around the Eucharist as the central, defining and obligatory action of Catholic worship.

The encyclical of 2003 also states the necessity of ecclesial communion in doctrine, sacramental life and Church governance before Christians may come together in Eucharistic celebration and communion (nos. 38–39 and 44). The Eucharist is an intensifying manifestation of ecclesial communion which presupposes that the celebrating community is visibly one, for example, that it is in true communion with the bishop and Pope named in every Catholic Eucharistic prayer. Still, in certain circumstances, the Catholic Eucharist may be extended, for their spiritual benefit, to properly disposed individual members of the other churches and communions (nos. 45–46).[68]

This chapter turns now to review the course of John Paul II's pontificate, especially the contacts just narrated, inserting accounts of how Lutherans, including their media, their church leaders and selected theologians responded to the Pope and his major actions during his long pontificate.

Section II – Lutherans view Pope John Paul II and respond to him and his pontificate

10.0 This account of Lutheran reactions to Pope John Paul II begins with a series of reports in the informative monthly journal, *Lutherische Monatshefte* (LM), which regularly informed its largely Lutheran readership of Catholic developments under Pope John Paul II. But some contributors to LM wrote in ways likely to awaken a sense of distance from the Catholic Church and even hostility toward the Pope for impeding what the writers took to be currents of reform and updating. Some LM writers did not observe Luther's teaching, on the 8th commandment, that a Christian should place a positive construction on what the neighbour says and does.[69] This, however, was not the only kind of response that appeared in the journal.

10.1 The LM issue for February 1980 offered two articles of stocktaking after the first year and some months of John Paul II's papacy.[70] The new Pope deals impressively with crowds and shows remarkable gifts in his teaching, for example, as he relates theological themes to Jesus Christ and social issues in his UN discourse of 1979, to human dignity and human rights. But the priority given to the Orthodox by his early visit to the Ecumenical Patriarch indicates that the Catholic Church judges evangelicals to be defective and most likely never to be recognized by Rome. All non-Roman churches should question their Catholic interlocutors whether the papal office can or cannot be reformed by purging it of the unacceptable claims, by Vatican I, of having universal jurisdiction and enjoying infallibility in teaching.

For LM, John Paul II's inaugural encyclical, *Redemptor hominis* (4 March 4, 1979) spoke weakly about ecumenical dialogue. His first Post-Synodal Apostolic Exhortation (*Catechesi tradendae*, 16 October 1979) seemed to locate the ecumenical dimension of catechesis in a clear and respectful presentation of doctrine to others – out of the fullness of truth and means of salvation entrusted to the Catholic Church.

The 15 December 1979 declaration by the Congregation for the Doctrine of the Faith that Hans Küng could no longer be considered a Catholic theologian shows a new readiness in Rome to discipline Catholics dissenting from the absolute claims of the Church. Rome does not value reform, but instead wants to make its system more secure. Lutherans should become more realistic in their ecumenical vision and not think that they can one day be reconciled with the Pope while remaining evangelical.

However, later in 1980, LM also published an essay underscoring, against Küng, that the truth does incarnate itself in affirmations, both in Scripture and in statements such as 'Jesus Christ is our sole bearer of salvation,' which Lutherans take as infallibly true. Further, Küng's functional Christology undermines the dogma of Nicea, professed in Art. 1 of the *Augsburg Confession*. Küng's account of Jesus Christ leaves redemption uncertain and undermines our consoling assurance that the Son of God died for us.[71]

10.2 The journal LM continued in a critical vein on the new Pontificate in the following years, with articles on the Special Synod in 1980 of the Dutch bishops ('Deep disappointment in Holland'),[72] on the demand that Edward Schillebeeckx clarify his Christology and theology of ordination,[73] on John Paul II's *Familiaris consortio*, found overconfident in discoursing about God's plan for marriage,[74] on the notification regarding the ecclesiology of Leonardo Boff,[75] and in a series of sharply worded comments by Roman correspondent Horst Schlitter on the 1990 Episcopal Synod on Priestly Formation (Catholic Church on the move – backwards! that is, on celibacy), on the 1991 Special Synod on Europe (ecumenically superficial) and on *Ordinatio sacerdotalis* (1994) with the added response in 1996 by the CDF (the granddaughter of the Holy Inquisition) that declared definitive the doctrine that only men may receive sacramental ordination.[76]

Still, some contrasting statements must be noted, for example, in H. Schlitter's admission that John Paul II consistently teaches on the basis of Vatican Council II,[77] and in LM's ample, respectful and appreciative presentations of John Paul II's social encyclicals, *Laborem exercens, Sollicitudo rei socialis* and *Centesimus annus*.[78]

11.0 LM's articles on John Paul II's pastoral visits to Germany and the Nordic lands, along with his 1983 letter on Martin Luther, merit special consideration, since some reports were not by religious journalists, but by office-holders in Lutheran churches. Personal meetings with the Pope elicited Lutheran appreciation for him and raised central ecclesiological questions.

11.1 In LM's December 1980 issue, the respected Territorial Bishop of Braunschweig, Gerhard Heintze, took stock of the ecumenical situation after John Paul II's first German visit in November of that year.[79]

John Paul II showed amazing vitality, as he moved through the stations of his very full programme. The encounter at Mainz (see section 2) constrained Protestant leaders to set aside the idea that the Pope from the traditional Catholic milieu of Poland would throw cold water on ecumenical hopes. He went beyond conventional words about the Protestant–Catholic situation in Germany and made his visit something other than a triumphal march by regularly showing consideration for non-Catholic Christians and non-Christians. All in all, evangelical Christians have many reasons for gratitude over this visit and for continuing to pray that its promise be fulfilled.

To be sure, the problems of our ecumenical relations have not been cleared away, but at least some of these were named in the Mainz meeting. Encountering John Paul II makes us face anew the issue of what we can say about the Catholic hierarchical system of Pope and bishops, for example, whether their claim to sole legitimacy is credible, from Scripture and history. John Paul II is impressive in his humanity, but we cannot see the Catholic structure as the only legitimate one, while admitting that our own structures leave much to be desired. But, still, the ecumenical effort is demanded by the Gospel.

11.2 In 1983, LM offered a comment on John Paul II's letter to Cardinal Willebrands on Martin Luther (see section 3.2).[80] The report began by recalling the Pope's words in Mainz in 1980 about positing a sign of union in the central mysteries of our faith. The Pope deals with preliminary historical issues, like Luther's deep religiosity, but also goes deeper to speak of 'fundamental questions about the correct interpretation and reception of the Christian faith'. The author wonders why John Paul II made no mention of the published results of the first two phases of dialogue on the world level. 'Could it be that he knows how deep is the difference over the true church, which for Luther lies hidden under the cross of Christ?'

Lutherans can be grateful that by his letter the Pope has alerted us to the danger connected with the notion of 'agreement in central and fundamental truths', since no Church union is acceptable which conceals the 'central fundamental difference' between ourselves and Catholics.

The last comment recalls the discussion during the 1980s of an alleged Catholic/Lutheran 'fundamental difference'. This broke out after the 1983 call for 'unity now' according to the 'Fries-Rahner plan', when some Lutheran responses claimed that such a difference, especially lying in opposed notions of the role of the church in mediating revealed truth and saving grace, prevented communion between the two traditions.[81] A 1987 conference in Puerto Rico was the venue for a Lutheran-sponsored ecumenical discussion of the issue, in which the notion of fundamental agreement, stated by Pope John Paul II regarding the *Augsburg Confession* in 1980 (see no. 11.1), found articulate defenders.[82]

11.3 Pope John Paul II's second visit to Germany in May 1987 was mainly for the beatifications of Rupert Mayer and Edith Stein. But it was treated in two LM articles, first, in a pre-visit interview with the Lutheran bishop of Lübeck, and second, in a balanced report in the wake of the visit.[83] The bishop countered the idea that the ecumenical atmosphere was cooling under John Paul II, by noting the Pope's declarations that the Catholic dedication to ecumenical effort is irrevocable. The visit did fulfil the hope of Bishop Wilckens that John Paul II would welcome the just completed study of the mutual doctrinal condemnations. Also, a positive step over the first visit was the holding of an ecumenical liturgy of the word in Augsburg, while the Pope's visit to the Marian shrine of Kevelaer posed a problem for evangelical Christians, which the dialogue about Mary should try to resolve.

John Paul II's third pastoral visit to Germany also included an ecumenical liturgy of the word in Paderborn on 22 June 1996, during which the Pope spoke again of Martin Luther, whose death 450 years earlier was being recalled that year. Historical work by evangelical and Protestant scholars, John Paul II said, enables us today to do portray more completely Luther's personality, while recent dialogues allow us to set aside old polemics. Then, a paragraph followed which drew attentive notice.

> Luther's thought was characterized by a strong emphasis on the individual, which weakened the awareness of the community's requirements. Luther's call for church reform in its original meaning was an appeal for repentance and renewal, which must begin in the life of every individual. Nevertheless, there are many reasons why division arose from this beginning. Among these is that failure in the Catholic Church for which Pope Adrian VI had already grieved in moving words; the interference of political and economic interests; and also Luther's own passion, which led him well beyond his initial intention to a radical criticism of the Catholic Church, her structure and her doctrine. We are all guilty. For this reason we are all invited to repentance and we all need to be purified again and again by the Lord.[84]

Soon after LM published two short articles, in one of which Reinhard Frieling claimed that the Pope's words about Luther were a distortion in his stress on the individual and his passion. For Luther the individual is a believer who has heard God's word, which presupposes both being in the community and being led to community. It was not his 'passion' that led Luther further but instead the basic theological issue of the Reformation, which is the relation of Faith, Scripture, Tradition and the Church, of which the Pope did speak elsewhere in his discourse at Paderborn.[85] But side-by-side with Frieling's comments, LM published a short piece by the Catholic historian, Rolf Decot, who saw John Paul II in movement towards a more satisfactory view of Luther, behind which the Pope could not conceal the traumatic impact of Reformation divisions. It was right that the Pope did not characterize central points of Luther's theology, since the ecumenical study of the condemnations is now pointing toward what could be reconciliation at a basic level.[86]

11.4 Earlier, section 5 of this chapter gave an account of the Pope's 1989 visit to the Nordic lands. The coverage of the visit in LM was partial, limited to Norway and Denmark, but it did express initial appreciation that the contacts with Lutherans were significant and not superficial.[87] However, the main part of the report told of shadows over the Pope's contacts with Scandinavian Lutherans.

In Norway, at the Cathedral of Nidaros, only four of the eleven Norwegian Lutheran bishops were on hand to greet John Paul II. In Denmark, the programme for the Vespers service at Roskilde bore on its cover an elegant reproduction of the medieval seal of the diocese, but the program itself made no mention of the presence of the Pope as the occasion for the service. After Vespers, the address directed to Pope John Paul II by the Lutheran Bishop of Copenhagen showed no sense of the well-known results of Catholic–Lutheran dialogues. Instead the Bishop rehearsed traditional points of difference between Catholics and Lutherans concerning Jesus Christ and his saving work, adding an observation that agreement over the visible institutions of ministry and church were not necessary to church unity.

In response, John Paul II's address pointed hopefully towards reconciliation by a process of dismantling the walls that had separated Lutherans and Catholics for half a millennium. Vatican II benefited from the presence and participation of the Danish Lutheran observer-theologian K. E. Skydsgaard and this began important efforts to evaluate afresh the questions raised by Luther and his message. We should be led towards a new relationship, motivated as Luther was by a desire to hear the Gospel and give credible witness to it. One could not miss John Paul II's sincere will to enter into dialogue, which contrasted with attitudes of his Danish hosts.

An American Lutheran of Scandinavian descent said that during John Paul II's visit he exemplified his sense of being chief pastor of all Christians, but that he expressed this toward Lutherans in a respectful, not presumptuous, way. He called on them to remember the faith and values of their ancestors, reaching back before the Reformation. In this he was opposing present-day secularism, and warning against reductions leading to denying the transcendent goal of human life.[88]

11.5 Finally, I cite a short but pointed report by the President of the Lutheran World Federation, the Bavarian Lutheran Bishop, Johannes Hanselmann, concerning his visit, with other LWF leaders, to Rome 3–5 May 1988.[89] They made the rounds, having good exchanges at the Unity Secretariat, the Commission Justitia et Pax, the Secretariat of State and the Congregation for the Doctrine of the Faith where they spoke with Cardinal Ratzinger.

With the Pope, Bishop Hanselmann spoke appreciatively of Catholic participation in events commemorating the *Augsburg Confession* in 1980 and Martin Luther in 1983. By these and other contacts the spirit of trust and mutual understanding is growing between Catholics and Lutherans. In response John Paul II spoke of the need to base our ecumenical hopes on ever deeper relations with Jesus Christ, which begins with our common baptism. 'Because we already share bonds of unity in Christ through baptism, we can never be satisfied with anything less than full communion.'[90]

Bishop Hanselmann summed up on the visit, 'This is the ecumenism one wishes for, open and objective, theologically precise and modest, in a brotherly atmosphere and based on the will clearly expressed to advance along the way towards more unity in practice.' The Bishop's words recall what Bishop Eduard Lohse said after his 1985 audience with Pope John Paul II, as cited at the end of section 4.2.

12.0 Lutheran reactions meriting mention were also called forth by the major texts for Catholic life that Pope John Paul II promulgated in 1983, that is, the revised Code of Canon Law, and in 1992, the *Catechism of the Catholic Church*. Then followed the Pope's two major encyclicals on moral issues, *Veritatis splendor* (1993) and *Evangelium vitae* (1995), on which a group of Lutheran theologians came together in an ecumenical symposium and published volume.

12.1 The Danish expert in church law, Peder Nørgaard-Højen, reported at length in LM on the new Code of 1983.[91] He noted the long period between the submission of an already revised text (October 1981) and the promulgation (January 25, 1983) during which the Pope himself, aided by a group of chosen experts, made final revisions.

The very existence of the Code rests on the complex nature of the Church, as both visible society and spiritual community (LG 8), with its indication of the two natures in Christ as a prime analogate. A church rejecting all law would represent a fall into ecclesiological docetism. The new Code is deeply rooted in Vatican II, even though in some areas the preferences of the Council minority have prevailed, as in the first-time inclusion of the papal title, 'Vicar of Christ' (can. 331), in the strong influence of the *Nota explicativa praevia* to *Lumen gentium*, and in the limited space given to the role of a general council.

The Code's fine specification of the rights and active roles of lay Catholics can serve to recall forgotten truths to Lutheran exponents of the priesthood of all believers. But the new law book has to disturb a Lutheran when it specifies that a Catholic pastor has to extend his care to even to 'those who do not profess the true faith' (can. 528.1, taken as indicating Protestants). Also, the norms regarding confessionally mixed marriages and joint worship, for example, with Eucharistic hospitality all but excluded, leave much for a Lutheran still to desire.

12.2 The *Catechism of the Catholic Church*, promulgated by Pope John Paul II on 8 December 1992, occasioned no less than three LM articles.

The Roman correspondent H. Schlitter offered an early report treating only the moral doctrine of the new catechism, noting that while it had been updated, drawing on John Paul II's social encyclicals and condemning genetic manipulation and actively induced euthanasia, it still rehearsed notions of sexuality that showed no change and remained distant from contemporary reality.[92]

Seven months later, LM offered comments on the new catechism by the Catholic systematic theologian Peter Hünermann and emeritus Lutheran Bishop Eduard Lohse.[93] The first singled out the difference between the new text and its predecessor, *The Catechism of the Council of Trent* (1566), in that the latter regularly evinced clear connections with the contemporary situation of the Reformation to which Catholic answers had to be given. The new exposition is a-historical, while receiving ample documentation from Scripture and broad currents of tradition.

In two critical reflections Hünermann noted, first, great simplicity in how the *Catechism* cites Scripture, which contrasts with the Pope's commendation of scholarly biblical study in his April address on the new document of the Pontifical Biblical Commission and with the sophisticated handling of the different New Testament texts on Jesus' resurrection in the recent German adult catechism.[94] Also Hünermann found in the *Catechism* a one-sidedly cultic-sacramental view of the priesthood, contrasting with the balance of the ministries of word, sacrament and pastoral leadership in Vatican II.

Bishop Lohse offered the general observation that the ample documentation of the new text shows the Catholic Church's sense of itself as responsible for articulating, protecting and magisterially advancing the whole of Christian tradition. All Christians, however, can and should learn from Part IV, where the *Catechism* teaches spirituality and prayer. One cannot say that the text sets aside Vatican II, far from it, but the style differs in the *Catechism*'s directness of teaching, which does not invite dialogue because it has behind it a magisterium claiming infallibility.

12.3 Because of limits of time and space, I only register here the fact that Pope John Paul II's major encyclicals on moral theology, *Veritatis splendor* (1993) and *Evangelium vitae* (1995), attracted sufficient attention among ecumenically minded Lutheran theologians that the two documents were taken up in a symposium in 1996 sponsored by the Lutheran World Federation's Strasbourg Institute for Ecumenical Research, which led to the publication of the papers 2 years later.[95]

13.0 Pope John Paul II's ecumenism encyclical *Ut unum sint* of 1995 (presented in section 7) called forth a number of different Lutheran responses.

13.1 The Roman correspondent of LM, Horst Schlitter began his report on *Ut unum sint* by indicating that the practice of giving Latin titles to papal documents already made them unattractive because this called up painful memories from the past.[96] From his reading, Schlitter concludes that this Pope gives no thought to removing even a single stone from the edifice of Roman doctrine. In fact the five points in *Ut unum sint* no. 79 that John Paul II euphemistically called 'areas in need of further study' (no. 79), really are 'the Roman essentials'. On papal primacy, when the Pope asks forgiveness for offenses leaving painful memories (no. 88) he goes right ahead to show that the primacy has to remain, even in its power for infallible teaching.

The following number of LM published a short statement by Hans Küng, listing what the Pope might have done for real ecumenical progress, such as recognizing Lutheran ordinations as valid and opening the way to intercommunion. The encyclical, however, really featured the Pope teaching on the Pope and by this he undercut his offer of a 'fraternal and patient dialogue' on the papacy.[97]

Neither of these LM reports took account of the extensive updating that *Ut unum sint* gave to Catholics in the whole world on the ecumenical advances of the previous 30 years. Neither noted its positive qualification of the ecclesial communities that reconfigured the Christian 'elements' during and after the Reformation. Neither noted its designation of Scripture, as 'highest authority', and tradition, as 'indispensable in interpretation', in the first of John Paul II's proposed dialogue points. But, fortunately, other voices spoke out in response to *Ut unum sint*.

13.2 Two ecumenical symposia, each including a Lutheran intervention, took up in considerable depth Pope John Paul II's invitation to dialogue on the exercise of the papal office and ministry.[98]

The experienced Lutheran ecumenist Harding Meyer spoke at Rome in 1997, offering first a clarification of the bases of Luther's qualification of the Pope as the Antichrist.[99] Study of the Reformer's polemic shows that it rested on particular papal claims and practices about interpreting Scripture, laying down new articles of faith and requiring obedience to himself as necessary to salvation. However, both Luther and Melanchthon spoke in other contexts of their readiness to accept papal primacy under certain conditions.

H. Meyer updated the Lutheran conditions concerning the primacy as *expectations* of 'a rightly exercised primacy', to serve church unity, which are in fact already being treated in Lutheran–Catholic dialogues today, after the Catholic entry into the ecumenical movement. Both Popes Paul VI and John Paul II have been aware of the problematic of their office and they have concretized new aspects of the papal ministry, especially with *Ut unum sint*. The relevant dialogues treating papal primacy were *The Gospel and the Church* (1972) and the US dialogues in Rounds 5 (1974) and 6 (1978), to which H. Meyer adds *Communio Sanctorum*, then nearing completion in Germany.[100]

The dialogues are important first steps, but the real centre of discussion will have to be efforts in dialogue (1) to interpret afresh the claim that papal primacy is necessary, but with greater sophistication in claiming that it rests on the *ius divinum* of God's founding of the church, and (2) to show that the Pope's infallibility in teaching is embedded in God's promise to *the church* to preserve it in the truth and that teachings at this level still admit the possibility of reform based on the perennially valid Scriptures and the central dogmatic tradition.

In the US symposium on *Ut unum sint*, Prof. David Yeago contributed the Lutheran paper.[101] He revisited and further developed the American dialogues, that of 1974, on the primacy and church unity, and of 1978, on teaching authority and infallibility. Neither dialogue made a great impact, probably because the issue goes well beyond the reconciliation of doctrines to deal with institutions existing in history. But the first dialogue made an important advance in treating 'the Petrine function' of all ministry, namely, the promotion of unity, communication, mutual help, and collaboration in the church's mission. This has been fruitful, appearing even in Pope John Paul II's description of his ministry in *Ut unum sint*, nos. 97–98. Yeago then developed a line of Lutheran reflection on the notion of a universal pastor.

But this discussion is weighed down immensely by the Catholic doctrine of the papacy culminating in Vatican I's definition of its 'supreme, full, ordinary, and immediate' power of rule. Lutherans repudiate this 'as leading to intolerable ecclesiastical tyranny'.[102] This indicates that the way ahead is not just movement towards doctrinal redefinition but much more a new form of papal practice to give the lie to such a Lutheran perception, for example, by care for legitimate diversity, collegiality and a wide diffusion of responsibility according to the principle of subsidiarity.

The US dialogue on teaching authority was, according to Yeago, burdened by being contemporaneous with Hans Küng's contestation of the very idea of irreformable teaching, which provoked inner-Catholic polarization in which Catholic members of the dialogue could not easily make fresh proposals. Also, the dialogue's treatment of infallibility hung in the air because it was not rooted in an account of magisterial ministry itself in the two traditions. The latter could have drawn on original themes of the Lutheran reformation, such as the account of the bishop's oversight of doctrine in the *Augsburg Confession*, (Art. 28), even though European and North American Lutheran churches do not show this in vigorous practice.

Realizing that ecumenical issues surrounding the papacy are beyond immediate solution, Yeago proposed small steps towards a better Lutheran–Catholic relationship, such as regular inclusion of each other's highest church leaders in the prayers of intercession of both churches. Also, the existing real communion between them could well be expressed in mutual consultation and conversation regarding matters of teaching, for example, between Lutheran and Catholic bishops in the same region.

13.3 Another Lutheran intervention on the papacy was the thematic issue of *Concordia Journal* in October 2003, in which theologians of the Lutheran Church – Missouri Synod offered six articles on the papacy, which move through early Christian history, Luther and the Lutheran confessional texts, and Vatican II on the papacy, to then treat John Paul II's *Ut unum sint* in two articles.[103]

Samuel Nafzger, who chairs the Missouri Synod's Commission on Theology and Church Relations, gave his readers an accurate summary of *Ut unum sint*, which highlighted the latter part of the text on the Catholic concept of church unity and the role of the Pope in this. No. 81 states the magisterium's responsibility for a definitive judgement on dialogues, and no. 86 has the one Church of Christ subsisting in the Catholic Church, while claiming that 'full unity will come about when all share in the fullness of the means of salvation entrusted by Christ to his Church.' In nos. 88–94 on Peter and the primacy, Nafzger highlighted how the description of papal ministry ends on the Pope speaking for all pastors, even in *ex cathedra* teaching about the content of the Christian faith (no. 94). These lines of John Paul II's encyclical raise the question for Nafzger whether the outcome of the desired 'patient and fraternal dialogue' has not already been decided.

For a dialogue going beyond *Ut unum sint*, Nafzger proposes beginning at the heart of the ecclesiological difference that becomes evident by juxtaposing, on the one hand, the Catholic Church's self-concept of subsisting as the one Church of Christ and, on the other hand, Art. VII of the *Augsburg Confession*, namely, that 'the church is the assembly of the saints in which the gospel is taught purely and the sacraments are administered rightly.' Thus situated, the dialogue could go on to review 'the Petrine function' in a ministry of unity and to explore the 'historical conditioning' of the relevant dogmatic formulations.[104]

The second Missouri Synod article on *Ut unum sint* drew important points from the interventions of Harding Meyer and David Yeago, related above, but also added in its final pages what the Lutheran Bishops of Sweden had said about the encyclical. They raised questions focused on the Catholic conviction of defective ecclesiality and orders among Protestants, namely, how this coheres with the Catholic recognition of baptism outside the Catholic Church. Can the papacy be made a constitutive element of *communio* between churches that practice the effective baptismal ingrafting of believers into the Body of Christ?

14.0 At this point, I pass over the intense Lutheran discussion prior to and following the signing of the *Joint Declaration on the Doctrine of Justification* (1999, see section 8), because references to Pope John Paul II played no role in that debate. But Lutheran reactions to the Instruction *Dominus Iesus* (2000) and to the encyclical *Ecclesia de Eucharistia* must be reviewed. The former did at times make connections with John Paul II's *Ut unum sint*. Also, they went beyond individual responses to take the form of a formal declaration, by the leadership of the Evangelical Church in Germany, setting forth in contrast to *Ut unum sint* the bases and aim of Lutheran-Protestant ecumenical efforts towards visible communion between the churches.

14.1 The American journal 'of evangelical and catholic theology', *Pro Ecclesia*, published short responses to *Dominus Iesus* early in 2001 from a rainbow of Christian traditions: by Avery Dulles (Catholic), Eugene Brand (Lutheran), Ephraim Radner (Anglican-Episcopalian), Geoffrey Wainwright (Methodist), Gabriel Fackre (Reformed) and Timothy George (Baptist-Evangelical).[105] Both the Methodist and Evangelical contributions lamented distortions of the document in media presentations. The Anglican-Episcopalian, Methodist and Reformed participants converged in praising *Dominus Iesus* as a confident, salutary word of conviction about Christ's universal saving work.

But G. Wainwright also cited *Ut unum sint*, no. 11, as a corrective to *Dominus Iesus*, Ch. IV, because in his encyclical Pope John Paul II spoke of how the presence and action of the 'elements' of sanctification and truth in the ecclesial communities ground the conclusion that the one Church of Christ is 'effectively present' in them, which *Dominus Iesus* does not cite.

E. Brand read *Dominus Iesus* carefully, leading to a critical question about its no. 16, note 56, where it cites a low-level 1985 CDF notification to clarify Vatican II's intended meaning in *subsistit in*, namely 'that there exists only one "subsistence" of the true Church,' which contrasts with 'only . . . *elementa*' outside the one subsisting church. This might seem minor, but the idea expressed in note 56 recalled to E. Brand's mind the undifferentiated identification of the Catholic Church with

Christ's Church, as taught by Pius XII, which Vatican II has been widely thought to have set aside. In an expression of his Lutheran self-understanding, Brand also objected to a simplistic account of church life outside the Catholic communion in terms only of 'elements', without recognition of the cohesion and configuration given to these gifts of Christ in the communities that are in real but imperfect communion with the Catholic Church.

14.2 The successor journal to LM, *Zeitzeichen*, formed by fusion with three other journals after German reunification, published, in late 2000, two substantial Lutheran responses to *Dominus Iesus*.[106]

Eberhard Jüngel noted that the Pope's effort to explain at a Sunday Angelus address the true intent of *Dominus Iesus* (see section 9.2) suggests that the doctrinal congregation had not done its work well. Actually, there is much for Jüngel to praise in the Instruction, beginning with the title, which is a central early confession of the Christian faith (cf 1 Cor. 12.3). Also, Lutherans have to sign on when the document asserts that human language *can* express the truth revealed by God.

But Jüngel says that Lutherans have to question the spousal imagery regarding Christ and the church in *Dominus Iesus*, no. 16, where it is not accompanied by a clear assertion of their distinction. He brings out two points on which he differs from the interpretation by Cardinal J. Ratzinger on *Dominus Iesus* in an interview in the *Frankfurter Allgemeine Zeitung*. First, it is an innovation beyond Vatican II to say that *subsistit in* means that the Church of Christ has the character of a 'subject' in the Catholic Church. Second, the same Ratzinger had earlier held that according to Vatican II the separated communities were, yes, churches, but not *the* Church. The challenge posed by *Dominus Iesus* was then for Jüngel the occasion to set forth in seven points an evangelical Lutheran understanding of the church.

Ulrich H. J. Körtner's essay, following that of E. Jüngel, expresses a basic 'I object!' to the Catholic ecclesiology expressed in *Dominus Iesus*, Ch. IV. The document is, for unrealistic ecumenists engaged in consensus-discovery, a wake-up call from their dreams after the signing of the *Joint Declaration* less than a year before. The claims of the new document are for many a surprise, but the reason is that the dialogues have bracketed fundamental ecclesiological issues and so allowed Catholics to remain silent regarding their claim to be the one church of Christ.

The Catholic view is not complementary but directly opposed to, the basic position advanced by Körtner as the evangelical starting point in ecclesiological dialogue. This has to start with mutual recognition of each other as churches of Christ amid a plurality of 'irremovable variety' of Christian bodies in the modern world. But the Catholic Church cannot do this, since it comes to dialogue to teach others out of its 'full possession' of the truth of God.

14.3 In 2000 and 2001 the Evangelical Church in Germany (EKD) articulated its position in response to the Catholic challenge in *Dominus Iesus*.[107] On 9 November 2000, just two months after the publication of *Dominus Iesus*, the EKD Synod issued a 'Declaration' (*Kundgebung*) on its participation in the movement of the churches towards greater unity. The aim for the EKD is unity in the form of sharing in word and sacrament, with mutual recognition of ministries, between churches which agree on the fundamental meaning of the Gospel of Christ, even while holding different confessional and doctrinal positions. The initial effort of the EKD has to be greater unity with the evangelical 'free churches' (Baptists, Mennonites, Methodists) and with the Anglican Churches.

Regarding the Catholic Church, the Declaration ascertains an opposition between its own and the Roman concept of unity, because the latter insists on unity 'with and under the Pope'. *Dominus Iesus*, with its affirmation of the precedence of the Roman Catholic Church and the Catholic refusal to acknowledge evangelical churches as 'sister churches', has to be judged a setback for efforts towards greater unity. It is a 'Roman' claim, not one that the EKD judges to be 'catholic'.

Ten months later, on 8 September 2001, the Council of the EKD approved and released to the public a more elaborate account of 'Church Unity (*Kirchengemeinschaft*) according to Evangelical Understanding,' which had been submitted by the EKD cabinet of theologians working under the leadership of Professors Eberhard Jüngel and Dorothea Wendebourg.

The theologians' text mentions *Dominus Iesus* in its opening paragraph as an expression of the self-understanding of the Catholic Church which now challenges evangelicals to give an account of the type of church unity they are seeking in their ecumenical efforts. The paper distinguishes the foundation (*Grund*) of the church, which is the Gospel preached and celebrated in sacraments, so as to make Christ present as the grace and truth of God to give believers the certainty of faith and form them into the body of Christ as the ecclesial community of Christian believers.

Particular churches, even though their doctrines differ in their confessions and teaching, have to work towards an ordered life together and communion with other churches, based on a common understanding of the Gospel, recognition of Jesus Christ as the foundation who gives himself in word and sacrament and mutual recognition as churches of Christ who practice fellowship in word and sacrament.

A later section of the EKD theologians' paper goes through the different areas of ecumenical engagement, for example, with the Anglican churches, Baptists, Roman Catholic Church and Orthodox Churches.

The concept of unity developed in the paper seems to its authors to be obviously incompatible with the Catholic conception of full, visible unity. Still, recent Catholic developments have shown movement regarding the foundations in faith, which make it necessary to seek further clarification and thus test whether the incompatibility is as deep as it seems. However, evangelical efforts have to aim at an agreement that a single, historically developed form of ministerial office cannot be made a condition of being in communion. Then the concluding word about Catholic forms is that evangelicals must contradict (1) the necessity of a 'Petrine office' and thus of papal primacy, (2) the Catholic understanding of apostolic succession, (3) the refusal to admit women to the ordained ministry, and (4) the major role in the Catholic Church that is played by canon law.

It will not surprise that Cardinal Walter Kasper made explicit mention, at the Pontifical Council's plenary meeting of November 2003, of this EKD position paper. Kasper did not go into detail on the list of contradictions, but explained the EKD paper as a sign of a fundamental ecclesiological problem presently inhibiting the Catholic dialogues with the ecclesial communities of Reformation traditions. This attempt to legitimate confessional pluralism creates a 'stalemate', which is especially evident in Protestant insistence on intercommunion – going against a fundamental element of Catholic identity.[108]

14.4 To complete this section, I select one Lutheran response to Pope John Paul II's last encyclical, *Ecclesia de Eucharistia* (2003), which came in George Lindbeck's contribution to an ecumenical symposium on it in *Pro Ecclesia*.[109]

Lindbeck's basis and criterion will not be the *Joint Declaration* of 1999, but another document from Augsburg, the *Confession* of 1530, which ranks as the principal statement of Lutheran faith and church reforms. Other Lutherans have lamented the restrictive norms of the encyclical on Eucharistic hospitality and claimed that John Paul II should have been more welcoming, now that the Lutheran–Catholic consensus has been formally declared regarding the central article of justification. But for Lindbeck such an outcome would run the risk of obscuring the distance remaining before Lutherans and Catholics are in full communion of faith and so are truly ready for visible church unity.

Lindbeck laments the unnuanced way John Paul II cited Vatican II on ministry being defective in non-episcopal communities, since the original term *defectus* in *Unitatis redintegratio*, no. 22, denotes a lack of perfection in something that is basically given, not a complete 'lack' or 'absence' that would be destructive of the sacramental reality.[110]

The Lutheran theologian, who attended Vatican II as an observer, notes that the great reforms of the Council are taken for granted by the encyclical and are not reversed, such as communion under both forms, wide use of the vernacular, upgrading of the liturgy of the word and a wider concept of Christ 'really' present in different ways, while there with 'unique intensity' in the elements received in Holy Communion. Lutherans should not claim that John Paul II's Eucharistic encyclical was going back on the very Vatican II reforms that met Lutheran concerns in ways beyond their expectations.

What concerned the Pope in no. 10 of the encyclical, that some take the sacrament as primarily celebrating the togetherness of the community, must also be a concern for Lutherans, who focus instead on the Lord's coming and self-gift in Communion as the central sacramental event that renews faith and certainty of God's saving grace in Christ.

Finally, Lindbeck has to register his concern over the Pope's emphatic recommendation of the pious practice of adoration of Christ present in the reserved sacrament (*Ecclesia de Eucharistia*, no. 25). One misses a sound Catholic indication that such tabernacle piety should at best have corporate forms. The practice was not known in the first millennium of Christianity, and the Pope's intent to foster it can, at best, be taken as a challenge that provokes Lutherans to reflect more deeply on the reasons for their critical reservations.

15.0 Pope John Paul II's death on 2 April 2005 occasioned several expressions of Lutheran appreciation for him and for his pontificate.

15.1 The General Secretary of the LWF, Dr. Ishmael Noko, said that even under a conservative Pope like John Paul II the Catholic Church during the years of his pontificate contributed substantially to major ecumenical processes, of which the *Joint Declaration on the Doctrine of Justification* was the great milestone. 'While for many churches the very institution of the Papacy lies beyond what they could adopt for themselves, many Christians would at the same time recognize that John Paul II truly exemplified a pastoral ministry of unity.'[111]

The President of the Lutheran Church, Missouri Synod, Dr. Gerald Kieschnick, said that John Paul II provided inspiration and leadership beyond the Catholic Church to the whole Christian world,

> with his uncompromising stances in favor of life and against the culture of death. Though historic differences between our churches remain, Pope John Paul II will also be remembered for his call for Christian churches to seek to work out their differences in faithfulness to their convictions and to their doctrinal heritage.[112]

The former ELCA Bishop of Metro New York, Dr. William H. Lazareth, listed the components of John Paul II's 'ecumenical legacy', mainly from *Ut unum sint*, with attention to its solidification of Vatican II's recognition of the Christian elements in church bodies not of the Catholic communion. The encyclical was important for praising the work of the Faith and Order Commission of the World Council of Churches, especially the Lima document, *Baptism, Eucharist, and Ministry* (1982). On John Paul II's watch, the valuable notion of 'reconciled diversity' was given expression in the *Joint Declaration on Justification*, which for Lazareth is a historical *novum* by the Catholic Church's approval in a binding manner of the outcome of ecumenical dialogue.[113]

Among individual Lutherans whom I contacted, one found the list of John Paul II's ecumenical initiatives towards Lutherans (cf Appendix 1, of this chapter) 'staggering'. On a wider scale, another individual remarked that

> John Paul II never tired of warning the West of the dangers of atheism, secularism, and all other ideologies that deny God and the transcendent goal of human life and history. He believed that the Church has an indispensable role in leading humanity to knowing truth in its fullness and thereby becoming truly human.

The author who summed up John Paul II for the German monthly on which I've drawn above, now called *Zeitzeichen*, singled out John Paul II's impact through the media on the whole world, which can make Protestants feel they belong to a small provincial church which is poorly equipped for the tasks of the future.[114] The Pope's claim to teach the truth is just one voice in the today's polyphony of such claims, but it also constrains Protestants to give more principled answers and draw clearer lines. Under pressure from John Paul II's impact, the writer has recourse to a strong passage from Luther's 1520 *Appeal to the Christian Nobility* against there being any Christian 'clerical-spiritual estate', for baptism makes all to be spiritual, although not all are called to minister. Still the late Pope was an exemplary man, in courage and consistency, with humour and affability – qualities that made him credible to millions. The final image comes from John Paul II's funeral, with the Gospel text lying on his coffin.

15.2 A more detailed Lutheran appreciation of John Paul II, by Dr. David Yeago, appeared in the journal *Pro Ecclesia*.[115]

John Paul II's teaching and church government was truly papal, in 'pulling to the center' against centrifugal efforts by progressive Catholics. But even decisions which most Protestants find wrong, as on women's ordination, were not stupid and ungrounded. More than anything else, Lutherans need to hear the central point of the message that John Paul II brought to the world, as he constantly insisted on what Vatican II's *Gaudium et spes* says about Christ the Redeemer (*Redemptor hominis*) ennobling human existence. Christ and no one else is at the centre of history in making our being human a 'wondrous thing, and every human being is a sacred mystery'.

John Paul II warned us all to avoid illusory kinds of freedom by taking seriously the threat of 'the culture of death' as it defines pragmatically the main arena of choice. But where freedom is responding to the truth, there our life is mysterious and wondrous, especially in other persons, each united in being to Jesus Christ, who thus draw forth our love, whatever be their capability or social utility.

All of the Pope's 'controversial teachings' on 'life-issues' arise from this profound philosophical and theological meditation on the wonder of human life and what fosters or threatens, respects or degrades it. Agree or disagree with him on this or that issue, it is a compelling

Christian social and cultural vision which it would be boorish for thinking Christians of any denomination to ignore.[116]

This can stand as an authentic Lutheran perception resting on consideration of John Paul II's teaching ministry, especially since the same author observed realistically in another context 'that we cannot assume that widespread Protestant admiration for the Pope as a man and Christian witness translates into a positive attitude toward the papacy as an institution and an order of church governance.'[117]

Conclusion

16.0 Turning now to a concise listing of components of John Paul II's theological legacy as this was expressed in exchanges with Lutherans, we can begin with what has just been articulated.

(1) Lutherans can gratefully appreciate Pope John Paul II's impressive theology of human dignity, as both an indicative in Christ and an imperative for human action, but this does not resolve the Lutheran–Catholic difference and opposition over the Petrine ministry itself of serving church unity at the universal level (section 15.2)

(2) Pope John Paul II, although lacking ecumenical experience before 1978, did become a major ecumenical figure, whose voice was distinctive in underscoring Catholic–Lutheran agreement on fundamental truths about God and Christ as held in 'creedal Christianity' (sections 1.2 and 2).

(3) John Paul II came to include central truths about justification as also being matters of consensus between Catholics and Lutherans, but he accompanied this with observations about differences remaining in ecclesiology which the soteriological agreement did not resolve (section 2).

(4) The personal contacts between this Pope and Lutherans were marked by a religious tone and by his encouragement of ecumenical processes then underway (sections 3.3, 4.1, 6 and 11.5).

(5) But John Paul II has also said regularly and clearly that common participation by Lutherans and Catholics in Holy Communion presupposed full consensus in faith and unity in visible church

government (sections 4.1, 5 [6th point], and 9.3 on *Ecclesia de Eucharistia* of 2003).

(6) John Paul II accepted in 1989 that the Catholic Church should begin processes looking towards official and possibly binding reception of Lutheran–Catholic dialogue results, which led to the *Joint Declaration on the Doctrine of Justification* in 1999 (sections 4.1, 5 [at note 27], and 8).

(7) This Pope took part in singular events in St. Peter's Basilica, where Lutheran episcopal primates joined him three times as co-presiders at Vespers services commemorating St. Birgitta/Bridget of Sweden (section 6.4).

(8) John Paul II's legacy of forthright assertions of both doctrine and church discipline exposed him to suffering journalistic mistreatment, by accounts putting him in what for Lutherans would be a bad light, although other Lutherans saw deeper and treated his actions and words with due seriousness (sections 10.2, 11.1, 11.5, and 13.1).

(9) *Ut unum sint* (1995) is a major confirmation by John Paul II of what Vatican II said about the ecclesial character of churches, like the Lutheran, which are in real but only imperfect communion with the Catholic Church. This character remains given in spite of such communities lacking ecclesial elements and areas of doctrinal difference still remaining to be clarified (section 7).

(10) In *Ut unum sint*, John Paul II formulated essential Catholic terms for a broad ecumenical discussion of the Petrine ministry of universal oversight and service of unity. This remains on the ecumenical agenda to this day (sections 7 and 13.2–3).

(11) In *Ut unum sint* Pope John Paul II set forth the Catholic vision of the ecumenical goal of unity, which some Lutherans have contested, since they hold and propose that confessional and doctrinal differences may subsist in ecclesial communion, even without working out reconciled diversities, as was done in formulating the Lutheran–Catholic *Joint Declaration* concerning justification (sections 14.2–3).

(12) In documents of Catholic doctrinal and disciplinary clarification, such as *Dominus Iesus* (2000) and *Ecclesia de Eucharistia* (2003), the pontificate of John Paul II contributed to a more intense ecumenical reflection, still going on, concerning the overall aim of the ecumenical movement (sections 9 and 14).

Appendix 1

Pope John Paul II and Lutherans – A Chronicle

1978, 16 Oct.: Cardinal Karol Wojtyła, Archbishop of Crakow, elected successor to Pope John Paul I.

1980, 25 June : Words at the General Audience on that day's 450th anniversary of the Augsburg Confession of 1530.

1980, 15 Nov.: During pastoral visit to Germany, met in Mainz with the Council of the German Evangelical Church, exchanging addresses with the Church President, Prof. Dr Eduard Lohse. Shortly after, a Joint Ecumenical Commission in Germany began work to study the divisive issues.

1983, 31 Oct.: Letter to Cardinal Jan Willebrands, Pres. of SPCU, on the upcoming 5th centenary of the birth of Martin Luther, Nov. 10, 1483.

1983, 11 Dec.: Visit to Christuskirche of the Lutheran Community in Rome.

1984, 2 Mar.: Audience for members of the International Lutheran–Catholic dialogue commission.

1985, May–July: Exchange of letters with Bishop James Crumley, President of the Lutheran Church in America (LCA), followed by audience with nine bishops of the LCA on 22 Sept..

1985, June 13: Audience with Bishop Eduard Lohse of the Evangelical Church in Germany, who came to Rome to report on the work of the Joint Ecumenical Commission formed after the papal visit to Germany in 1980.

1986, 2 Oct.: Audience for a group of LCA bishops on ecumenical pilgrimage in Europe.

1987, 4 May: During 2nd visit to Germany, ecumenical service in Augsburg, with reference to Luther/Cajetan meeting in 1518 and to the submission of Augsburg Confession in 1530.

1989, 1–10 June: Pastoral Visit to the Nordic lands, with several ecumenical services and meetings in Norway, Iceland, Finland, Denmark and Sweden.

1990, 13 Jan.: Letter to Bishop Johannes Hanselmann, President of the Lutheran World Federation (LWF), sending greetings to the Eighth LWF Assembly in Curitiba, Brazil.

1991, 5 Oct.: Ecumenical vespers in St. Peter's Basilica commemorating the 6th Centenary of the Canonization of St. Bridget of Sweden, celebrated together with the Lutheran Archbishops of Uppsala and Turku, Finland.

1991, 7 Oct.: Audience with Lutheran and Catholic participants in International Study Conference on St. Bridget.

1992, 23 April: Audience for LWF delegation, led by Pres. G. Brakemeier and Gen. Secy. G. Stallsett, on the 25th anniversary of the International L/RC

Dialogue , concluding with prayer service in Redemptoris Mater chapel in the Apostolic Palace.

1995, 14 March: Audience for participants in a conference on Lutheran–Catholic relations, held at the Bridgetine Centre, Farfa, Italy.

1995, 30 May: Publication of *Ut unum sint*, Pope John Paul II's encyclical on commitment to ecumenism.

1997, 19 April: Address to Episcopal Conference of Scandinavia, during ad limina visit, with mention of their ecumenical initiatives, the L/RC dialogue commission, and recent admission of women as bishops in Lutheran Churches.

1998, 28 June: Reflection at Sunday Angelus to the 'important ecumenical achievement' of the *Joint Declaration on the Doctrine of Justification*, on which the CDF and PCPCU had just issued 'The Response of the Catholic Church.'

1999, 18 Jan.: Welcome to the Lutheran Archbishop of Turku and Finland, who was leading delegation to Rome for feast of Finland's patron St Hendrik.

1999, 4 June: Letter to the Archbishop of the Lutheran Church of Sweden, on occasion of ecumenical celebration in Uppsala of the 10th anniversary of the papal visit to Sweden.

1999, 31 Oct.: Expression, at Sunday Angelus, of satisfaction over the signing that day in Augsburg, Germany, of the *Joint Declaration on the Doctrine of Justification*, by Cardinal E. I. Cassidy, for the Catholic Church, and the President and Vice-Presidents of the LWF.

1999, 13 Nov.: Ecumenical vespers in St Peter's Basilica, honoring St. Bridget of Sweden, recently proclaimed co-patroness of Europe, with the Lutheran Bishops of Uppsala and Turku, Finland, joining the Pope in presiding.

1999, 9 Dec.: Audience with Dr Christian Krause, LWF President, and the delegation he led to Rome.

2000, 5 Sept.: Publication by the Congregation of the Doctrine of the Faith of the Declaration *Dominus Iesus*, On the Unicity and Salvific Universality of Jesus Christ and the Church, ratified and confirmed by Pope John Paul II, and treating in Ch. IV, nos. 16–17, 'The Unicity and Unity of the Church.'

2000, 1 Oct.: Words at Sunday noon Angelus on the true intent of *Dominus Iesus*.

2002, 4 Oct.: Ecumenical celebration of Vespers in St. Peter's Basilica, commemorating the 7th centenary of the birth of St. Bridget of Sweden, with participation of Lutheran bishops of Northern Europe and prayers by the Emeritus Lutheran Archbishop of Uppsala and by Bishop Eero Huovinen, Lutheran Bishop of Helsinki.

2002, 16 Nov.: Audience for Bishop Finn Wagle, Lutheran bishop of Nidaros/ Trondheim, Norway, and a delegation come to Rome for the feast of St Olav, patron of Norway.

2003, 20 Jan.: Audience for Bishop Erik Vikström, Bishop of Porvoo, Finland, with a delegation come to Rome for the feast of St. Hendrik, patron of Finland.

2003, 24 Mar.: Audience with a delegation of bishops and members of the Evangelical Lutheran Church in America, led on their ecumenical pilgrimage by the newly elected presiding bishop, Mark Hansen.

2003, 11 April: Audience with Dr. Christian Krause, LWF President, leading small delegation.

2004, 19 Jan.: Welcome to the ecumenical delegation from Finland, led by Bishop Eero Huovinen Lutheran bishop of Helsinki, in a visit to Rome for the feast of Finland's patron St Hendrik.

2005, 2 April: Death of Pope John Paul II at age of 84.

Appendix 2

Lutheran–Catholic (L/RC) Ecumenical Texts Issued during John Paul II's Pontificate

1980: L/RC International Joint Commission, *All under One Christ*, Statement on the Augsburg Confession; and 'Ways to Community'. Feb. 23, 1980.

1981: L/RC International Joint Commission, *The Ministry in the Church*. March 13, 1981.

1983: L/RC International Joint Commission, *Martin Luther, Witness to Jesus Christ*. May 10, 1983.

1984:L/RC International Joint Commission, Facing Unity: Models, Forms and Phases of Catholic–Lutheran Church Fellowship. March 3, 1984.

1984: Bilateral Working Group of the German Catholic Bishops' Conference and the Leadership of the United Evangelical Lutheran Church of Germany, *Kirchengemeinschaft in Wort und Sakrament*.

1985: US Lutheran–Catholic Dialogue, *Justification by Faith*.

1986: Ecumenical Working Group of Evangelical and Catholic Theologians, *Lehrveurteilungen – kirchentrennend*? I, *Rechtfertigung, Sakramente und Amt im Zeitalter der Reformation und heute*. Eds. Karl Lehmann and Wolfhart Pannenberg (Freiburg: Herder, and Göttingen: Vandenhoeck & Ruprecht, 1986). In English as *The Condemnations of the Reformation Era:*

Do They Still Divide? Eds. K. Lehmann and W. Pannenberg (Minneapolis: Fortress, 1990).

1992: US Lutheran–Catholic Dialogue, *The One Mediator, the Saints, and Mary.*

1993: L/RC International Joint Commission, *Justification and the Church.*

1995: US Lutheran–Catholic Dialogue, *Scripture and Tradition.*

1999: LWF & the Catholic Church, *Joint Declaration on the Doctrine of Justification.* October 31, 1999.

2000: Bilateral Working Group of the German Catholic Bishops' Conference and the Leadership of the United Evangelical Lutheran Church of Germany, *Communio Sanctorum. Die Kirche als Gemeinschaft der Heiligen.* In English as *Communio Sanctorum. The Church as the Communion of Saints* (Collegeville: Liturgical Press, 2004)

2005 (Jan.): US Lutheran–Catholic Dialogue, *The Church as Koinonia of Salvation: Its Structures and Ministries.*

Notes

1. On the Council observers and guests, Thomas F. Stransky gave precious accounts based on his own experiences as a worker of the first hour in the Unity Secretariat. 'Paul VI and the Delegated Observers/ Guests to Vatican Council II,' in *Paul VI e l'ecumenismo.* Pubblicazioni dell'Istituto Paolo VI, 23 (Rome: Ed. Studium, 2001), 118–158, and 'The Observers at Vatican II. A Unique Experience of Dialogue,' in Centro pro unione (Rome), *Bulletin,* no. 63 (Spring 2003), 8–14. Apart from their reports on the Council by letter and by addresses at LWF meetings, the Lutheran observers contributed chapters to the volume *Dialogue on the Way: Protestants Report from Rome on the Vatican Council* (ed.), George Lindbeck (Minneapolis MN: Augsburg, 1965).

2. The report's 75 numbered paragraphs are divided into these chapters: I. The Gospel and Tradition, II. The Gospel and the World, III. The Gospel and the Office of Ministry in the Church and IV. The Gospel and the Unity of the Church. The report included this prophetic but challenging claim, 'Today . . . a far-reaching consensus is developing in the interpretation of justification' (no. 26). For the text: *Growth in Agreement* (eds), Harding Meyer and Lukas Vischer (New York: Paulist, and Geneva, World Council of Churches, 1984), 168–189.

3. The original text is *Das Herrenmahl* (Paderborn: Bonifatius and Frankfurt: Lembeck, 1978), which came out as *The Eucharist* (Geneva: Lutheran World Federation, 1980), with the English text also given in *Growth*

in Agreement, 190–214. – In the United States, the Catholic Bishops' Committee on Ecumenical Affairs and the Lutheran National Committee of the LWF appointed members to a dialogue commission in the USA which began meeting in 1965, producing reports on: (1) The Status of the Nicene Creed as Dogma of the Church (1965), (2) One Baptism for the Forgiveness of Sins (1966), (3) The Eucharist as Sacrifice (1967), (4) Eucharist and Ministry (1970), (5) Papal Primacy and the Unity of the Church (1974), and (6) Teaching Authority & Infallibility in the Church (completed in September 1978).

4. *All Under One Christ* is given in *Growth in Agreement*, 241–247. The statement could base itself on joint studies under way before the anniversary year, such as *The Role of the Augsburg Confession. Catholic and Lutheran Views* (ed.), Joseph A. Burgess (German original 1977; Philadelphia: Fortress Press, 1980), and *Confessing One Faith: A Joint Commentary on the Augsburg Confession by Lutheran and Catholic Theologians* eds), G. W. Forell and J. F. McCue (German original 1980; Minneapolis: Augsburg Publishing House, 1982).

5. Citing from *Growth in Agreement*, 243. The text goes on to reaffirm the 'broad consensus' on understanding justification 'solely by grace and by faith in Christ's saving work and not because of any merit in us that we are accepted by God and receive the Holy Spirit who renews our hearts and equips us for and calls us to good works' (no. 14), a passage which will be central to the *Joint Declaration* of 1999.

6. Speech of 25 June 1980, cited from *Information Service*, no. 44 (1980/ III–IV), 91. This is the documentary publication of the Vatican Secretariat (from 1989, 'Pontifical Council') for Promoting Christian Unity. The Pope's words on 25 June were not isolated remarks, as John A. Radano shows in *Lutheran und Catholic Reconciliation on Justification* (in press: Grand Rapids: Eerdmans, 2008), 69–70, on further words by John Paul II on the *Augsburg Confession* in 1980, 1984 and 1987.

7. 'All Under One Christ, No. 14, cited in note 5.

8. Before the papal visit, the German Bishops' Conference had a concise one-volume history of the church in Germany published, for use in parishes, which contained a sharply critical section, by Prof. Remigius Bäumer (Freiburg), on Luther as the irresponsible fomenter of discord and false doctrines among Christians, while omitting Luther's insistence on the central and fundamental truths about God and Christ. A Lutheran historian, Gerhard Müller offered a pointed rebuttal in 'Martin Luther im Zerrspiegel. Antwort auf die Behauptungen von Remigius Bäumer', *Lutherische Monatshefte* 19 (1980) 708–711. The *Time* report on the papal visit said that the Pope spoke about Luther and the Reformation 'with

considerably more grace than Bäumer' (1 December 1980), including acknowledgments that Catholics also had their part in causing the division of the churches in the sixteenth century.

9. Meeting of 17 November 1980; texts from *Information Service*, no. 45 (1981 / I), 5–6.

10. See Section 9.3 in text on the passages of Pope John Paul II's *Ecclesia de Eucharistia* (2003) which take up the first and third of Bishop Lohse's requests.

11. Martin Luther – Witness to Jesus Christ, cited from Information Service, no. 52 (1983 / II), 84–88, from p. 85.

12. The letter is cited here from *Information Service*, no. 52 (1983 / II), 83–84.

13. Citing *Information Service*, no. 52 (1983 / II), 94–95. The Pope preached in German, the main language of the Christuskirche, which serves families of German Lutherans living and working in Rome. In the sentence cited, the Pope is echoing Vatican II's Pastoral Constitution, *Gaudium et spes*, no. 10, para. 2, which some call 'the Christological credo' of the Council.

14. See the list of U.S. dialogue documents given in note 3. As Bishop Crumley wrote, a seventh text, completed in 1983, was about to come out in booklet-form from the U.S. Lutheran–Catholic Commission, *Justification by Faith* (eds), H. George Anderson, T. Austin Murphy, and Joseph A. Burgess. *Lutherans and Catholics in Dialogue*, VII (Minneapolis, MN: Augsburg Publishing House, 1985).

15. Letter of Bp. Crumley, cited from Information Service, no. 59 (1985 / III–IV), 18. The same number of Information Service gives both Bp. Crumley's letter of May 22, 1985, and Pope John Paul II's response of July 22, 1985, on pp. 17–20. The two texts also come out in a booklet with annotations published by the Department of Ecumenical Relations of the Lutheran Church of America (New York, 1985).

16. In 1982, three national Lutheran churches in the USA voted to come together as a single church in 1988. These were the Lutheran Church in America, the American Lutheran Church, and the Association of Evangelical Lutheran Churches. The new church, the ELCA, has nearly 5 million baptized members.

17. *Information Service*, no. 59 (1985 / III–IV), 21.

18. E. Lohse, 'Schritte ökumenischer Verständigung. Zum Besuch bei Papst Johannes Paul II. in Rom', *Lutherische Monatshefte* 24 (1985), 340–342, in the August issue. The timing of the visit was due to the fact that in 1985 Bishop Lohse would complete his term as President of the Council of the

EKD, which would also end his co-chairmanship of the Joint Ecumenical Commission.

19. Lohse, 'Schritte ökumenischer Verständigung', 341.
20. Address to the Norwegian ambassador to the Holy See, 17 February 1983; citing *Information Service*, no. 51 (1983), 6. Radano gathers this and other ecumenical-theological points from these meetings of 1980 to 1988 in his *Lutheran and Catholic Reconciliation* (as in n. 6), 78–80.
21. Address at the National Shrine of Thingvellir, Iceland, 3 June 1989 (*Information Service*, 71 [1989 / III–IV], 93), and 9 June service in the Lutheran Cathedral of Uppsala, Sweden (ibid., 108). Also, the prayer service in Oslo, 1 June (ibid., 85).
22. Address to the Danish Lutheran bishops, 7 June, after a service at the cathedral of Roskilde, citing UR 4 (ibid., 101), and words on Scripture later that day at an ecumenical meeting in Copenhagen (ibid., 104).
23. On St. Olav, at an ecumenical service in Oslo, 1 June (ibid., 85), and again on 2 June in the Lutheran Cathedral of Nidaros at Trondheim, Norway (ibid., 88). On Sts. Erik and Birgitta at Uppsala on 9 June (ibid., 108).
24. Citation of Hadrian VI at the meeting of 7 June at Roskilde, Denmark (ibid., 102), and of UR 7 at Uppsala (ibid., 108).
25. Words at the 7 June meeting with Danish Lutheran bishops at Roskilde (ibid., 101).
26. Ecumenical Service at Oslo, 1 June (ibid., 86), and the meeting at Roskilde on 7 June (ibid., 102)
27. This recurred in the addresses cited here, with reference to the need of authoritative reception at Oslo on 1 June (ibid., 86) and at Turku, Finland on 5 June (ibid., 98).
28. June 7 meeting with Danish Lutheran bishops at Roskilde (ibid., 101).
29. This dimension of the journey has been set forth by John A. Radano in '*Ut unum sint*: The Ministry of Unity of the Bishop of Rome', *Angelicum* 73 (1996), 325–359, at 348–357
30. Words at the General Audience on 14 June 14 1989. *Information Service*, no. 71 (1989 / III–IV), 110.
31. Cited from *Information Service*, no. 75 [1990 / IV], 131.
32. *Information Service*, nos. 61 (1986 / III), 126; 78 (1991 / III–IV), 157; 82 (1993 / I), 20 and 113 (2003 / II–III), 72–73. These visits regularly included discussions at the Unity Secretariat (or Pontifical Council), where, for example, during 1988 it was decided to hold annual joint staff meetings between officers of the Secretariat and the LWF, which continue to this day, as a way to keep each other up to date on developments in their respective communions.

33. *Information Service*, no. 82 (1993 / I), 20. The first sentence makes implicit reference to the work of the third phase (1986–1994) of the Lutheran–Catholic international dialogue commission, which would publish its results in *Church and Justification: Understanding the Church in the Light of the Doctrine of Justification* (Geneva: Lutheran World Federation, 1994).

34. *Information Service*, nos. 55 (1984 / II–III), 51; 64 (1987), 62 and 75 (1990/ IV), 133–134, including the reply to the Pope from Dr G. Stallsett, General Secretary of the LWF, after the Curitiba Assembly, on 2 April 1990. The presidents of the Unity Secretariat or Pontifical Council, Cardinals Willebrands, Cassidy and Kasper addressed the LWF General Assemblies, in 1984 (Budapest), 1997 (Hong Kong), and 2003 (Winnipeg, Canada). Cardinal Cassidy spoke on the work in progress towards the *Joint Declaration*, as given in *Information Service*, no. 95 (1997 / II–III), 99–101, while Cardinal Kasper's address is given in, no. 113 (2003 / II–III), 73–74.

35. Radano lists the LCA visits of 1981–1986, in *Lutheran and Catholic Reconciliation* (as in n. 6), 73. The Pope's words to the 1986 pilgrim-visitors are in *Information Service*, no. 75 (1986 / IV), 182. At Bishop Crumley's invitation, Cardinal Willebrands spoke on Lutheran–Catholic relations in a major address at the LCA Assembly at Toronto, on 3 July 1984, which is given in the special issue of *Information Service* no. 101 (1999 / II–III), 140–143 , on the occasion of the Cardinal's 90th birthday.

36. See Radano, *Lutheran and Catholic Reconciliation*, 79–80, and Pope John Paul's brief addresses of 1999, 2003 and 2004 in *Information Service*, nos. 102 (1999 / IV), 235; 112 (2003 / I), 25 and 115 (2004 / I–II), 10.

37. The outline of the service is given in *Information Service*, no. 80 (1992 / II), 19–21, with the Pope's homily on pp. 21–22 (cited) and addresses of the two Lutheran Archbishops on pp. 22–24. On 6 October, Pope John Paul II celebrated mass at Piazza Farnese, with some 50,000 attending, including the King and Queen of Sweden and numerous Lutheran bishops from the Nordic lands, mentioning in his homily how St Bridget is equally loved and venerated by Lutherans and Catholics (ibid., 25).

38. Ibid., 27. The introductory note to Archbishop Vikström's presentation notes that lead to a 'lively discussion'.

39. *Information Service*, no. 102 (1999 / IV), 235–238, and no. 111 (2002 / IV), 215–217. The Pope's homily on 13 November 1999, naturally singled out the signing two weeks before of the *Joint Declaration* (no. 102, 236). Through Archbishop Hammar of Uppsala, Luther was heard in St. Peter's, as the Archbishop included in his address a long paragraph based on Luther's 1521 commentary on Mary's Magnificat (ibid., 237). At the 2002

Vespers, Archbishop Emeritus Werkström (Uppsala) and Bishop Eero Huovinen (Helsinki) offered the prayers after Psalms 140 and 84, respectively (no. 111, 216).

40. Previous passages of this chapter have referred to indicators of movement towards the *Joint Declaration* in notes 2 and 5 and in text-sections 2 (at the end), 4.2 (Bishop Lohse's report), 6.1 (papal address of 1993 to the LWF President) and 6.4 (John Paul II's homily of 5 October 1991, at Vespers in commemoration of St. Bridget). Some works on the genesis of the *Joint Declaration* are J. Wicks, 'The Lutheran–Catholic Joint Declaration on the Doctrine of Justification', *Ecumenical Trends* 27 (1998), 85–89, Paweł Holc, *Un ampio consenso sulla dottrina della giustificazione*, Tesi Gregoriana, Serie Teologia, 53 (Rome: Gregorian University Press, 1999) and Dorothea Wendebourg, 'Zur Enstehungsgeschichte des "Gemeinsame Erklärung,"' *Zeitschrift für Theologie und Kirche*,Beiheft 10 (1998), 140–206. These will be complemented by the publication by Radano of *Lutheran and Catholic Reconciliation* (as in n. 6) which relates the genesis with attention to the Holy See especially the Pope and the Unity Secretariat or Pontifical Council.

41. The papers of that conference came out in *Le relazioni cattolico-luterane a tre decenni dal Vaticano II* (ed)., Mario Russotto, Studia Œcumenica Farfensia, 1 (Vatican City: Libreria Editrice Vaticana, 1997).

42. Address of 14 March 1995, cited from *Information Service*, no. 90 (1995 / IV), 128.

43. *Justification by Faith* (as in n. 14), nos. 4 and 157, on pp. 16 and 72.

44. Ibid. no. 156, pp. 71–72.

45. *Lehrverurteilungen—kirchetrennend?* (eds), K. Lehmann and W. Pannenberg (Freiburg/B.: Herder, and Göttingen: Vandenhoeck, 1988); in English as *The Condemnations of the Reformation Era. Do They Still Divide?* (Minneapolis, MN: Fortress Press, 1990).

46. 'Final Report of the Joint Ecumenical Commission on the Examination of the Sixteenth-Century Condemnations', issued by the co-chairmen, Bishop Eduard Lohse and Bishop Paul-Werner Scheele (who succeeded Cardinal Ratzinger upon the latter's transfer to Rome as Prefect of the Congregation for the Doctrine of the Faith), in *The Condemnations of the Reformation Era*, 178–187, citing 179–180.

47. Ibid., 182–183, with emphasis added.

48. *Church and Justification*, as in n. 33, pp. 89–115, on ecclesial institutional continuity, the ordained ministry, binding church doctrine and ecclesial jurisdiction, that is, that these realities do not undercut the gratuity of God's gracious gift and work in justifying the sinner. Heinz-Albert Raem,

official of the Pontifical Council and co-secretary of the third-phase commission, recounted the commission's work in 'The Third Phase of the Lutheran/Roman Catholic Dialogue (1984–1993)', *Information Service*, no. 86 (1994 / II–III), 189–197.

49. On this text, see Raem, 'The Third Phase', 190–191. The original title: 'Feststellung des weitreichenden Konsenses in der Rechtfertigungslehre', accepted at the Commission's third meeting, Versailles, France, on 11 March 1988, published as the Appendix to P. Holc's account (as in n. 40), 377–389. Its sections are: Die Zeugnisse des erreichten Konsenses (including the passage from *All Under One Christ*, no. 14, given in n. 5, as a Lutheran–Catholic common 'short formula'), *Die Erörterung der einzelnen Problemfelder der Rechtfertigungslehre* (8 sub-sections drawing on the US text *Justification by Faith* and the German study of the condemnations), and *Der erreichte Konsens – spanningsvolle Gemeinsamkeit im Glauben* (on agreement in reconciled diversity, in which positions remain diverse but not church-dividing).

50. This section digests what Radano sets forth in detail in his *Lutheran and Catholic Reconciliation* (as in n. 6), Chapters 9–11. An early indicator is the 1991 paper of the joint staff group of the Pontifical Council and LWF, 'Strategies for Reception. Perspectives on the Reception of Documents Emerging from the Lutheran-Catholic International Dialogue', in *Information Service*, no. 80 (1992 / II), 42–45.

51. The main drafters were Prof. Harding Meyer (LWF Institute for Ecumenical Research, Strasbourg) and Prof. Lothar Ullrich (Catholic Theology Faculty, Erfurt).

52. The 'Final Proposal' sent for official responses is found in *Information Service*, no. 98 (1998 / III), 81–90.

53. For the LWF response of 16 June 1998, see ibid., 90–93.

54. The 'Response', released on 25 June, the day on which Lutherans commemorate the anniversary of the *Augsburg Confession*, is given in ibid., 93–95, from which I cite from no. 1 (p. 93) and no. 5 (p. 94).

55. From Dr. Noko's 'Reflection', ibid., 97–98.

56. Words before praying the Sunday noon Angelus, cited from ibid., 100.

57. Radano presents the responses, in their variety, in Ch. 11 of his *Lutheran and Catholic Reconciliation* (as in n. 6).

58. One factor at the origin of the Hanselmann-Ratzinger meeting was the information given to Pope John Paul II by Bishop Alfons Nossol (Opole, Poland) about deep disappointment over the Catholic Response of June. Bishop Nossol had hosted a meeting of the Lutheran–Catholic world-level commission, 28 August–3 September 1998. The Pope then asked Cardinal Ratzinger to work toward a resolution, which led to the Regensburg meeting with Bishop Hanselmann. The Bishop and Cardinal were

assisted by the theologians Dr Joachim Track (Lutheran) and Heinz Schütte (Catholic) who laid before the two church leaders a draft text of elucidations which then was revised at the Regensburg meeting.

59. The 'Annex' is given in *Information Service*, no. 103 (2000 / I–II), 4–6, and appears in all editions of the *Joint Declaration*, for example, that brought out by Eerdmans of Grand Rapids in 2000, pp. 43–47.

60. The 'Offical Common Statement' is given in *Information Service*, no. 103 (2000 / I–II), 4, and in all editions of the *Joint Declaration*.

61. Before his study of the reconciliation on justification now in the press, John A. Radano presented these and further statements of the Pope from 1991 to 1997 in 'Towards Rapprochement on the Doctrine of Justification: Pope John Paul II's Contribution', *Ecumenical Trends* 27 (1998), 90–94.

62. Citing the Pope's talk from *Information Service*, no. 93 (1996/IV), 154–156, specifically 154 and 155. The Pope spoke again of the rapprochement on justification in his letter of July 1997 to Dr Gottfried Brakemeier, President of the LWF, on the occasion the Hong Kong Assembly of the Federation: *Information Service*, no. 95 (1997 / II–III), 98.

63. Radano reports this at the end in Ch. 11 of his *Lutheran and Catholic Reconciliation*, as it was reported in *Lutheran World Information*, May/June 1999. Further, the Council of the LWF gave its full support to the signing during its meeting 22–29 June 1999, as conveyed to Cardinal Cassidy in Dr Noko's letter of July 2, in *Information Service*, no. 103 (2000 / I–II), 4.

64. Ibid., 34, where it is followed on pp. 34–35 by further words on the *Joint Declaration* in addresses by Pope John Paul II on 13 November (celebration of St. Bridget as co-patroness of Europe), 9 December (to a LWF delegation led by Dr. Christian Krause, the Federation President and first Lutheran signer at Augsburg), and 21 December 1999 (pre-Christmas address to the Cardinals and staff of the Roman Curia).

65. This passage of *Dominus Iesus*, no. 17, para.. 1, contains an echo of Vatican II's Decree on the Pastoral Ministry of Bishops, *Christus Dominus*, no. 11, which defines a diocese or particular church as

> a portion of God's people entrusted to a bishop to be guided by him with the assistance of his clergy so that, loyal to its pastor and formed by him into one community in the Holy Spirit through the Gospel and the Eucharist, it constitutes one particular church in which the one, holy, catholic, and apostolic church of Christ is truly present and active (inest et operatur).

Thus a bishop in apostolic succession and valid celebration of the Eucharist are essential components of a church 'in the proper sense' according to Catholic doctrine.

66. The paragraph contained references to Vatican II's *Unitatis redintegratio*, no. 22, on the connection between valid orders and the Eucharist; no. 3, on baptism affording a certain but imperfect communion; and no. 22, again, on the inner dynamic of baptism. My own attempt to be theologically helpful is 'The Significance of the "Ecclesial Communities" of the Reformation', *Ecumenical Trends* 30 (2001), 170–173.

67. Cited from *Information Service*, no. 106 (2001 / I), 19. The reference to the Catholic Church's suffering from the separation of the others echoes the final paragraph of no. 17 of *Dominus Iesus*, a point which had been made first in the CDF Letter *Communionis notio* in 1992.

68. Thoughtful comments on John Paul II's encyclical appeared in 'A Symposium on the Encyclical Letter *Ecclesia de Eucharistia* of Pope John Paul II', *Pro Ecclesia* 12 (2003), 394–416, by Susan Wood (Catholic), David Wagschal (Orthodox), George Lindbeck (Lutheran), and William Stacy Johnson (Reformed). Section 14.4 will relate considerations raised in G. Lindbeck's comparison of the encyclical with Lutheran confessional positions.

69. It is a particularly fine, noble virtue to put the best construction on all we may hear about our neighbors . . . and to defend them against the poisonous tongues of those who are busily trying to pry out and pounce on something to criticize in their neighbor. (*Large Catechism*, no. 289, cited from *The Book of Concord. The Confessions of the Evangelical Lutheran Church* (eds), Robert Kolb and Timothy J. Wengert (Minneapolis, MN: Fortress Press, 2000), 424)

70. 'Um einige Illusionen ärmer: Bilanz nach der Küng-Krise', LM 19 (1980), 61–63; 'Atmosphäre der Reglementierung. Nach dem ersten Amtsjahr Papst Johannes Pauls II', Ibid., 82–83.

71. Horst Georg Pöhlmann, 'Solidarität unter Vorbehalt', LM 19 (1980), 525–527. Pohlmann, Professor of Lutheran theology in the University of Osnabruck, published annotated popular editions of the *Lutheran Confessions* (1987), Luther's *Large Catechism* (1995) and Melanchthon's *Loci communes* (1993).

72. E. Kleine, 'Tiefe Enttäuschung in Holland. Die Bischöfe passen sich der Gegenreform an', LM 19 (1980), 137–138.

73. H.-V. Herntrich, 'Nach dem Debakel um Küng: Rom contra Schillebeeckx', LM 20 (1981), 417–418 and H. Schlitter, 'Kirche von oben oder von unten? Rom bremst den belgischen Theologen Edward Schillebeeckx', LM 24 (1985), 99–101.

74. G. Isermann, 'Ökumenische Ehe-Seelsorge', LM 21 (1982), 105-106.

75. H. Brandt, 'Kirche von den Armen her. Zur Befreiungstheologie bei Leonardo Boff,' LM 24 (1985), 8–11.

76. H. Schlitter, 'Ein Aufbruch in die Vergangenheit. Bischofssynode baut den Zölibat zur Festung aus', LM 29 (1990), 529–531; 'Die beiden Lungenflügel Europas. Eine römische Bischofssynode der Defizite', LM 31(1992), 64–65 and Höhere Treue. 'Rom bliebt dabei: Keine Priesterinnen', LM 35 (1996), 33.

77. H. Schlitter, 'Strategie genen Rebellen', LM 27 (1988), 340–341, an article on the excommunications following the illicit episcopal ordinations carried out by Archbishop Marcel Lefebvre.

78. M. Plathow, 'Mensch und Arbeitswelt. Von Leo XIII. zu Johannes Paul II', LM 21 (1982), 426–428; H. Schlitter, 'Eine Utopie zur Rettung der Welt. Der Papst als Sprecher des unterentwicketen Südens', LM 27 (1988), 145–146; D. Seeber, 'Neue Fragen, alte Antworten. Eine Sozialenzyklika der vielen Themen', LM 30 (1991), 307–309, followed by H. Schlitter, 'Päpstliche Kritik am Konsumismus. Überwiegende Zustimmung zur neuen Sozialenzyklika', ibid., 809–810.

79. G. Heintze, 'Ökumene nach dem Papstbesuch. Eine Bilanz der Begegnung mit Johannes Paul II.', LM 19 (1980), 706–708. Bishop Heintze was at the time the presiding bishop of the association of strictly Lutheran territorial churches within the Evangelical Church in Germany.

80. Joachim Lell, 'Zum Lutherfest: Grüße seiner Heiligkeit', LM 22 (1983), 537–538.

81. Heinrich Fries and Karl Rahner, Unity of the Churches – an Actual Possibility (Philadelphia: Fortress Press, and New York: Paulist Press, 1985). Eilert Herms, Einheit der Christen in der Gemeinschaft der Kirchen. Die ökumenische Bewegung der römischen Kirche im Lichte der reformatorischen Theologie: Antwort auf den Rahner-Plan (Göttingen: Vandenhoeck & Ruprecht, 1984). André Birmelé, Le salut en Jésus-Christ dans les dialogues oecumeniques (Paris: Éd. du Cerf, 1986). A mixed Catholic–Protestant commission in France treated the issue with uncommon depth: Consensus œcuménique et différence fondamentale (Paris: Le Centurion, 1987). I called upon Luther's catechetical instructions to show that the notion of the church as instrument of sanctification by the Holy Spirit had a place in Lutheran doctrine. 'Holy Spirit – Church – Sanctification: Insights from Luther's Instruction on the Faith', Pro Ecclesia 2 (1993), 150–172; also in J. Wicks, Luther's Reform: Studies on Conversion and the Church (Mainz: Philipp von Zabern, 1992), 197–220.

82. The papers came out in the volume, *In Search of Christian Unity. Basic Consensus / Basic Differences* (ed.), Joseph A. Burgess (Minneapolis, MN: Fortress Press, 1991).

83. 'Die Anzeichen der Erneuerung sehen. Fragen zum Papstbesuch an Bischof Ulrich Wilckens (Lübeck),' LM 26 (1987), 215–218 and E. Emmerich, 'Der Besuch aus Rom,' ibid., 242–243.

84. Cited from the Pontifical Council's *Information Service*, no. 93 (1996/ IV), 157. John Paul's reference to Pope Adrian VI points to the latter's 'Instruction' to the Nuncio Francesco Chieregati on what to say in the Pope's name at the German Imperial Diet of Nürnberg in September 1523. For the text: *The Catholic Reformation: Savonarola to Ignatius Loyola* (ed.), John C. Olin (New York: Harper & Row, 1969), 122–127.

85. R. Frieling, 'Des Papstes schiefes Lutherbild', LM 35 (1996), 18–19.

86. R. Decot, 'Zögernde Annäherung', ibid., 19–20.

87. Peder Nørgaard-Højen, 'Vorstoß gen Norden. Zur Skandinavien-Reise des Papstes, LM 28 (1989), 292–293. The author will reappear below as a critical reader of the 1983 Code of Canon Law.

88. Personal letter of 19 February 2008.

89. J. Hanselmann, 'Auf dem Weg zu mehr Gemeinschaft', LM 27 (1988), 153. This is the same Johannes Hanselmann who worked with Cardinal Ratzinger in 1998 to overcome the obstacles blocking the way of adopting the Joint Declaration on Justification, as related above towards the end of section 8.2.

90. Cited from the account of the visit in the Secretariat's *Information Service*, no. 67 (1988 / II), 90–91. LM cited the Pope's words in German, set off in a box beside Bishop Hanselmann's report.

91. 'Das Papstamt bleibt bestimmend. Zur Revision des katholischen Kirchenrechts', LM 24 (1985), 129–134.

92. 'Wie sie war und wird. Die katholische Lehre im neuem Katechismus', LM 32, no. 1 (January 1993), 3.

93. P. Hünermann, 'Mangel an Gegenwart. Der neue katholische Katechismus', LM 32, no. 8 (August 1993), 13–15, and E. Lohse, 'Erschwerte Ökumene. Doch der Katechismus sollte das Gespräch nicht hindern', ibid., 15–16.

94. The Pope's 'Address on the Interpretation of the Bible in the Church' is given in *The Biblical Commission's Document 'The Interpretation of the Bible in the Church'. Text and Commentary* (ed.), Joseph A. Fitzmyer, Subsidia Biblica, 18 (Rome: Pontifical Biblical Institute, 1995), 1–10.

95. *Ecumenical Ventures in Ethics: Protestants Engage Pope John Paul II's Moral Encyclicals* (eds), Reinhard Hütter and Theodor Dieter (Grand Rapids, MI and Cambridge: Eerdmans, 1998). The ten papers by non-Catholic

participants were engaged at the symposium and in the published volume by two Catholic theologians, Eberhard Schockenhoff and James F. Keenan, S.J.

96. 'Der Papst und das große Ö. Die Enzyklika "Ut unum sint" laßt keinen Raum für Kompromisse', LM 34, no. 7 (1995), 31–33.

97. 'Nur zu römischen Bedingungen. Zur Ökumene-Enzyklika Papst Johannes Paul II.', LM 34, no. 8 (1995), 21.

98. The Centro pro unione of the Franciscan Friars of the Atonement gathered scholars in Rome, 4–6 December 1997, with the papers coming out in *Petrine Ministry and the Unity of the Church* (ed.), James F. Pulisi (Collegeville: Liturgical Press, 1999), while the Center for Catholic and Ecumenical Theology held a conference in 1999, leading to the volume, *Church Unity and the Papal Office* (eds), Carl E. Braaten and Robert W. Jenson (Grand Rapids and Cambridge: Eerdmans, 2001). Also, the Pontifical Council for Promoting Christian Unity gathered responses to *Ut unum sint* in a study document discussed at the November 2001 Plenary of the Council, given in *Information Service*, no. 109 (2002 / I–II), 29–42.

99. "Suprema auctoritas ideo ab omne errore immunis": The Lutheran Approach to the Primacy,' in *Petrine Ministry* (ed.), Puglisi, 15–34.

100. See notes 2 and 3. *Communio Sanctorum* came out in 2000 (see Appendix 2, of this chapter).

101. Yeago, 'The Papal Office and the Burdens of History: A Lutheran View', in *Church Unity* (eds), Braaten and Jenson, 98–123.

102. *Papal Primacy and the Unity of the Church* (eds), Paul C. Empie and T. Austin Murphy (Minneapolis: Augsburg Publishing House, 1974), 13.

103. The two relevant articles are Samuel H. Nafzger, '*Ut unum sint* and What It Says about the Papacy: Description and Response', *Concordia Journal* 29 (2003), 447–462 and Edward J. Callahan, 'Papacy as a Constitutive Element of *Koinonia* in *Ut Unum Sint?*,' ibid., 463–482.

104. The last issue entered this article via Raymond Brown's presentation of the 1973 text of the Congregation of the Doctrine of the Faith, *Mysterium ecclesiae*, no. 5, on the factors which make it necessary to update past expressions of Catholic doctrine because of the limits of language and the impact of circumstances on texts of Church teaching. Nafzger, 461–462, in reference to the CDF text given in *The Christian Faith in the Doctrinal Documents of the Catholic Church* (ed.), Jacques Dupuis, 7th edition (Bangalore: Theological Publications in India, 2001), 63–65 (nos. 160–162).

105. 'A Symposium on the Declaration *Dominus Iesus* . . .,' *Pro Ecclesia* 10 (2001), 5–16. Another US journal in the Lutheran tradition, *Dialog*,

responded to *Dominus Iesus*, but it did this with an article by a Reformed theologian from Heidelberg who focused on Eucharistic theology: Michael Welker, '*Dominus Iesus* as Ecumenical Shock,' *Dialog* 41 (2002), 73–76.

106. Eberhard Jüngel, 'Paradoxe Ökumene. Ende der Höflichkeiten bei wachsender Nahe', *Zeitzeichen* 1, no. 11 (2000), I–VI and Ulrich H. J. Körtner, 'Ökumenischer Einspruch. Das katholische Kirchenverständnis untergräbt christliche Mission', ibid., VI–VIII. The Roman numbers were for the eight-page insert, on gray paper, giving these responses in the journal's November issue.

107. 'Kirchengemeinschaft nach evangelischem Verständnis. Ein Votum zur geordneten Miteinander bekenntnisverschiedenen Kirchen', *Ökumenische Rundschau* 51 (2002), 87–91, which circulated earlier as *EKD-Text*, no. 69 (Hannover: EKD, 2001), giving the *Kundgebung* of November 2000 in an appendix.

108. 'Introductory Report of the President Cardinal Walter Kasper', PCPUC, *Information Service*, no. 115 (2004 / I–II), 28–29, delivered 3 November 2003.

109. 'Augsburg and the *Ecclesia de Eucharistia*', *Pro Ecclesia* 12 (2003), 405–414.

110. This problematical aspect of *Ecclesia de Eucharistia*, namely an all-or-nothing framework for assessing the Lutheran and Protestant Lord's Supper, was also noted by the Catholic ecumenical theologian, Susan Wood, in same *Pro ecclesia* symposium (ibid., 397–398).

111. Cited in PCPCU, *Information Service*, no. 118 (2005 / I–II), 13.

112. Text furnished by Dr. Samuel Nafzger out of documentation of the Lutheran Church – Missouri Synod.

113. 'The Ecumenical Legacy of Pope John Paul II', *Lutheran Forum* 39 (2005), 12–13.

114. 'Provinzspieler und Weltmeister. Die Faszination des Papstamtes, der Protestantismus und die Intellektuellen', *Zeitzeichen* 6, no 5 (May 2005), 54–56.

115. 'Reflections on the Legacy of Pope John Paul II', *Pro Ecclesia* 14 (2005) 270–275. Dr Yeago's reflections began as a letter circulated among his colleagues at Lutheran Theological Southern Seminary, Columbia, South Carolina. He added to the letter the recommendation to read John Paul's Trinitarian trilogy of encyclicals, *Redemptor hominis*, *Dives in misericordia*, and *Dominum et vivificantem*.

116. D. Yeago, 'Reflections', 274.

117. D. Yeago, 'The Papal Office' (as in note 101), 109, n. 22.

Chapter 8

John Paul II and Islam

Christian W. Troll S.J.

During my years in India when I was living and teaching at Vidyajyoti Institute of Religious Studies in Delhi, I used to accept the frequent invitations to breakfast at the home of my friend Dr. Khwaja Ahmad Faruqi, Professor of Urdu Literature at the University of Delhi. Now, when I arrived at Faruqi Sahib's home on the morning of 15 May 1981, two days after the attempted murder of Pope John Paul II, he looked strangely bewildered and excited. Upon my enquiry about his health, he told me that from the previous day on he had not been able to do any work. And he explained:

> I heard on the BBC World Service yesterday that the first words the Pope spoke after regaining consciousness were words of forgiveness for his assassin Ali Agça. This has impressed me so deeply that all the time now I have been chained as it were to the one emotional thought: this act of immediate forgiveness was truly Christ-like! Indeed, Pope John Paul II has brought home to me the very mind of Jesus.

Introduction

In the mid-eighties Fr. Thomas Michel S.J., a pioneer and veteran in the field of Christian–Muslim Relations, published two important essays directly dealing with our subject. An essay written in 1985 is entitled: 'Christianity and Islam: Reflections on Recent Teachings of the Church'. Sixteen of the 22 pages of this essay deal with the teachings on Islam by John Paul II. A year later Michel published an essay 'John Paul II's

Teaching about Islam in his Addresses to Muslims'. Finally, in 1994, together with Michael Fitzgerald, then Secretary of the Pontifical Council for Interreligious Dialogue, he edited and partly wrote the richly illustrated and documented volume: *Recognize the Spiritual Bonds Which Unite Us: 16 Years of Christian–Muslim Dialogue.* These three publications remain of primary importance regarding our subject.

Thomas Michel from 1981 to 1988 served on the Asia desk of the Pontifical Council for Interreligious Dialogue, and from 1988–1994 was Head of the Office of Islam in the same Vatican Department (PCID). He is now Secretary of the Jesuit Secretariat for Interreligious Dialogue in Rome, and Ecumenical Secretary for the Federation of Asian Bishops' Conferences. Hence the following statement carries weight:

> It can be asserted without fear of contradiction that no Pope in history has devoted so much attention to the relations between Christians and Muslims as has Pope John Paul II. Both in his addresses to Christians living in the midst of Muslims in Asia, Africa, the Middle East and Europe, as well as in his speeches to Muslims in the context of his travels to various Islamic countries, the present Pope has attempted to lay the bases for Christian–Muslim dialogue and the principles for living together among the followers of those two monotheistic faiths.[1]

In the other essay just mentioned, Michel points out that for a complete evaluation of the teachings of Pope John Paul II about Islam, one would need to study the following documents (and they are not few):

1. Teachings for Christians, especially Catholics, about other Religions (e.g. *Redemptor hominis, Redemptoris missio,* the repeated addresses to the staff of the PCID).
2. Teachings for the whole human family on matters which touch upon interreligious relations (e.g. World Day of Peace Messages, Radio Talks to the Peoples of Asia).
3. Teachings for Christians about Islam and Relations with Muslims (e.g. Address to the Christians in Ankara, Homily at the Eucharistic Celebration at Casablanca).
4. Addresses to Muslims.
5. Addresses to Muslims and Others. (Michel, 1986, 182–183).

To this should be added a few relevant pages in the book *Crossing the Threshold of Hope* (1994), where John Paul II answers questions which the journalist Vittorio Messori had submitted to him in writing.

However, the objective of this conference is clearly to explore the *theological* dimension of the heritage of the late Pope, and I have been asked to speak about 'John Paul II and Islam' in this specific context. Hence, presumably I am not supposed to describe and analyse his remarkably innovative ideas and initiatives in the field of interreligious, and more specifically, Christian–Muslim relations and dialogue. Also, I guess, I am not supposed here to try to throw light on John Paul II's perception of dialogue in its relation to mission or to proclamation. Nor is it the aim of this chapter to explore, in more detail and genetically, his basic insights about a Christian theology of non-Christian religions in general, although this theme will be touched at the end of the chapter. Rather, we intend here to enquire into his perception of Islam as a distinct religious vision and as a body of normative practices and beliefs. Also we are interested to see how the late Pope perceived the living reality of the Muslim community worldwide, its great diversity with regard to a broad spectrum of sects, movements, tendencies and ideological trends and the fact of it being in the process of constant change.

Islam in *Crossing the Threshold of Hope*

As far as I know, we have no evidence that John Paul II at any period of his life has made a distinct effort to study Islam as a religion and culture.[2] In spite of the presence in Poland of an ancient small group of Tatars, Muslim religion and culture do not play a significant role in the secular and religious discourse of modern Poland, except for the memory of the brilliant role King Jan Sobieski III (1629–1696) played in the successful battles against Ottoman aggression.

One can safely presume that John Paul II began to take an interest in, and started to think more deeply about, Islam and the Muslim world only in the context of Vatican II discussions about the Muslims and Islam which resulted in the relevant passages in *Lumen gentium,* no.16 and *Nostra aetate* 3.

In the course of the 1994 interview by Vittorio Messori with the late Pope, *Crossing the Threshold of Hope*, we find four pages under the title

'Muhammad?' (pp. 91–94). I deliberately start my analysis with the statements on Islam made in this text. Here we are sure to have the Pope's own deeply reflected thinking, uninfluenced by any draft or sketch provided by another hand. This contrasts with virtually all the other texts that will be quoted and discussed later in my chapter. On these few pages John Paul II, after due reflection, answers in writing the gist of his theological thought on Islam, Islam as one of 'these great monotheistic religions', as he himself puts it.

The Pope first recalls an event from his younger days

> In the convent of the Church of Saint Mark in Florence, we were looking at the frescoes of Fra Angelico. At a certain point a man joined us, who after sharing his admiration for the work of the great religious artist, immediately added: 'But nothing can compare to our magnificent Muslim monotheism.' His statement did not prevent us from continuing the visit and the conversation in a friendly tone. It was on that occasion that I got a kind of first taste of the dialogue between Christianity and Islam, which we have tried to develop systematically in the post-conciliar period.

I guess John Paul II mentions this experience in order to underline the central position which the idea of the unique and one God, that is, 'pure monotheism', occupies in the Muslim vision of faith. In order to demonstrate furthermore that the Muslims see themselves always in a relationship of competition and emulation with other visions of faith [not least the Christian] and their doctrines and practices, he quotes the words the Muslim on a visit in St. Marks' added to his words of admiration for the painting of Fra Angelico.

The following remark of the Pope is also significant: 'This did not prevent us from continuing the visit and the conversation in a friendly tone.' It is as if he wants to tell us: differences in faith and doctrine and potentially conflictual opposition of doctrines and truth claims on the normative level are one thing, the pursuit of continuing a 'friendly' dialoguing and visiting another. Thus we have here through this succinctly told episode his thinking and outlook on this matter – in a nutshell as it were. John Paul II considered it essential to hold together simultaneously the clear perceiving of the doctrinal differences between the teaching of both religions and the Christian duty to pursue mutual visiting and friendly conversations between the adherents of the two faiths.

The following two paragraphs of *Crossing the Threshold* indicate where exactly John Paul II considers the key difference between the two faiths lies. Reading the Koran and comparing it with the central message of the biblical Scriptures, he detects first of all '*the process by which it [the Koran] completely reduces Divine Revelation.*' (emphasis his). In what does this 'complete reduction' consist? It consists in moving 'away from what God said about Himself, first in the Old Testament through the Prophets, and then finally in the New Testament through His Son'. This statement is further radicalized in the statement that follows immediately: 'In Islam *all* the richness of God's self-revelation, which constitutes the heritage of the Old and New Testaments, has *definitely* been set aside' (emphasis mine). It is commonly said that revelation in the understanding of the Koran consists in a revelation of God's Will not his Being.

However, one could well argue that the Koran in naming God in manifold ways, describing him, for example, as merciful, clement and all-knowing, does in effect truly reveal qualities of God's nature in the sense of God revealing in these koranic phrases aspects of Himself which mere reason would not be able to reach. Hence one could query John Paul II's statement that in Islam *all* of God's self-revelation has been set aside. However, even then one can hardly fail to agree that the Koran has indeed set aside the richness of the specifically biblical understanding of God's self-revelation. Presumably John Paul II thinks here of the manifold ways, in which the God of the Hebrew scripture reveals Himself by effectively engaging with his chosen people and by identifying Himself with the maligned and suffering prophet in whose message and suffering (see the songs of the suffering servant in Isaiah) He reveals Himself as forgiving, healing and redeeming. Be this as it may, the Pope does not spell out here the specific points he has in mind. Furthermore, in stressing God's initiative in the act of revelation – in an ultimate way through His Son – John Paul II could be hinting at the answer of Christian faith to the koranic accusation that the Christians by way of exaggeration have elevated Jesus to the position of divinity and thus have obscured the utter purity of the monotheistic faith as proclaimed by the Koran.

In the following paragraph John Paul II writes: 'some of the most beautiful names in the human language are given to the God of the Koran, but he is ultimately a God outside of the world, a God who is *only Majesty, never Emmanuel*, God-with-us.' (emphasis his) This statement would seem to indicate that the late Pope does not in any way attribute to the Koran a revelatory quality of any kind. He seems to say: The God of the Koran, who is not the God of the Bible, is given 'some of the most beautiful names *in the human language*'. Put this way, the phrase seems categorically to wish to exclude the idea that at least certain statements of the Koran about God's *sifāt* (qualities, names) might be understood as partial revelations on the part of the One God of the Bible – the idea, in other words, that some enunciations of the Koran contain elements of genuinely revealed truth.

It may well be questioned whether one is justified in stating, as John Paul II does, that 'the God of the Koran' 'is ultimately a God out-side of the world'. There exist 'readings' by Muslims, past and present, of the text of the Koran, that stress God's active presence or, if you want, God's present activity in the world of created beings. Here countless texts by Muslim mystics could be quoted. These claim that God is at work in and through the world of creation, and that this belief is firmly based on unambiguous statements of the Koran. John Paul II here seems to lack a sufficiently differentiated knowledge of Islam, in consequence of which he has arrived at a too undifferentiated assessment of the Muslim image – or better – of the different Muslim images of God. Fur-thermore, one misses the distinction between, on the one hand, the 'nearness' and even 'presence' of God to his creatures, especially to the human person ('closer than the jugular vein', Sura 50, 16), and, on the other hand, the issue of how the nature of this infinitely near God would have to be described koranically . Even when taking into account the wide range of Koran-based conceptions of God, one will hardly ever come across the idea of God's love being genuinely self-giving and unconditional, extending to the sinner and to the enemy of God.[3]

John Paul II is on safe ground with a further statement: 'There is no room for the Cross and the Resurrection. Jesus is mentioned, but only as a prophet who prepares for the last prophet, Muhammad. There is also mention of Mary, His Virgin Mother, but the tragedy of redemp-tion is completely absent.' It is of interest to compare the Pope's words here with the third paragraph of *Nostra aetate*, where we read: 'Although not acknowledging him as God, they [i.e. the Muslims] venerate Jesus as prophet, his virgin Mother they also honour, and even at times devoutly invoke.' Clearly, in obvious contrast to this comparable text of *Nostra aetate,* John Paul II's *Crossing the Threshold* deliberately stresses the essential differences between Christian and Muslim belief concerning Jesus and his mother Mary. The Council points out the veneration of Jesus as a prophet and the honouring of Mary his mother as shared elements of Christian and Muslim belief. John Paul II, in contrast, points out the hiatus between the doctrines: here 'only a prophet' who 'prepares for the last prophet', *there* in *Nostra aetate* 'veneration of Jesus as prophet' as something positive to be affirmed together; *here* 'veneration and even devout invocation of Mary, the virgin Mother' as shared elements to be commonly affirmed, *there* affirmation of the fact that 'His Virgin Mother' is 'mentioned' linked immediately with 'the complete absence' on the side of Muslim faith of 'the tragedy of redemption'.

The phrase 'the tragedy of redemption' may at first sound unusual to the theologian. However, the event of Christ's redeeming suffering and death on the cross, when looked at from a human perspective, surely can be described in terms of tragedy. John Paul II seems to want to emphasize here the human side of the divine–human event of redemption, in contrast to Islam's stress upon God alone and His utter transcendence. Furthermore, the phrase brings to the fore the dramatic and 'costly' aspect of the Christ event. In this way the short conclusion to these two paragraphs does not come as a surprise: 'For this reason not only the theology but also the anthropology of Islam are very distant from Christianity.'

From a paragraph that follows, John Paul II speaks of *'the religiosity of Muslims'* which *'deserves respect'*. He singles out *'their fidelity to prayer'*.

The image of believers in Allah, who, without caring about time or place, fall to their knees and immerse themselves in prayer remains a model for *all those who invoke* the true God, in particular, for those Christians who, having deserted their magnificent cathedrals, pray only little or not at all.

The theme of Christian respect for Muslim religiosity, as it finds special expression in prayer, fasting and almsgiving, dominates as it were the Pope's addresses to Christians as well as to Christian–Muslim audiences. In the text quoted we notice the use of the term 'Allah' when John Paul II speaks of the Muslims as 'believers in Allah', on the one hand, and the use of the term 'the true God', when he speaks of the non-Muslims who invoke him, on the other. Does this indicate that he would not subscribe to the view that Christians and Muslims pray to the same God?

John Paul II affirms the Church's engagement in dialogue with Muslims and quotes the final part of the relevant paragraph 3 in *Nostra aetate*, where Vatican II 'urges all to forget the past and to work toward mutual understanding'. He mentions explicitly the prayer meetings held in the Assisi tradition and his own frequent meetings with Muslims during his numerous apostolic journeys. He mentions the 'great hospitality' he experienced from Muslims and the fact that Muslims listened to him. Among the meetings with Muslims he gives pride of place to the 'unforgettable' encounter with the young people at Casablanca Stadium in 1985. He makes it a special point to mention the 'openness of the young people to the Pope's words', 'when he spoke of faith in the one God'. Finally, he speaks of concrete difficulties in countries where 'fundamentalist movements come to power, human rights and the principle of religious freedom come to mean freedom to impose upon all citizens the 'true religion'.

In the third part of my chapter I shall select a few passages from the central speeches or addresses of John Paul II, in which he has addressed in some detail some of the central aspects of Islam (understood as religious faith and practice): (1) the quality of Muslim faith, (2) the key values and spiritual ideals that Islam teaches, thus offering a basis for Christian–Muslim religious fellowship and, (3) the importance of liturgical prayer and of churches as well as mosques insofar as they (hopefully) foster and forge a kind of religious group identity.

John Paul II on key beliefs and values of Islam

The Quality of Muslim Faith

In his address to the Catholic Community of Ankara on 29 November 1979, during his first visit to a country with a Muslim majority, the Pope chose to take his lead from the first letter of St Peter, addressed 'to the exiles of the Dispersion in Pontus, Galatia and Cappadocia . . . ' (1 Pet. 1. 1–2).

Michel has shown, how this Ankara address and a number of further statements of John Paul II during his travels explicate with regard to Catholic teaching about the faith of Muslims what had remained ambiguous in the Vatican II documents, *Nostra aetate* and *Lumen gentium*. Michel wisely comments: 'The conciliar decrees cautiously declared that Muslims "associate themselves with the faith of Abraham" (*NA*, no. 3) and "profess to hold the faith of Abraham" (*LG*, no. 16). Both phrases leave open the possibility for a "restrictive" interpretation which would hold that although Muslims consider themselves in the line of Abraham, in fact we as Christians do not consider them as such' (Michel 1985, p. 12)

Quoting from various papal addresses, Michel shows how John Paul II draws in each case a 'parallel . . . between the Islamic self-identification as descendants of Abraham and that of Christians' (Michel 1985, p. 13). He writes: 'In his discourse to the Catholic community in Ankara the Pope states unequivocally: "They have, therefore, like you, the faith of Abraham in the one almighty and merciful God." In his message to the president of Pakistan, the Pope referred to Abraham, "to whose faith Christians, Muslims, and Jews alike, eagerly link their own". (quoted in ibid.). In Lisbon he said to a gathering of Jews, Muslims and Christians: "Abraham, our common ancestor, teaches everyone – Christians, Jews and Muslims – to follow this way of mercy and love." (Gioia 2006, no. 403). In each case a parallel is drawn between the Islamic self-identification as descendants of Abraham and that of Christians.'

Reflecting theologically on these papal statements, Michel remarks:

The soteriological implications of this position in the light of Pauline theology that "*Abraham was saved through his faith*" are great, and have not been thoroughly explored by theologians of religions. One might ask, whether Muslims are not saved, in a manner, analogous to the Jews, as children in faith of Abraham who are inheritors of the promises made to the patriarch. In any theological evaluation made of Islam by Roman Catholics, the relevance of such papal teachings is apparent and must be taken into consideration.

'John Paul II seems to point into this direction', Michel continues, 'when – again to the Catholic community in Ankara – he declares:

> Faith in God, professed by the spiritual descendants of Abraham – Christians, Muslims, and Jews – when it is lived sincerely, when it penetrates life, is a certain foundation of the dignity, brotherhood, and freedom of men and a principle of uprightness for moral conduct and life in society. (Gioia 2006, no. 339)

'In affirming the societal and moral effects of this faith, the Pope seems to be presuming', Michel states, 'that such faith is genuine and not a relationship to God which Muslims merely impute to themselves . . . It is precisely this shared faith which is the foundation of dialogue and cooperation between Christians and Muslims . . . It would seem that the Holy Father has intuited an important point of contact between Christian's faith in God and that of the Muslim. A comparative study of the Qur'anic understanding of faith with that expressed in the New Testament, particularly in the Petrine writings, might enrich believers in each religion (Michel 1985, pp. 13–14).

Shared Values and Essential Differences

In the passage from *Crossing the Threshold* quoted earlier, we have seen the exceptional importance John Paul II attached to his Address 'To the Young Muslims of Morocco' of 19 August 1985 (Gioia 2006, nos. 465–475). In this speech the Pope went out of his way in stressing the Church's recognition of 'the spiritual wealth of the Muslims':

> The Church regards with respect and recognizes the quality of your religious approach (*demarche religieuse*) and the wealth of your spiritual tradition. I believe that we, Christians and Muslims, must recognize with joy the religious values that we have in common, and give thanks to God for them . . . We believe in one God, the only God, who is all justice and all mercy; we believe in the importance of prayer, of fasting, of almsgiving, of repentance and pardon: we believe that God will be a merciful judge to us at the end of time, and we

hope that after the resurrection he will be satisfied with us and we know that we will be satisfied with Him. (ibid., no. 474)

At the same time John Paul II adverts to the importance of recognizing and respecting the differences between the two confessions of faith: 'Obviously the most fundamental [difference] is the regard that we have for the person and work of Jesus of Nazareth. You know that, for Christians, Jesus causes them to enter into an intimate knowledge of the mystery of God and into a filial communion by his gifts, so that they recognize him and proclaim him Lord and Saviour. Those are important differences, which we can accept with humility and respect in mutual tolerance; this is a mystery about which, I am certain, God will one day enlighten us' (ibid.).

Churches and mosques as symbols for distinct but compatible identities

On 6 May 2001, only 4 years before his death, as part of his 'Jubilee Pilgrimage' to Cairo, Jerusalem and Damascus, John Paul II visited the Umayyad Great Mosque in Damascus. The speech held in the mosque on this occasion may be regarded as a last testament concerning his vision of Islam and its relationship to Christianity in a globalized world. The Great Mosque of Damascus, which in fact is the converted ancient Cathedral of John the Baptist, contains the tomb of John the Baptist, known as Yahya in the Muslim tradition. The saint is venerated by both Christians and Muslims. The Pope began his speech (Gioia 2006, nos. 1110–1113) by evoking the memory and legacy of St. John the Baptist for Christians and Muslims: 'John's life, wholly dedicated to God, was crowned with martyrdom. May his witness enlighten all who venerate his memory here so that they – and we too – may understand that life's great task is to seek God's truth and justice' (ibid., no. 1111).

Then, as befits a speech held in and from a mosque, the Pope underlined the centrality of prayer for both Christians and Muslims as a sign of the fact 'that man is a spiritual being, called to acknowledge and respect the absolute priority of God in all things. Christians and Muslims agree that the encounter with God in prayer is the necessary nourishment of our souls, without which our hearts wither and our will no longer strives for good but succumbs to evil' (ibid.). John Paul II went on (implicitly) to recommend the practice of Christians and Muslims to be present in silence on privileged occasions: 'When, on the occasion of weddings or funerals or other celebrations Christians and Muslims remain in silent respect at the others' prayer, they bear witness to what unites them, without disguising or denying the things that separate' (ibid.).

But probably the most significant point of the Pope's speech at the Umayyad Great Mosque of Damascus is the unambiguously positive way in which he speaks about the function of mosques and churches as the places where 'Muslim and Christian communities shape their religious identity . . . and the young receive a significant part of their religious identity' (ibid.). He asks both sides to acknowledge one another as distinct religious communities that build, and further their respective, visible and distinct places of worship and their related religious institutions. At the same time, however, he shows concern as to 'what sense of identity is instilled in young Christians and young Muslims in our churches and mosques'. He expresses his

> ardent hope that Muslim and Christian religious leaders and teachers will present our two great religious *communities as communities in respectful dialogue, never more as communities in conflict?* (italics of the Pope). And he conjures up the spectre of the 'misuse of religion itself to promote or justify hatred and violence.

He adds: 'violence destroys the image of the Creator in his creatures, and should never be considered as the fruit of religious conviction' (ibid.).

A vision of Islam as part of the 'Radical' unity of mankind

John Paul II's theological view of Islam was embedded in his wider theological vision of the 'the profound unity of those who seek in religion spiritual and transcendent values that respond to the great questions of the human heart, despite concrete divisions' (Gioia 2006, no. 562; cf. NA, no. 1). It was his genius that conceived of the Assisi event, that is, the World Day of Prayer for Peace at Assisi on 27 October 1986. He repeatedly pointed out that for him the 'Assisi' 'event' gave visible expression to this 'profound unity', and prophetically anticipated a world united in the yearning for peace as a spiritual gift.

The Pope's customary address to the Roman Curia shortly before the celebration of Christmas, which in 1986 took place on 22 December was wholly given to an extended theological reflection on the Assisi event and its theological implications. In the light of evident doubts and criticisms of this bold papal initiative on the part of certain circles, including some from within the Curia itself, this theologically significant address can be considered also as a kind of defence of the Assisi event.

Since 'the Church finds her identity and task as "universal sacrament of salvation" precisely in being "a sign and instrument of intimate union with God and of the unity of the whole human race" (*LG*, no. 1)' it belongs to the essence of the Church's mission to highlight and strengthen the universal unity of all humankind that is based on the event of creation and redemption and leaves its trace in the lived reality of all peoples, even as they belong to different religions. The significance of the event of Assisi as part of the Church's mission thus becomes evident. Because it is precisely this orientation towards the unity of the one People of God – which is often hidden from our eyes – that can be glimpsed anew in the day of prayer at Assisi (Gioia, no. 567).

The whole address of 22 December 1986 must be understood as John Paul II's passionate effort to impress upon the Cardinals and through them upon the whole Church what he considers to be the essence of the good news and the gist of the message of Vatican II:

> There is *only one* divine plan for every human being who comes into this world (cf. Jn 1, 9), one single origin and goal, whatever may be the colour of his skin, the historical and geographical framework within which he happens to live and act, or the culture in which he grows up and expresses himself. The differences are a less important element, when confronted with the unity which is radical, fundamental, and decisive. (Gioia 2006, no. 564)

And as there is no human being that does not 'bear the sign of his or her divine origin, so there is no one who can remain outside or on the margins of the work of Jesus Christ . . ..We must therefore', John Paul II concludes, 'hold that the Holy Spirit gives to all men the possibility of coming into contact with the paschal mystery, in the way God knows (GS 22)' (Gioia 2006 no. 565).

The Pope did not deny that there exist 'those differences between religions and cultures, in which there are revealed the limitation, the evolution and the falls of the human spirit which is undermined by the spirit of evil in history (LG 16)' (Gioia, no 566). Indeed, again and again he insisted on not minimizing these differences, and he emphasised the task of the Church to address these differences in the work of dialogue and proclamation.

What, in the view of John Paul II, the Church and all human people need in the first place is the consciousness that all humankind belongs together to the one order of unity: 'The order of unity goes back to creation and redemption and is therefore, in this sense, "divine"' (Gioia, no. 566). With regard to Islam this implies that Christians heed the teaching of *Lumen gentium* 16 that '. . . the plan of salvation also embraces those who acknowledge the Creator, and among these the Moslems are first. They profess to hold the faith of Abraham and along with us they worship the one merciful God who will judge humanity on the last day.'

Postscript: two Muslim Responses

The collective volume *John Paul II and Interreligious Dialogue*, (Sherwin and Kasimow, 1999), contains two Muslim 'responses' to the collections of texts by John Paul II on interreligious dialogue.

The eminent Schiite scholar Mahmoud Ayoub sees as 'the ultimate goal of dialogue to achieve a fellowship of faith, a sort of "religious consensus" that would see in the diversity of expressions of this common faith a divine blessing' (p.178). He also holds that the Church like other religions is 'only one of many ways to salvation' (p. 180). Since he finds John Paul II persistently opposed to these ideas and, furthermore, takes note of the fact that the Pope does not believe that the idea of evangelization and of proclamation of the Christian truth in itself is opposed to sincere dialogue, Ayoub concludes that he does not stand for 'true dialogue' but rather for 'simply condescending tolerance aimed at facilitating evangelization' (p. 179).

Ibrahim M. Abu-Rabi is a Sunnite scholar teaching at Hartford Theological Seminary, Connecticut. In contrast to Ayoub he does not concentrate so much on John Paul II's ideas about Islam as a theological system. He rather looks at the Pope's approach in sociohistorical terms. He remarks, for instance, that he 'does not encounter Islam and the Muslims as the estranged other, like the secular press, but as a spiritual community that has deep religious roots and whose fate is highly intertwined with that of the Catholics.' (p. 199) The Pope even thinks, Abu-Rabi remarks, 'that contemporary Christians have to learn from the Muslim religious experience.' (p. 200). The Pope seems to be concerned about the loss of spiritual and religious values in the contemporary Western world. Although he does not oppose modernity in principle, he would like the modern world to open its arms to basic traditional values. Also, 'John Paul II defends human rights – those of the Muslims and the Christians – and in this he challenges the modern Muslim world to come up with its own version of human rights that is congruent with both the lofty principles of Islam and the current situation in the Muslims' world' (p. 200).

So, in Abu-Rabi's perception, the Pope sees Islam as a different religion than Christianity and that is has to be treated as such. In marked difference from Ayoub, Abu- Rabi sums up John Paul II's basic attitude to Muslims thus: 'Dialogue and not conversion, is the only true method to reach out to Muslims and peoples of other faiths' (ibid., pp. 200–01.).

Bibliography

I. M. Abu-Rabi, 'John Paul II and Islam', in B.L. Sherwin and H. Kasmow (eds.), *John Paul II and Interreligious Dialogue* (Maryknoll, NY: Orbis, 1999), pp. 185–204.

Ayoub, M. 'Pope John Paul II on Islam', in ibid., pp. 169–184.

F. Gioia, (ed.), *Interreligious Dialogue. The Official Teaching of the Catholic Church from the Second Vatican Council to John Paul II* (1963–2005), (Boston, MA: Pauline Books, 2006).

John Paul II, *Crossing the Threshold of Hope*, (London: Jonathan Cape, 1994).

J. M. McDermott, *The Thought of Pope John Paul II: A Collection of Essays and Studies.* (Rome: Editrice Pontificia Università Gregoriana, 1993).

T. Michel, 'Christianity and Islam. Reflections on Recent Teachings of the Church', *Encounter* (Documents for Muslim–Christian Understanding. PISAI, Rome), No. 112 (February 1985).

T. Michel, 'John Paul II's Teaching about Islam in his Addresses to Muslims', in *Secretariatus pro non-Christianis*, Bulletin. no. 62 (1986), vol. XXI/2, pp. 182–191.

T. Michel, and M. Fitzgerald (eds), *Recognize the Spiritual Bonds which Unite Us*. (Vatican City: Pontifical Council for Interreligious Dialogue, 1994).

B. L. Sherwin, and H. Kasimow (eds), *John Paul II and Interreligious Dialogue* (Maryknoll, NY: Orbis Books, 1999).

Notes

1. Pontifical Council for Interreligious Dialogue, (Vatican City: Libreria Editrice Vaticana, 1994).
2. I have not found in the comprehensive biography of John Paul II by George Weigel, *Witness to Hope*. (New York: Cliff Street Books, 1999), any reference to the late Pope's interest in Muslims and Islam pior to the time of his taking part in the discussions of Vatican II.
3. Even in the 2007 'Open Letter' of the 138 Muslim intellectuals, which goes to great lengths in showing that the double commandment of love constitutes the core message of the Koran and of Islam, does not speak of God's love in terms of self-giving, self-sacrificial love.

Response to Chapter 8 Professor Christian Troll's paper John Paul II and Islam

Simonetta Calderini

I thoroughly enjoyed reading Professor Troll's paper and I particularly commend its well-structured, multi-layered, balanced and clear argument and thorough references. To write about *Pope John Paul II and Islam* could have resulted in focusing on one of the following issues:

1. the theological and doctrinal arguments, that is the similarities and differences, between the two religions, the ways to approach them and, if possible, the identification of some common ground for a meaningful doctrinal exchange;
2. the political and diplomatic relations between the Vatican and individual Islamic countries and the meetings and exchanges between the Pope and various Islamic leaders;
3. the Pope's statements in response to events relating to Islam and Islamic countries and the work on the ground of organizations which pursue dialogue and inter-communal relations between Muslims and Christians.

Professor Troll makes it clear that the intent of his chapter is not to focus on John Paul II's understanding of and initiatives related to inter-faith dialogue or his insights into a Christian theology of non-Christian religions. However, after reading his chapter, the above were the very issues that intrigued me and I was left with a number of unanswered, crucial, theological questions (about salvation, Christology, the mission of the Church and, ultimately, how to interpret the process of divine revelation) as well as about the scope of interfaith dialogue.

In a recent chapter on alternative voices in Islam[1], I analysed the works of a Muslim pioneer of interfaith dialogue, Hasan Askari. He discussed the concept of progressive revelation which is fundamental to Islam but also developed it by acknowledging that progressive revelation continues to evolve, and explained this by making a distinction between historical Islam and universal Islam. Thus, Askari controversially maintained that those Muslims who 'stop or start with Muhammad, are locked up in one step of the ongoing divine revelation',[2] and clarified that the universal quality of a Muslim (i.e. one who submits to God) goes beyond chronological and even religious boundaries. The archetypical example of the universal Muslim which Askari, along with all Muslim theologians, provides is that of Abraham. Askari's understanding of the 'universal Muslim', it seems to me, has a parallel with the statement, cited by Professor Troll in his chapter, coming from Pope John Paul II at his 1986 address to the Roman Curia concerning the Church's identity and task as 'universal sacrament of salvation' and the understanding of the whole of humankind as partaking, in potentiality, in the work of Jesus Christ. To what extent can 'the universal unity of humankind' be reconciled with the different historical religions? Can the doctrinal differences be overcome only by positing a non-historical (or a sacred history) approach to revelation resulting in the concept of 'universal Muslim' or 'universal Christian' (with, in the latter case, non-Christians being perceived as, to use the well known expression by inclusivist theologian Karl Rahner, 'anonymous Christians')?

Hence, with regard to salvation the question needs to be clearly addressed: about 'who is saved?' As Thomas Michel put it: what are the soteriological implications of the Pope's emphasis on the objective nature of Muslims sharing with Christians the faith of Abraham? In other words: if Abraham was saved through his faith, are Muslims and Jews saved as children of Abraham? Have claims of finality of a specific religion been superseded or is the Pope's emphasis on the Abrahamic tradition of faith instead a strong reminder of shared moral and social values among the religions of 'the children of Abraham?'

Another unresolved issue is that of the nature of the Qur'an: is it a sacred text? Is it scripture, or does it just contain elements of revelation? The latter interpretation seems to be implied in the Ankara speech when

John Paul II quotes similar passages from the Bible and the Qur'an referring to the creation of humankind.

However, not being a theologian and hoping for theologians to answer some of these questions, I would rather highlight the extent to which Professor Troll's chapter portrays the developments in John Paul II's attitude towards Islam, by contextualizing them through brief mentions of historico–political events related to Islam which occurred during John Paul II's pontificate.

To concur with Thomas Michel, there is no doubt that John Paul II devoted more attention to Christian–Muslim dialogue than any other Pope who preceded him. It is reported that, apart from mentions in speeches, letters and documents, he held over 50 formal meetings with Muslim leaders during his pontificate. It would have been even more surprising, though, if the leader of the Catholic Church had not been influenced by, and had not responded to, the political and social events unfolding during his pontificate. It began at a time when the oil boom had made the oil rich Islamic countries in the Persian Gulf financially and politically visible to the rest of the world.

The 1979 Iranian revolution was to spark a revival of political Islam in different continents and further increase the visibility and expansion of Islam in Africa (Nimeiri's Sudan, for example), in Indonesia and elsewhere. Sadat's assassination of 1981 was one of the dramatic political consequences of some radical interpretations of such revival. The issue of radicalization and politicization of religion, as well as the confrontation between religions, was spelt out, almost prophetically, in May 2001 when in his address at the Umayyad mosque in Damascus John Paul II stated:

> [I]t is crucial for the young to be taught the ways of respect and understanding, so that they will not be led to misuse religion itself to promote or justify hatred and violence. Violence destroys the image of the Creator in his creatures, and should never be considered as the fruit of religious conviction.[3]

In the Middle East the year 1987 marked the beginning of the first Intifada, with Arafat recognizing, a year later, Israel's right to exist. The Palestinian–Israeli peace process was to unfold in 1991, with the Madrid-Oslo 'peace process' and the UN Security Council Resolution 242, to develop further in the 2000 Camp David Agreements. The Pope had controversially received Yasser Arafat in 1982 (the Vatican formally recognized the state of Israel only in 1993). One of the Pope's strongest references to the Palestinian issue was made in his speech in Damascus, on 5 May 2001, when he stated that it was time 'to return to the principles of international legality: the banning of acquisition of territory by force, the right of people to self-determination, respect for the resolutions of the United Nations and the Geneva convention.'[4] Whether the Pope could have done more in support of the Palestinian cause, and specifically for the Christian Palestinian people, remains an open issue.[5]

One of the positions for which Pope John Paul II is most admired by Muslims is his stance against war. The Pope opposed the 1991 Gulf war and he reiterated his condemnation of war immediately before the inception of the 2003 Iraq war. On this occasion his criticism was unabated, he stated: 'No to war! War is not always inevitable. It is always a defeat for humanity,'[6] and he strongly supported recourse to the upholding of UN resolutions and to diplomacy. He raised his voice on behalf of 'the people of Iraq, the land of the Prophets, a people already sorely tried by more than twelve years of embargo.'[7] Finally, another significant example of the Pope's response to historical events is his convening, a few months after 11 September 2001, of a meeting in Assisi, Italy, with the motto 'Terrorism never again' and a joint condemnation by all participants of all violence in the name of religion.

Professor Troll's chapter traces the development in John Paul II's attitude towards Islam on the basis of his own words and then of his speeches. He does so by way of an insightful analysis of the Pope's statements during a 1994 interview with journalist Vittorio Messori, with his acknowledgment of differences (at a theological and doctrinal level) which, the Pope believes, should nevertheless not hinder dialogue and cooperation between the two religions. Expressions of differences are the Pope's early statements about 'the Qur'an reducing divine revelation' and about the emphasis on the transcendence of God, rather than his immanence. Professor Troll convincingly shows that, in time, John Paul II refined his language and examples and his speeches exhibit more sophisticated nuances with much deeper understanding and assessment of Islam and of Christian–Muslim issues. However hard it is or ultimately impossible, to reconcile, the doctrinal differences between the two religions, that does not take away the admiration and respect that the Pope voices for Muslims' ritual expression of their religious commitment through prayer and fasting – a theme which would recur in several of the Pope's speeches during his visits to Islamic countries. The example of rituals is indeed much more direct, uncontroversial, easier to relate to and with a hightened practical resonance for the audiences, both Christian and Muslim, that the Pope was addressing during his visits.

For instance, when in 1979 he visited Turkey, his speech to the Catholic community focused on the commonalities between Islam and Christianity: the Abrahamic monotheistic faith, one creator God, Jesus as prophet, devotion to Mary, judgement day and upholding morality through the performance of rituals. Again in 1985 when, invited by the king of Morocco, he paid a visit to that country, the Pope reiterated his respect for Muslims, praising them for their performance of prayer, for their obedience and acts of charity. In his celebrated speech to the youth in Casablanca he used a shared terminology such as 'God the Forgiving and the Compassionate', he called Muslims 'brothers and sisters in the faith of one God in a true sense'; he listed in a nutshell the common doctrines: monotheism, divine justice, the day of reckoning. This mini-doctrinal statement is directly comparable to a number of passages from Qur'anic suras (such as 4.136 or 9.29). At the same time, he referred to the controversial issue of the status of Jesus as 'a mystery'.

Indeed, as clearly pointed out by Professor Troll, a central statement by the Pope with reference to Muslims concerns their partaking in the Abrahamic tradition. While in previous Vatican documents, Muslims were portrayed as 'striving to submit to divine decrees' (*Nostra aetate*) or as professing 'to keep their faith in Abraham' (*Lumen gentium*), Pope John Paul II's speech in Ankara, in which he stated 'we are all part of the Abrahamic tradition' and 'they [Muslims] share with you the faith of Abraham in the one omnipotent and compassionate God,' marks a clarification which made the Polish theologian Alexander Mazur remark in his 2004 book that John Paul II was the first Pope to state that Muslims 'share objectively the Abrahamic faith'.[8]

However, to what extent can we adequately discuss the personal vision of a Pope and the historical and political developments which shaped or influenced his positions and statements, without acknowledging the institutions and organizations set up during his pontificate and the careful work of several eminent scholars and theologians, who helped to refine the Pope's understanding of doctrines and his interpretation of events? Both the product of, and the force behind, the Pope's emphasis on ecumenical interreligious dialogue and actions, has been the work of the Pontifical Council for Interreligious Dialogue, which had originally been set up in 1964 by Paul VI, but was then renamed and reshaped by John Paul II in 1988. Of considerable impact on interfaith dialogue as a whole, and specifically on the Vatican's relations with Islam, over the pontificate of John Paul II, has been the towering figure of the Council's secretary, Archbishop Michael Fitzgerald.

Among the outcomes of the Pope's emphasis on interreligious dialogue was his convening of the 1986 and the 2002 International Peace Prayer Conference in Assisi. Some conservative sections of the Catholic Church voiced their criticism over what they perceived as excessive syncretism shown during the conferences. Notwithstanding the critical remarks, such conferences were enduring legacies of John Paul II and, with particular regard to Islam, so were his visits to Islamic countries, not only for the speeches he gave there but also for the meetings he held with religious and political leaders, some of which were to lead to lasting cooperation, such as his unprecedented meeting in Egypt in 2001 with the Sheikh of the University of al-Azhar and the continued cooperation that ensued in interfaith dialogue.

The Pope's work in interreligious dialogue and related events give rise to yet another set of questions: what are the aims, the scope and the use of interfaith dialogue?

Professor Troll's chapter does not address this question directly. However, from some of the references in his paper, it could be deduced that dialogue is to be understood as a necessary acknowledgment of other faiths and of commonalities. The aims of dialogue are tolerance, peace (*Redemptionis anno*, 1984), or peaceful communal living and social and human growth, as the Pope himself stated in 1992 to the Pontifical Council for Interreligious Dialogue: 'inter-religious contacts and ecumenical dialogue now seem to be obligatory paths, in order to ensure that the many painful wounds inflicted over the course of centuries will not be repeated . . . and those wounds remaining will soon be

healed'.[9] Some further developments in the understanding of what
dialogue entails can be detected in a later speech in Jerusalem in 2000:

> Such a dialogue is not an attempt to impose our views upon others.
> What it demands of all of us is that, holding to what we believe, we
> listen respectfully to one another, seek to discern all that is good and
> holy in each other's teachings, and cooperate in supporting every-
> thing that favours mutual understanding and peace.[10]

An alternative key of interpretation could be proposed when interfaith dialogue is linked to proclamation or mission, as argued by
Mahmud Ayoub in Professor Troll's postscript. Could dialogue be seen
in any way as an instrument of mission? How is the Christological doctrine with reference to salvation to be interpreted? Furthermore, could
it not be argued that the 'obligatory path' of interfaith dialogue with
Islam be seen as a response from one major universalistic missionary
religion to another, whose increased missionary activity (*da'wa*) has
led to continued expansion with numerous conversions to Islam?

Finally, with the premise that identity, hence also religious identity, is
relational in nature, could interfaith dialogue become yet another way
to address the self: that is, to provide messages for Christians, as the
Pope explicitly or implicitly has done in several of his speeches when
referring to, and praising, Muslims performing their rituals? Could
such references be seen as a wake up calls for Christians to abide by
their own ritual requirements? In this light we can read the Pope's
remarks about the positive impact Muslim immigration is producing in
Western countries. In addressing Muslims in the West John Paul II
stated: 'When you are not embarrassed to pray publicly, you thereby
give us Christians an example worthy of respect'.[11] On the basis of this
and similar papal statements Ibrahim Abu-Rabi' infers that the Pope's
opinion is that 'Muslims, especially those who live in Europe, can serve
as a religious model for the Christians to emulate. The Pope seems to
be concerned about the loss of spiritual and religious values in the contemporary Western world'.[12]

I realize that more than a response to Professor Troll's fine chapter,
my contribution has given rise to more questions other than providing
answers. Nevertheless, I hope that, to an extent, it might have contributed

to partly contextualizing and partly expanding on Troll's insightful analysis of John Paul II and Islam.

Notes

All the URLs in this section were active on 18 April 2008.

1. 'Islam and Diversity: Alternative Voices within Contemporary Islam', *New Blackfriars* 89 (2008), pp. 324–336.
2. Askari, Hasan (1985), 'Within and beyond the Experience of Religious Diversity', in Hick, J and H. Askari (eds), *The Experience of Religious Diversity*, (Aldershot: Gower), p. 199.
3. http://www.vatican.va/holy_father/john_paul_ii/speeches/2001/documents/hf_jp-ii_spe_20010506_omayyadi_en.html. and http://www.rcab.org/EandI/muslim/bulletinQuotes.html, from the Pope's address on his visit to the Umayyad Great Mosque 6 May 2001.
4. http://www.vatican.va/holy_father/john_paul_ii/speeches/2001/documents/hf_jp-ii_spe_20010505_president-syria_en.html on the occasion of the Pope's address at the welcome ceremony in Damascus, and quoting an earlier speech made by him on 13 January 2001.
5. See for instance the controversial 1987 book by Livia Rokach, *The Catholic Church and the Question of Palestine*, (London: Saqi Books), written prior to the Vatican's recognition of the state of Israel in 1993.
6. http://www.vatican.va/holy_father/john_paul_ii/speeches/2003/january/documents/hf_jp-ii_spe_20030113_diplomatic-corps_en.html, on occasion of the Pope's address of diplomats on 13 January 2003, 2 months before the US-led invasion of Iraq.
7. http://www.vatican.va/holy_father/john_paul_ii/speeches/2003/january/documents/hf_jp-ii_spe_20030113_diplomatic-corps_en.html.
8. *L'insegnamento di Giovanni Paolo II sulle altre religioni*, (Rome: Gregorian University Press, 2004), p. 96.
9. http://www.vatican.va/holy_father/john_paul_ii/speeches/1992/november/documents/hf_jp-ii_spe_19921113_dialogo-interreligioso_en.html , 13 Nov 1992.
10. http://www.vatican.va/holy_father/john_paul_ii/travels/documents/hf_jp-ii_spe_20000323_jerusalem-notre-dame_en.html on the occasion of his address during an interreligious meeting on 23 March 2000 at the Notre Dame Pontifical Institute of Jerusalem.
11. Quoted from the Pontifical Council for Interreligious Dialogue, *Recognize the Spiritual Bonds*, (1994) by Ibrahim M. Abu-Rabi', in 'Pope John Paul II

and Islam', *The Muslim World*, 88, 3–4 (July–October1988), p. 289.

12. Ibrahim M. Abu-Rabi', 'Pope John Paul II and Islam', *The Muslim World*, 88, 3–4 (July–October1988), p. 296.

Chapter 9

John Paul II and Catholic–Jewish Dialogue

Margaret Shepherd, nds

When Cardinal Karol Wojtyla accepted the heavy responsibility of the papacy, the two names by which he chose to be known were significant for the path he was to follow for the next 27 years. He is now recognized and acclaimed as the Pope who did more than any other Pope before him to foster and develop the new relationship between Catholics and Jews. By choosing to be called John Paul II, he was intending far more than honouring the memory of his immediate predecessor, John Paul I, whose reign had been so brief. He was surely indicating that he wished to follow in the footsteps of Pope John XXIII, who, as part of the work of renewal of Vatican II, had begun the task of rethinking the Church's relationship with the Jews. Pope John Paul II was also to follow closely and encourage the continuation of the the work of Pope Paul VI, who established the Holy See's Commission of Religious Relations with the Jews.

In his first encyclical, *Redemptor hominis* (1979), he said:

> By following the example of my venerable Predecessor in choosing (the two names, John and Paul), I wish like (Pope John Paul I) to express my love for the unique inheritance left to the Church by Popes John XXIII and Paul VI and my personal readiness to develop that inheritance with God's help.

> John XXIII and Paul VI are a stage to which I wish to refer directly as a threshold from which I intend to continue, in a certain sense together with John Paul I, into the future, letting myself be guided by

unlimited trust in and obedience to the Spirit that Christ promised and sent to his Church.[1]

Already, in this encyclical, Pope John Paul II was looking to lead the Church towards becoming 'more mature in her spirit of discerning, better able to bring out of her everlasting treasure "what is new and what is old" [Mt 13:52], more intent on her own mystery'.[2]

There are echoes here of Vatican II *Declaration on the Relationship of the Church to Non-Christian Religions, Nostra aetate*, with its fourth section on Judaism: 'As this Sacred Synod searches into the mystery of the Church it remembers the bond that spiritually ties the people of the New Covenant to Abraham's stock'.[3]

In *Redemptor hominis*, John Paul II recognized the importance for the Church of dialogue:

This awareness – or rather self-awareness – by the Church is formed 'in dialogue'; and before this dialogue becomes a conversation, attention must be directed to 'the other', that is to say: the person with whom we wish to speak. The Council gave particular attention to the Jewish religion, recalling the great spiritual heritage common to Christians and Jews.[4]

The contribution which Pope John Paul II was to make in this area was to be considerable.

John Paul II and *Nostra aetate*

The Catholic world was astounded in 1978 when a Pole was elected Pope, a clear break with tradition. With the all too recent memory of the decimation of its people in the trauma of the Shoah, much of it taking place on Polish soil, the Jewish world was fearful. A Polish Pope? What might the future hold? However, there was no need for fear, as Pope John Paul II's personal history up to that point had provided the necessary formation which would determine the decisive role he would take in reshaping the Church's position vis-à-vis the Jewish people, both at the level of doctrine and personal relations.

What is now well known, Pope John Paul II's closest friend as a child growing up in Wadowice, had been Jerzy Kluger, a Jew. It was a friendship which would endure throughout his life. On 30 March 1989, on the occasion of the unveiling of a plaque on the site of the synagogue in Wadowice, commemorating the Jews of that town who had been killed by the Nazis, Pope John Paul II wrote to Jerzy Kluger:

> Many of those who perished, your coreligionists and our fellow-countrymen, were our colleagues in our elementary school and, later, in the high school where we graduated together, fifty years ago. All were citizens of Wadowice, the town to which both you and I are bound together by our memories of childhood and youth.
>
> I remember very clearly the Wadowice Synagogue, which was near to our high school. I have in front of my eyes the numerous worshippers, who during their holy days passed on their way to pray there.
>
> If you are able to be there, in Wadowice, on the ninth of May, tell all who are gathered there that, together with them, how I venerate the memory of their cruelly killed coreligionists and compatriots and also this place of worship, which the invaders destroyed.[5]

In this same letter, John Paul II chose to recall and repeat the words he spoke to the representatives of the Jewish community of Warsaw 2 years earlier, on 14 June 1987:

> The Church and all peoples and nations within this Church are united with you . . . . Indeed, when they speak with warning to people, nations, and even to the whole humanity, they place in the forefront your nation, its suffering its persecutions, its extermination. Also the pope raises his voice of warning in your name. This has a special significance to the pope from Poland, because together with you, he survived all that happened in this land.[6]

Time and again, Pope John Paul II spoke of the terrible fate of the Jewish people during the Nazi era. He had witnessed it at first hand. He had lived through those years and had lost friends and colleagues. This was not mere history to him. He was therefore in a unique position to empathize at the deepest level with the Jewish community in their suffering, their persecution, degradation and attempted annihilation. It is important to note that when he became Pope in 1978, survivors of the

Shoah were only just finding the courage to speak of what they had been through during those years; wounds, memories and feelings were still very raw.

Groundbreaking though it was, the fourth section of *Nostra aetate*,[7] in speaking of the Church's relationship with the Jews made no mention of the Shoah, which was one of the Jewish criticisms to the document. It was to be addressed in the 1974 *Guidelines*[8], issued under Pope John Paul, where it says, 'the step taken by the Council finds its historical setting in circumstances deeply affected by the memory of the persecution and massacre of Jews which took place in Europe just before and during the Second World War.' Far more was to be said of the tragedy of the Shoah and the duty of remembrance in *We Remember*, issued in 1998 as part of the preparation to mark the millennium.

Intrinsic to the Shoah was, of course, the whole issue of anti-Semitism and its integral links with anti-Judaism. This had been initially addressed in *Nostra aetate*, where it is stated: 'in her rejection of every persecution against any man, the Church, mindful of the patrimony she shares with the Jews and moved by the spiritual love of the Gospel and not by political reasons, decries hatred, persecutions, manifestations of anti-Semitism, directed against Jews at any time and by anyone.'[9] 'Decries' was strengthened to 'condemns' in the 1974 *Guidelines*, just one small but significant indication of the progress which was gradually to be made.[10]

Pope John Paul II never missed any opportunity, whomever he was addressing, of expressing repeatedly both this now official teaching of the Church and his own personal feelings about it. He went out of his way, moreover, to stress the origins of the Church in Judaism which had been initially acknowledged in *Nostra aetate*: 'As the Sacred Synod searches into the mystery of the Church it remembers the bond that spiritually ties the people of the New Covenant to Abraham's stock.'[11]

Again, Pope John Paul II was to speak of this unique 'bond' repeatedly, thereby alerting the Church to the new understanding of what lies at the heart of its very being (as it 'searches into the mystery' of its identity) and also sending out a clear signal to the Jewish community that the Church attaches the highest importance and significance to this newly rediscovered relationship.

The few examples I have given so far are but a small indication of how far Pope John Paul II went, throughout his papacy, to put into practice the teaching of Vatican II on the bond with Judaism, to make it a reality for the Church at every level, and to encourage others to make it a reality in their own lives. In this he was living out what he said in 1980, commenting on the Constitution on Divine Revelation, *Dei verbum*: 'as the centuries go by, the Church is always advancing towards the plenitude of divine truth' (*DV*, 8). Reflecting on this he declared: 'The enrichment of faith is nothing else than increasingly full participation in divine truth. This is the fundamental viewpoint from which we must judge the reality of Vatican II and seek ways of putting it into practice.'[12] As a philosopher he had already stressed the value of action when he posed the rhetorical question: 'does man reveal himself in thinking or, rather, in the actual enaction of his existence?'[13] He maintained that it was imperative that a person 'has to take an active stand upon issues requiring vital decisions and having vital consequences and repercussions'. [14]

Having participated in Vatican II from its inception to its conclusion, Pope John Paul II was to ensure throughout his pontificate that he demonstrated in action, in his very person, the teachings of the Council, including, and in particular, the new understanding of the Catholic–Jewish relationship, which was to follow its own special trajectory. The truth of this is borne out in the particular ways he was to respond actively to deeply felt Jewish concerns. Sensitive, especially from his experience as a child and young man, to the trauma of the Shoah, he made a pilgrimage to Auschwitz in June 1979, where he said in his homily:

> In particular, I pause with you dear participants in this encounter, before the inscription in Hebrew. This inscription awakens the memory of the people whose sons and daughters were intended for total extermination. This people draws its origin from Abraham, our father in faith [Rom. 4.12], as was expressed by Paul of Tarsus. The very people who received from God the Commandment, 'thou shalt not kill,' itself experienced in a special measure what is meant by killing. It is not permissible for anyone to pass by this inscription with indifference.[15]

On 13 April 1983, Pope John Paul II was to recall and repeat these words to those ordinary members of the faithful who were present at his General Audience and went on to say:

'Today, I want to call those words to mind again, remembering with all the church in Poland and the whole Jewish people the terrible days of the uprising and of the destruction of the Warsaw ghetto forty years ago . . . It was a desperate cry for the right to life, for liberty, and for the salvation of human dignity.'[16]

Personal meetings

During a later pastoral visit to Poland, Pope John Paul II, as he did wherever he went in the world, made a point of meeting the Jewish leaders of the country. For him, in his native land, this meeting took on a more personal tone when he recalled the suffering the Jews of Poland had undergone during the Nazi period:

[T]his meeting . . . recalls much to my memory, many experiences of my youth – and certainly not of my youth alone. Memories and experiences were good, and then terrible, terrible. Be sure, dear brothers, that the Poles, this Polish Church, is in a spirit of profound solidarity with you when she looks closely at the terrible reality of the extermination – the unconditional extermination – of your nation, an extermination carried out with premeditation . . . In your name, the pope, too, lifts up his voice in this warning. The Polish pope has a particular relationship with all this, because, along with you, he has in a certain sense lived all this here, in this land.[17]

On 27 August 1989, in a section of his Apostolic Letter on the 50th anniversary of the outbreak of the Second World War, Pope John Paul II said: 'Among all these antihuman measures, however, there is one which will forever remain a shame for humanity: the planned barbarism which was unleashed against the Jewish people.'[18]

Having spoken in some detail of the atrocities endured by the Jews, as well as other groups, 'whose crime was to be "different" or to have rebelled against the tyranny of the occupier,' he went on to say:

On the occasion of this sorrowful anniversary, once again I issue an appeal to all people, inviting them to overcome their prejudices and to combat every form of racism by agreeing to recognize the fundamental dignity and the goodness that dwell within every human being, and to be ever more conscious that they belong to a single human family, willed and gathered together by God. I wish to repeat here in the strongest possible way that hostility and hatred against Judaism are in complete contradiction to the Christian vision of human dignity.[19]

Just over a year later, on 26 September 1990, when Pope John Paul II delivered the annual meditation at the Polish place of Marian pilgrimage, Jasna Gora, he said during the General Audience, with the approaching millennium in mind:

There is yet another nation, a particular people: the people of the patriarchs, of Moses and the Prophets, the heirs of the faith of Abraham. 'The Church keeps ever before her mind the words of the Apostle Paul about his kinsmen: 'to them belong the sonship, the glory, the covenant, the giving of the Law, the worship and the promises; to them belong the patriarchs, and of their race according to the flesh, is the Christ' [Rom 9:4–5] [Vatican II, *Nostra aetate*, 4].

Christ and the Apostles, and you yourself, O Virgin Mother, Daughter of Sion.

This people lived arm in arm with us for generations on that same land which became a kind of new homeland during the Diaspora.

This people was afflicted by the terrible deaths of millions of its sons and daughters. First they were marked with special signs, then they were shoved into ghettos, into isolated quarters. Then they were carried off to the gas chambers, put to death – simply because they were the sons and daughters of this people.

The assassins did all this on our land, perhaps to cloak it in infamy. However, one cannot cloak a land in infamy by the death of innocent victims. By such deaths the land becomes a sacred relic.

The people who lived with us for many generations has remained with us after the terrible death of millions of its sons and daughters. Together we await the Day of Judgment and Resurrection.[20]

The delicate matter of the location of a convent of Carmelite nuns at Auschwitz which had caused consternation in some sections of the Jewish community was eventually resolved in April 1993 by a personal intervention of Pope John Paul II, who asked them to move to another place in the town. His letter to them showed the greatest sensitivity and pastoral care. [21]

On 8 November 1990, Pope John Paul II was to receive Hans-Joachim Hallier, the new ambassador of the Federal Republic of Germany to the Holy See. It is significant that in the course of his address, he chose to recall the fate of so many innocent people during the Second World War:

> In this context we should also mention the tragedy of the Jews. For Christians the heavy burden of guilt for the murder of the Jewish people must be an enduring call to repentance; thereby we can overcome every form of anti-Semitism and establish a new relationship with our kindred nation of the Old Covenant. The Church, 'mindful of her common patrimony with the Jews, and motivated by the Gospels' spiritual love and by no political considerations, . . . deplores the hatred, persecutions, and displays of anti-Semitism directed against the Jews at any time and from any source' [*Nostra aetate*, 4]. Guilt should not oppress and lead to self-agonizing thoughts, but must always be the point of departure for conversion.[22]

The Pope's reference to an 'enduring call to repentance' was to be made a concrete reality in the important document of March 1998, *We Remember: A Reflection on the Shoah*, prepared by the commission for Religious Relations with the Jews and endorsed by Pope John Paul II. It contained a strong call to Christians to repentance:

> We cannot know how many Christians in countries occupied or ruled by the Nazi powers or their allies were horrified at the disappearance of their Jewish neighbours and yet were not strong enough to raise their voices in protest. For Christians, this heavy burden of conscience of their brothers and sisters during the Second World War must be a call to penitence.[23]

> We deeply regret the errors and failures of those sons and daughters of the Church. We make our own what is said in the Second Vatican Council's Declaration *Nostra aetate,* which unequivocally affirms: 'The Church . . . mindful of her common patrimony with the Jews,

and motivated by the Gospel's spiritual love and by no political considerations, deplores the hatred, persecutions and displays of anti-Semitism directed against the Jews at any time and from any source.'

This was to find its culmination in the prayer for forgiveness Pope John Paul II offered during Mass in Rome on the first Sunday of Lent in the Jubilee Year of 2000. But more of this later.

Two prophetic gestures

I have been trying to demonstrate Pope John Paul II's determination to live out the Church's teaching – which developed significantly during his pontificate – on its relationship with the Jewish people. Two key moments were to stand out as seminal; each signified the power of *gesture* to convey genuine conviction. The first was Pope John Paul II's visit in 1986 to the Synagogue of Rome and the second was his visit to Israel and the Palestinian Territories in 2000. Both were pilgrimages of the spirit, just as his whole life was a pilgrimage.

There has been a Jewish community beside the Tiber, in Rome, since before the time of Christ. Pope John Paul made history on 13 April 1986. He entered the Synagogue of Rome, the first Pope ever to do so. At the conclusion of his address there to the Jewish community of Rome – and with the wider audience of the world in mind – he noted that his presence there marked the beginning of a new era in Catholic–Jewish relations. The event itself had great symbolic significance, with its evocative image of the warm embrace of the Pope in his white robes and Chief Rabbi Elio Toaff, also clad in white. But the occasion, rich as it was in symbolism, was also significant for the opportunity which Pope John Paul II took to make a clear declaration of his – and the Church's – position on Jews and Judaism. Many years had now passed since the epoch-making Declaration of the Second Vatican Council, *Nostra aetate*, in 1965. The *Guidelines*[24] of 1974 had, in the light of 'fraternal dialogue' developed the thrust of *Nostra aetate*, deepening some aspects and opening new avenues of exploration. The third document from the Holy See, *Notes* [25], had explored more key issues, including that of Israel. It is significant that this last document, far-reaching as it was, had been entitled '*Notes*' – '*Sussidi*', as if indicating that this would not be the last, definitive word on the subject to be said by the Church, as indeed it has not been. So, in 1986, when Pope John Paul II took this historic step of visiting the Synagogue of Rome, he could draw on these three key documents which had by that time been issued, defining the Church's new theology in this relationship, so integral to its own being and self-understanding.

In the strongest terms, the Pope reiterated the teaching of *Nostra aetate* about anti-Semitism , and made his own addition: 'I repeat; "by anyone"' – to *Nostra aetate*'s decrying of hatred, persecution and anti-Semitism. The specific suffering of the Jews in the Shoah, which had been referred to in the 1974 *Guidelines* was lamented and decried by the Pope. The denial of the centuries-old accusation of deicide, refuted in *Nostra aetate*, was strongly repeated. The deep, essential relationship between Jews and Catholics was dwelt upon, made explicit and developed in four significant sentences:

> The Church of Christ discovers her 'bond' with Judaism by 'searching into her own mystery' [cf. *Nostra Aetate*]. The Jewish religion is not 'extrinsic' to us, but in a certain way is 'intrinsic' to our own religion. With Judaism, therefore, we have a relationship which we do not have with any other religion. You are our dearly beloved brothers and, in a certain way, it could be said that you are our elder brothers.[26]

Pope John Paul II reinforced here the teaching in *Notes*, which incorporated his own words three years prior to that:

> Because of the unique relations that exist between Christianity and Judaism – 'linked together at the very level of their identity' (John Paul II, 6 March 1982) – relations 'founded on the design of the God of the Covenant' (ibid.), the Jews and Judaism should not occupy an occasional and marginal place in catechesis; their presence there is essential and should be organically integrated.[27]

There is a brief reference in the Pope's address in the Rome Synagogue to the fact that God's call, God's Covenant with the Jewish people is irrevocable. Such a conviction, now the teaching of the Church, overturning centuries of supercessionist theology, had been expressed more forcibly by Pope John Paul II six years earlier in Mainz, in his address to the Jewish community there, when he spoke of the dialogue in terms of the meeting 'between the people of God of the Old Covenant, which has never been revoked' (Rom. 11.29), and the people of the New Covenant. This is at the same time a dialogue within our Church, that is to say, between the first and the second part of her Bible.[28]

The visit of Pope John Paul II to the Synagogue in Rome was significant for many reasons, not least for its powerful linking of his remarkable gesture to the importance of the words he spoke – and those spoken by Chief Rabbi Elio Toaff in response. History had been made.

History was to be made again in 2000, when Pope John Paul II made his long-awaited pilgrimage to the Holy Land, fulfilling a personal dream and effecting a fitting climax to all the years of his long pontificate, during which the key issues of the Catholic–Jewish relationship had been addressed, including that of the links of the Jewish community to the land of Israel, central to their understanding of themselves. Jewish leaders had persistently and consistently raised the matter of the State of Israel in their meetings with Pope John Paul II.

This had eventually been addressed in the 1985 *Notes*: The history of Israel did not end in AD 70 (cf. *Guidelines*, II). It continued, especially in a numerous Diaspora which allowed Israel to carry to the whole world a witness – often heroic – of its fidelity to the one God and to 'exalt Him in the presence of all the living' (Tob. 13.4), while preserving the memory of the land of their forefathers at the heart of their hope (Passover Seder).

> Christians are invited to understand this religious attachment which finds its root in Biblical tradition, without however making their own any particular religious interpretation of this relationship (cf. Declaration of the U.S. Conference of Catholic Bishops, 20 November 1975).
>
> The existence of the State of Israel and its political options should be envisaged not in a perspective which is in itself religious, but in their reference to the common principles of international law.
>
> The permanence of Israel (while so many ancient peoples have disappeared without trace) is a historic fact and a sign to be interpreted

within God's design. We must in any case rid ourselves of the traditional idea of a people punished, preserved as a living argument for
Christian apologetic. It remains a chosen people, 'the pure olive on
which were grafted the branches of the wild olive which are the gentiles' (John Paul II, 6 March 1982, alluding to Rom 11:17–24).[29]

In 1993, against a background of apparent progress towards a Middle
Eastern peace, the Vatican felt able to recognize Israel formally. The
long-awaited *Fundamental Agreement Between the Holy See and the
State of Israel* was signed on 13 December 1993, with its opening words,
quite extraordinary for a document of this nature:

The Holy See and the State of Israel,

Mindful of the singular character and universal significance of the
Holy Land;

Aware of the unique nature of the relationship between the Catholic
Church and the Jewish people, and of the historic process of recon-
ciliation and growth in mutual understanding and friendship between
Catholics and Jews;

Having decided on July 29, 1992 to establish a 'bilateral permanent
Working commission', in order to study and define together issues of
common interest, and in view of normalizing their relations;

Recognizing that the work of the aforementioned commission has
produced sufficient material for a first and Fundamental Agreement;

Realizing that such agreement will provide a sound and lasting basis
for the continued development of their present and future relations
and for the furtherance of the commission's task,

Agree upon the following articles . . . [30]

With this Agreement, a major hurdle in the ongoing developing relationship had been cleared.

However, when Pope John Paul II's longing and 'fervent wish' to visit
the Holy Land became a reality, it was to be in a special league of its
own. Many words were spoken during the visit, of course, but it was the
powerful *image and gesture* which spoke even more forcibly, just as they

had when John Paul II visited the Synagogue of Rome. A friend and colleague, Yossi Klein Halevi, an Israeli journalist, wrote before the Pope's visit to Israel:

> When Pope John Paul II lands at Ben Gurion Airport . . ., he will be embodying the Vatican's new theology, whose key point is that the Jews are not rejected but still blessed by God . . . Indeed, in 2,000 years, no individual has done more to foster reconciliation between Christians and Jews than this Polish pope . . . now he will be the first pontiff to come to Israel with the benefit of full diplomatic relations – which he initiated in 1993 . . ..[31]

This was indeed true of this unforgettable visit, even though it was intended by Pope John Paul II to be primarily, as he put it, 'both a personal pilgrimage and the spiritual journey of the Bishop of Rome to the origins of our faith in 'the God of Abraham, of Isaac and of Jacob'. During it he was to acknowledge both the State of Israel and also the difficult situation of the Palestinians, when he visited Deheisheh, the refugee camp south of Bethlehem.

With regard to Catholic–Jewish relations, there were two very special moments in this spiritual journey which stand out and which, again, showed Pope John Paul II demonstrating by his very actions the changed understanding and relationship between the Church and the Jewish people. The first was his visit to *Yad Vashem*, the Israeli Memorial to the Shoah, which was to be one of the most moving moments in this journey. There he greeted survivors of the Shoah, going to each one in turn. As Fr. Michael McGarry commented:

> Here the image of the Pope – frail, hobbling, himself a survivor of the Shoah – going to each survivor at *Yad Vashem*, stunned and moved the country who were all watching. When the Holy Father met survivor Edith Tzirer who squeezed and held his hand for more than a few moments, tears streaming down her cheek, the country experienced a corporate gasp of emotion.[32] This electric moment eclipsed his speech which was to follow.[33]

The second iconic moment was on the seventh day of the pilgrimage, in Jerusalem. This was Pope John Paul II's memorable visit to the Western

Wall, all that remains of the Jerusalem Temple, and sacred to the Jewish people. Rabbi Michael Melchior, former Minister for Diaspora Affairs and the newly appointed Deputy Foreign Minister in Israel, greeted the Pope with these words: 'We welcome your coming here as the realization of a commitment of the Catholic Church to end the era of hatred, humiliation and persecution of the Jewish people . . .'[34] Fr. McGarry describes what happened next:

> After accepting from Rabbi Melchior a specially inscribed Bible, Pope John Paul shuffled away from the clique of dignitaries to the Wall itself where in its cracks he placed a request for forgiveness for all the ways Christians through the ages have hurt the Jewish people. In his note, he used the same text proclaimed two weeks before in the Mass of forgiveness at St Peter's Basilica in Rome. In this simple, untrumpeted gesture – the first time a Pope has prayed at the Western Wall – provided, I think, the most profound and lasting catechesis of the Israeli people about contemporary Catholic teaching about Jews and Judaism that has occurred in fifty years. There at the Wall he prayed, not as a Jew, but as a Christian at the Jews' most sacred site. Rabbi Melchior later reflected, 'As I accompanied the Pope to the podium my perception was that the Pontiff was as if magnetized by the power of the Western Wall. When he touched the Wall I sensed that the Wall was indeed moving in the Pontiff's direction and was coming to touch Him'.[35]

The note that Pope John Paul II placed in the Wall is now preserved and displayed in *Yad Vashem*. Its moving words convey simply and directly the significant shift which had taken place between Catholics and Jews since the tentative beginnings of dialogue which *Nostra aetate* had initiated:

> God of our fathers, you chose Abraham and his descendants to bring your Name to the Nations. We are deeply saddened by the behaviour of those who in the course of history have caused these children of yours to suffer, and asking your forgiveness, we wish to commit ourselves to genuine brotherhood with the people of the Covenant.

242 The Legacy of John Paul II

As he sums up the impact of Pope John Paul II's visit to the Holy Land, Fr. McGarry admits that before it took place he did not have particularly high expectations, but then goes on to say:

But, like the Palestinian and Israeli expectations reflected in the English-language press, I began to change as his arrival got close. Hard-core Jewish and Muslim religious sentiments seemed to be ready not to be influenced in any way. And one might ask, Why should they have been? The centrality of the Pope as a religious leader is certainly well known, even overplayed in the West. Here in the Middle East other and more complex dynamics hold sway so one would have had to be unaware of these factors to think that a papal visit would substantially change realities on the ground . . . Nonetheless I must say that certain moments in the Papal visit were overwhelmingly moving, not only to me but also to those around me. Many – though not *all* – Palestinian Christians I know felt that Pope John Paul had lifted up their concerns for the world to see. Israeli Jews open to dialogue and new expressions of understanding were incredibly moved by the three iconic moments I have already enumerated: the handshake with Prime Minister Barak at the airport, the meeting with Shoah survivors at Yad Vashem, and the Holy Father's placing the expression of Catholic regret for all transgressions of the Christian people against Jews in the Western Wall. As one rabbi eloquently put it, 'He touched the wall and the wall touched him.' Like his visit to the Rome Synagogue in 1986, what was remembered by those who live here in the Holy Land – whether in Palestine, Jordan, or Israel – were not so much the words as his actions.[36]

Fr. McGarry had been responsible for some of the media coverage of the papal visit and was therefore in a position to observe the reactions of others similarly involved:

I was amazed by the reaction of highly professional but furiously busy media people, many of whom were still exhausted from the recent American presidential campaign. In the cramped, cluttered rooms that passed for television studios in the Jerusalem Hilton, people conscientiously went about their work. But when the Pope approached the Holocaust survivors or when he shuffled toward the

Wall or as his helicopter circled over the Old City Jerusalem on its way to Ben Gurion airport, a hush descended on the otherwise bustling engineers. They listened intently to this old man, this pilgrim, as they keenly yearned for signs of hope in their own world often surfeited by the superficial, the slick, and the spin. I was dumb-founded. Maybe *this* was the effect of the trip: for people from all walks of life and many religious traditions to be moved by a man obviously overwhelmed by his own faith, beyond the suasions of trends and fads, seeking understanding, peace, and justice.[37]

At the end of his life, now physically frail, Pope John Paul II was still living out his own words written 30 years earlier: 'does man reveal himself in *thinking* or, rather, in the actual *enacting* of his existence?'[38]

The Jewish people and their Scriptures

I would like to refer to one more important moment between the year of Pope John Paul II's historic pilgrimage to the Holy Land and his death in 2005. This was the publication, in November 2001, of a new document of the Pontifical Biblical Commission, *The Jewish People and their Sacred Scriptures in the Christian Bible*. This is a remarkable document and reflects not only the steady development of the Church's understanding of its relation to the Jewish people, as it continues to 'search into its mystery' and its very identity, which Pope John Paul II had assiduously promoted, but also the mindset of his own theological reflection expressed in his writings and addresses.

In the final section of the document, some conclusions are drawn, beginning with this statement:

At the end of this exposition, necessarily all too brief, the main conclusion to be drawn is that the Jewish people and their Sacred Scriptures occupy a very important place in the Christian Bible. Indeed, the Jewish Sacred Scriptures constitute an essential part of the Christian Bible and are present, in a variety of ways, in the other part of the Christian Bible as well. Without the Old Testament, the New Testament would be an incomprehensible book, a plant deprived of its roots and destined to dry up and wither.[39]

This continuity has deep roots and manifests itself at many levels. That is why in Christianity the link between Scripture and Tradition is similar to that in Judaism. Jewish methods of exegesis are frequently employed in the New Testament. The Christian canon of the Old Testament owes its formation to the first century Jewish Scriptures. To properly interpret the New Testament, knowledge of the Judaism of this period is often necessary.

In the past, the break between the Jewish people and the Church of Christ Jesus could sometimes, in certain times and places, give the impression of being complete. In the light of the scriptures, this should never have occurred. For a complete break between Church and Synagogue contradicts Sacred Scripture.[40]

In the section on Pastoral Orientations, the document pays tribute to the initiative taken by Pope John Paul II in developing the initial Vatican Council Declaration, *Nostra aetate*, as well as the documents which were to follow: *Guidelines*, *Notes* and *We Remember*. It cites a speech he made in 1997 during a meeting on the roots of anti-Jewish feeling among Christians, when he said:

This people has been called and led by God, Creator of heaven and earth. Their existence then is not a mere natural or cultural happening . . . It is a supernatural one. This people continues in spite of everything to be the people of the covenant and, despite human infidelity, the Lord is faithful to his covenant.[41]

The Biblical Commission goes on to speak of God's union of love with His people, both paternal and spousal, which is affirmed in perpetuity and never renounced, notwithstanding Israel's infidelities. The importance of this is that it no longer regards the relationship of God and Israel as a purely formal or legal construct (the covenant) but talks in terms of God's eternal love for His people.

What is remarkable is that Pope John Paul II himself had made this explicit as early as 1980 in his encyclical, *Dives in misericordia*. There, he speaks of the tenderness and generous love of God for those who are His own which overcome His anger. These are reciprocated by the spontaneous words of 'love, tenderness, mercy and fidelity' of the psalmists:

> Thus, in deeds and in words, the Lord revealed His mercy from the very beginnings of the people which He chose for Himself; and, in the course of its history, this people continually entrusted itself, both when stricken with misfortune and when it became aware of its sin, to the God of mercies. All the subtleties of love become manifest in the Lord's mercy towards those who are His own: He is their Father [cf. Isa. 63.16], for Israel is His firstborn son [cf. Exod. 4.22]; the Lord is also the bridegroom of her whose new name the prophet proclaims: Ruhamah, 'Beloved' or 'she has obtained pity.' [cf. Hos. 2.3]
>
> Even when the Lord is exasperated by the infidelity of His people and thinks of finishing with it, it is still His tenderness and generous love for those who are His own which overcomes His anger. [cf. Hos. 11.7–9; Jer. 31.20; Isa. 54.7ff] Thus it is easy to understand why the psalmists, when they desire to sing the highest praises of the Lord, break forth into hymns to the God of love, tenderness, mercy and fidelity. [cf. Ps 103 (102) and 145 (144)]
>
> From all this it follows that mercy does not pertain only to the notion of God, but it is something that characterizes the life of the whole people of Israel and each of its sons and daughters: mercy is the content of intimacy with their Lord, the content of their dialogue with Him. Under precisely this aspect, mercy is presented in the individual books of the Old Testament with a great richness of expression. It may be difficult to find in these books a purely theoretical answer to the question of what mercy is in itself. Nevertheless, the terminology that is used is in itself able to tell us much about this subject.

In the lengthy and important footnote to this last paragraph of *Dives in misericordia* (footnote 52), John Paul II makes clear that the covenantal relation is not only juridical but also rooted in a relationship of grace and love which transcends its formal, contractual content. These important and very touching comments are not usually quoted in the context of Jewish–Catholic relations because the encyclical is about different matters, but they are a clear indication of Pope John Paul II's views being both richer and more profound than most realize or appreciate.[42]

The Jewish People and their Sacred Scriptures in the Christian Bible concludes with these words:

> The example of Paul in Rom 9–11 shows that . . . an attitude of respect, esteem and love for the Jewish people is the only truly Christian attitude in a situation which is mysteriously part of the beneficent and positive plan of God. Dialogue is possible, since Jews and Christians share a rich common patrimony that unites them. It is greatly to be desired that prejudice and misunderstanding be gradually eliminated on both sides, in favour of a better understanding of the patrimony they share and to strengthen the links that bind them.[43]

Conclusion

Pope John Paul II's relationship to Jews had a number of different facets, and if it is to be described as dialogue it is dialogue in a sense that is unusually rich:

- He described Jews in terms that would ensure that they had a valid and respected place in Catholic theological understanding, without in any way compromising or diluting that understanding.
- He actively responded to deeply felt Jewish concerns.
- He expressed himself in symbolic gestures that could be very eloquent.
- He showed friendship, engagement and personal warmth whenever possible, in letters, speeches and meetings with Jewish communities in many different countries. His continued relationship with his boyhood friend, Jerzy Kluger is also significant.
- He sought to nurture a new understanding in the Catholic community: the prayer for the Jews that he composed for the Polish church is particularly remarkable.[44] One strand of the canonization of Edith Stein can be seen in this context – it was not why she was canonized but it was clearly important, albeit that Jewish commentators understandably saw the matter rather differently.

- His pontificate is notable for important episcopal documents relating primarily to the war years, published in Germany, France and Poland, as well as for ongoing work of the bishops in the USA.
- He maintained his relationship with Jews without compromising other relationships or becoming politicized. His visit to the Holy Land took in Palestinian refugee camps as well as significant Jewish places. He sought to develop relations with Muslims as well as Jews. His stand on the Auschwitz Convent in no way affected his relationship with Polish Catholics, and he staunchly defended Pope Pius XII on his war time record.
- He approached theological or communal difficulties with wisdom, care and delicate balance, able to speak both to his own Catholic faithful and to Jews, aware of and hearing the needs and concerns of both these and other communities. This was especially so when the context was one of conflict and the mending of human relations promised to be difficult.[45]

The work of dialogue between Catholics and Jews which Pope John Paul II encouraged at all levels in the life of the Church has continued, although its truths, so necessary, and fundamental, have yet to be known, accepted and lived by all members of the Church, whether clergy, religious or lay. Its implications are far-reaching and should affect every aspect of church life. I pray earnestly that, in God's good time, this may eventually be the case. As a Sister of Sion, I feel privileged to have played some small part in trying to make this a reality, which has been based on and rooted in precious friendships with those in the Jewish community, as was the case with Pope John Paul II himself. His challenge of April 1993 remains:

As Christians and Jews, following the example of the faith of Abraham, we are called to be a blessing for the world [cf. Gen. 12.2ff]. This is the common task awaiting us. It is therefore necessary for us, Christians and Jews, to first be a blessing to each other. This will effectively occur if we are united in the face of the evils which are still threatening: indifference and prejudice, as well as displays of anti-Semitism.

For what has already been achieved by Catholics and Jews through dialogue and cooperation I give thanks with you to God; for what we are still called to do I offer my ardent prayers. May God further guide us along the paths of his sovereign and loving will for the human family.[46]

Acknowledgement

I would like to record my thanks to Dr. Eugene Fisher[47] for taking the time to read this paper and make valuable corrections and suggestions for its improvement.

Note

1. *Redemptor hominis*, 4
2. Ibid.
3. *Nostra aetate*.
4. *Redemptor hominis*, I.
5. Eugene J. Fisher and Leon Klenicki (eds), Spiritual Pilgrimage: Pope John Paul II – Texts on Jews and Judaism 1979–1995, (New York: Crossword, 1996), p. 129.
6. Ibid.
7. *Nostra aetate*, Declaration on the Relationships of the Church to Non-Christian Religions.
8. Vatican Commission for Religious Relations with the Jews – Guidelines and Suggestions for Implementing the Conciliar Declaration *Nostra aetate* (no. 4),
9. *Nostra aetate*, 4.
10. The reason *Nostra aetate* did not use 'condemns' was that Pope John XXIII did not want the Council to be an anathematizing one, like Vatican I or Trent, but positive in tone. The only time Vatican II used 'condemns' was with regard to nuclear war, for obviously good reason. I am indebted to this observation to Eugene Fisher in a personal communication.
11. *Nostra aetate*, 4.
12. Karol Wojtyla, *Sources of Renewal: Study of the Implementation of the Second Vatican Council* (London: Collins, 1980), p. 15.
13. Karol Wojtyla, The Acting Person, 1969, (Dordrecht: Reide, 1979), pp. vii, viii.
14. I am indebted to Paul McPartlan, for these references in his article, 'The Legacy of Vatican II in the Pontificate of John Paul II', New Catholic

Encyclopedia, Jubilee Volume (Washington DC: Catholic University of America, 2001), pp. 63–70.

15. Fisher and Klenicki, Spiritual Pilgrimage, p. 7.
16. Ibid. p. 28.
17. Ibid. pp. 98–99.
18. Ibid. p. 131.
19. Ibid.
20. Ibid. p. 138.
21. Cf. http://www.vatican.va/holy_father/john_paul_ii/letters/1993/documents/hf_jp-ii_let_19930409_suore-carmelo_it.html
22. Ibid. p. 139.
23. cf. Pope John Paul II, Address to the New Ambassador of the Federal Republic of Germany to the Holy See, 8 November 1990, 2; AAS 83 (1991), pp. 587–588.
24. Vatican Commission for Religious Relations with the Jews – Guidelines and Suggestions for Implementing the Conciliar Declaration *Nostra aetate* (No.4), 1 December 1974.
25. Vatican Commission for Religious Relations with the Jews – Notes on the Correct Way to Present the Jews and Judaism in Preaching and Catechesis in the Roman Catholic Church (24 June 1985).
26. Fisher and Klenicki, Spiritual Pilgrimage, p. 63.
27. Notes 1:2.
28. Ibid. 1:3.5.
29. Ibid. VI:1.
30. Fisher and Klenicki, Spiritual Pilgrimage, p. 203.
31. Yossi Klein Halevi, 'Pilgrimage into the Lion's Den', in The Jerusalem Report of 27 March 2000, p. 16, quoted by Revd Michael McGarry, Rector, Tantur Ecumenical Institute, Jerusalem, in Yehezkel Landau & Michael McGarry, John Paul II in the Holy Land: In His Own Words, (Mahwah, NJ: Paulist Press, 2005), p. 20.
32. Yad Vashem described Edith Tzirer in these words: On the day of liberation, Edith [Tzirer] was lying next to the camp fence, suffering from tuberculosis and totally drained of strength. A young priest, Karol Wojtyla, gave her first piece of bread and a cup of hot tea. He carried her on his back for 3 km, from the camp to the railway station where she joined other survivors. After staying in an orphanage in Cracow, Edith was sent to a sanatorium in France to recuperate. In 1951 she emigrated to Israel, where she married and raised a family. Karol Wojtyla later became Pope John Paul II. See *John Paul II in the Holy Land: In His Own Words*, p. 26, footnote 23.
33. John Paul II in the Holy Land: In His Own Words, pp. 26–27.

34. Ibid, p. 34.
35. Ibid. pp. 34–35. Rabbi Melchior'ss words are from a column in L'Osservatore Romano, 22 March 2000.
36. Ibid., pp. 37–38.
37. Ibid.,pp. 38–39.
38. cf. note 12.
39. The Jewish People and Their Sacred Scriptures in the Christian Bible, 84. Vatican city: Liberia Editrice Vaticana, 2002.
40. Ibid. 84,5. Cf. also www.bc.edu/cjlearning and www.sidic.it
41. Ibid., 86. Quote is from Documentation Catholique 94 (1997), 1003.
42. I am indebted for these observations to Jonathan Gorsky of Heythrop College, London.
43. The Jewish People and their Sacred Scriptures in the Christian Bible, 87.
44. Prayer of Pope John Paul II for the Jewish People:

God of Abraham
God of the Prophets
God of Jesus Christ.
You in Whom all is included,
You towards Whom everything moves,
You, Who are the end of everything.
Hear our prayers for the Jewish People,
whom you still consider dear because of their forefathers.
Awaken in them a constant and ever-more-vital desire
to fathom Your truth and Your love.

Assist them, so that their search for peace and justice
may reveal to the world the power of Your blessing.

Support them, so that they may know love and respect
from those who still do not understand the extent of their sufferings,
and from those who out of concern and solidarity
do share their pain of the wounds that have been inflicted on them.

Let new generations, young people and children,
understand that your plan of redemption includes all humanity

and that You are the beginning and the ultimate goal for all peoples.
Amen
John Paul II

45. I am again indebted to Jonathan Gorsky for these observations.
46. Fisher and Klenicki, Spiritual Pilgrimage, p.169.
47. Former Associate Director, Secretariat for Ecumenical and Interreligious Affairs, National Conference of Catholic Bishops, USA.

Chapter 10

'Mohammed – Prophet for Christians also?'

Christian W. Troll, S.J.

'We Muslims recognize Jesus as a prophet and revere him. Why do you Christians not accept Mohammed as a prophet in the same way?' Among Christians with Muslim friends and acquaintances who talk about religious issues, there are unlikely to be many who have not encountered this question before. Often it will have been pointed out that the West even to this day insolently and hurtfully denigrates Mohammed in images and words, libeling his character and his name in an unspeakable manner.

In reply to these accusations of injury and libel Christians will express with deep regret the enormous extent of ignorance of past generations in terms of other cultures and religions. This ignorance was often linked with fear and deep discontent about 'the Muslims': that is, the Saracens, the Turks, etc. The renewed flaring up of such vilification is, at least in part, connected to the subliminal fears of large groups of society in Europe about Islamist terrorist attacks. It is also connected with the rapidly increasing visibility of Muslim groups and movements as a consequence of specifically Islamic dress and the construction of widely visible mosques in the centres of Western European cities.

However, this first question of Muslims with its implied request for the mutual recognition of Jesus and Mohammed as prophets goes even deeper. At first it ostensibly appears to have some degree of plausibility. After careful analysis, however, it becomes apparent that the stated parallel between the Muslim's reverence of Jesus and the Christian rejection of Mohammed is deceptive. Because where Muslims revere Jesus as a prophet in the sense of their Qur'an based faith, they simply follow their creed. The Jesus depicted in Islam identifies with the Qur'an's message and lives in accordance with the rules laid down in the Qur'an. To recognize this Jesus does not cost Muslims anything, because the role of the Jesus of the Qur'an is precisely that: to support the belief in Mohammed as the final true prophet, and therefore the veracity of the Qur'an. If, on the other hand, Christians seriously accept Mohammed's claim they turn away from everything laid down in Christianity's most important creedal documents.

What is it, therefore, that Muslim partners are asking of Christians? The faithful Muslim is convinced that Islam is the true religion, 'the religion of the truth' (*dīn al-haqq*, *sura* 9, 33). On the basis of this conviction Muslims know themselves to be instructed to invite Christians to recognize the truth of Islam, and to enter by conversion into the community of Muslims.

The term 'Prophet' in Islam

For believing Muslims a true prophet is someone who brings a message from God and who works with absolute determination towards the effective implementation of this message. The Islamic belief in the unchanging message of true prophets has at its core the doctrine of God's uniqueness and unity and of the responsibility each individual has before God, the creator and judge. It is the message that has been proclaimed by all true prophets since Adam. It is written into the nature of each human being (see also sura 30, 30), and each person is now obliged to recognize and accept this message. It is contained in its final, complete and utterly clear form in the text of the Qur'an as it was faithfully delivered by Mohammed. Today this message reaches everyone through the faithful witness of the *umma* as a whole, as well as of its single members. Each person is asked to become a Muslim, to publicly become a member of the Islamic community and therefore to walk the 'straight path' of the revealed law. That path is laid down in great detail in the text of the Qur'an, the reliable statements of Mohammed ('sound' Hadiths), and in the sharia, derived from these two sources. In following this path the Muslim witnesses to the truth and struggles for the 'clear victory' (*al-fath al-mubīn*, for example, 48, 1) of Islam in this world.

Christians find the request to recognize Mohammed as a prophet difficult, when Mohammed and his teachings are presented as the final and universal norm. Muslims never tire of assuring Christians that Mohammed is the last messenger from God and the seal of the prophets, whose coming was predicted by Moses and Jesus. Furthermore, they state that it is one of the central teachings of Islam that Mohammed is the prophet God sent to *all* nations. The Qur'an, they say, is the unchanged, verbatim message Mohammed over a period of 21–22 years received bit by bit through the Angel Gabriel from God, and which he wrote down faithful to each letter. The Qur'an is thus said to be binding for all nations of all times. All other messages proclaimed by any other authentic prophet are *only valid for a certain nation for a certain period in time*. According to Islamic faith the prophets before Mohammed, including Jesus (*Īsà ibn Maryam*) are Mohammed's harbingers or representatives. Practically all forms of Islam teach that these prophets accepted Mohammed's prophetic leadership and his superiority quasi in advance.

Christians don't find even a hint of a prediction about the coming of the prophet Mohammed in their sacred writings, although some Muslims are convinced that the verses from St. John's Gospel (14,16–17) in which Jesus promises the coming of a comforter, the paraclete, are to be interpreted as the prediction of the future coming of Mohammed.

Furthermore, Christians do not share the Muslim belief that Jesus, like Mohammed, had received revelatory scripture, the *injīl*, from God through the angel *Jibrīl* (Gabriel). On the contrary, Christians believe that the person of Jesus himself is the final revelation from God, which cannot be superseded.

If one wants to carry out such a structural comparison at all, one could say: The position Jesus occupies in Christian faith as the timeless and uncreated Word co-existent with God, can be compared to the position the Qur'an occupies in the Muslim faith, in as far as it is believed to be the uncreated Word of God. It would be possible to say that, according to Muslim faith, in the Qur'an the Word of God as it were has become book ('inlibration' as against incarnation).

Because of their faith Christians are therefore unable to agree to the Qur'an's claim, and thus the Muslim claim, that Jesus is a representative of Mohammed, and that he had been commissioned to bring a message to one specific nation at one specific time in history. Rather, in the Christian faith Jesus is the decisive revelation of God for all people at all times and in all places. In him God, in sovereign freedom, has created solidarity with mankind. This shows that the above-mentioned Muslim beliefs about Mohammed and the Qur'an are not acceptable to Christians, and that they cannot be a mutual playing field between Christians and Muslims.

Is there a middle ground in this question?

From the beginning of the last century some Catholic theologians have been developing certain new perspectives and attempting to uncover principles which might make it possible to recognize Mohammed as a prophet. In terms of the powerful *prophetic experience* that marks the beginning of this major movement of Islam, it was argued that it is possible to call Mohammed a prophet.

From this perspective, however, the term prophet assumes a new meaning, which I believe to be different from the biblical as well as the Qur'an's meaning of the word. The question to be asked is: do those who understand the word of the prophet as explained above, also support absolute obedience to the prophet and his teachings? Or do they leave it to the individual to select at will from the prophet's teachings and leave the rest alone?

Much depends on how we deal with the undeniable fact that, from the Christian point of view, the message of the Prophet of Islam contains obvious theological errors. Certainly there exists the opinion that ultimately the message of the Qur'an would not contain anything that contradicts the Christian message. In other words, the rejections and condemnations of the Qur'an would refer only to distorted depictions of Christianity, which Christians also reject. Also, there are those who don't mind that a prophetic message contains doctrinally dubious statements. Furthermore, some occasionally ask: do doctrinal statements still matter in this day and age?

One point must be made without a doubt: Muslims react in a very emotional and negative way when the term prophet is devalued in whatever shape or form. Let me give an example: At the second congress in

Cordoba (21–27 March 1977) a Christian speaker, Prof. Gregorio Ruiz, presented an overview of the meanings of the word prophet. He explained that today the term has a rather broad meaning. It describes a person with extraordinary insight and intuition, who is sensitive to specific situations in society and who has left a lasting impression in history. In this sense, for example, Karl Marx (1818–1883) could be called a prophet. He added that he personally had no problem with calling Mohammed a prophet in this sociological sense. It is not surprising that the majority of Muslims present at this large conference could not agree with this view and the parallels depicted. On the contrary, they were rather offended.[1]

Would it then be preferable to speak of Mohammed as a prophet more or less akin to the great prophets of the Old Covenant? It is hardly likely that Muslims would be happy with this option. Many of them say: if a Christian says that Mohammed is a prophet, without subsequently becoming a Muslim, then he either does not understand his own (Christian) faith or he is a hypocrite.

Critical openness to Mohammed's life and teachings

Our question does not simply concern a word or the title 'prophet', but the confession and the acceptance of the truth the title 'prophet' describes and which is the second part of the Muslim creed. For Christians Mohammed cannot be a 'prophet' in the sense this title has in the Qur'an and therefore in the Muslim faith. To accept Mohammed in the sense of the Qur'an and of Islam as a prophet means simply: to accept the teachings of the Qur'an about Mohammed and about Mohammed's claim to be a prophet, and therefore also to consider the life of Mohammed to be a 'beautiful and good model' (*uswa hasana*, 33, 21) for ones own life and the life of all people.

At the same time, and as already indicated, Christians will distance themselves decisively from any libel and condemnation of Mohammed, but will attempt to recognize and honour his exceptional historic persona, his role as the founder of Islam and his place in the faith, the piety and the religious thinking of Muslims. They will then explain whether, as faithful Christians, they can only reject Mohammed's teachings and his life, or whether these may, after all, powerfully bring to light major aspects of God's truth – that truth which Christians for their part see reflected in the light of human reason, made visible through faith in the person and the teachings of Jesus Christ.

Ultimately, this essay therefore follows the Qur'an's own request (5, 47) to the 'people of the gospel' to 'discern what God has sent down in him (*liyahkum ahl al-indschīl bimā anzala Allāhu fīhi*)', in other words, to discern which aspects of Mohammed's life and teachings are acceptable for believing Christians, maybe even exemplary and worthy of admiration, and which aspects, from the point of view of the Christian faith, appear questionable, unacceptable and requiring salvation.

The option of the Qur'an and of Mohammed for political power

Our statements about the life and the teachings of Mohammed are based on the text of the Qur'an, which we read in the context of the fundamental information provided in the classical biography Mohammed's (*sīra*, especially the book: *Sīrat Rasūl Allāh by Ibn Ishāq* [ca. 704-767] ed. by Ibn Hishām [died. 833][2]), and the earliest Qur'an commentaries discussing the occasion of revelation (*asbāb al-nuzūl*). No evaluation of the phenomenon of the messenger (*rasūl*) can avoid engagement with his message (*risāla*) as it is given to us in the text of the Qur'an. We take the Qur'an to be the text which Mohammed believed to be revealed by God, the statements of which wholly reflect his beliefs. In other words, whatever the Qur'an says we take to be Mohammed's message and teaching.

Everything in the Qur'an is to be understood as revelation in the name of the Lord (see sura 96). From the first sura revealed in AD 609 and 610 to the last ones revealed in 632 the Qur'an represents claims and challenges for those it addresses. It requires of them to believe in Mohammed's appointed mission from God and defends the origin of this mission as directly from God against any possible question and doubt.

The Christian observer and student must primarily consider the quality of the confrontation, even the enmity, between the prophet and his audience. It is important to comprehend the breadth of the truth that defines the battleground, as well as the factors which cause the hostile argument. It is not about the 'whether' but the 'how' of the confrontation. The question is: to what extent does the Qur'an's message as given by Mohammed correspond with the means Mohammed chose to achieve the supremacy of his message in his times and in his sphere of influence. The *hijra* in 622 is the linchpin in the prophet's history, the corner stone of the Qur'an and of the prophetic career: the *hijra* initiates Mohammed's prophetic leadership.

What is the core of the message, which caused the antagonism, even the open enmity, between the prophet and the people in Mecca? The basic tenets of this message are easily named. First, the request for unconditional recognition of the one and only God and, implied in this, the condemnation of polytheism and idolatry as foolishness; second, the proclamation of the reality that all people without exception will be subject to God's judgment, and thus their call away from comfortable forgetfulness and away from any other form of irresponsible living. His audience accused Mohammed of being 'crazy' (81, 22), no longer a mere 'soothsayer' (52, 29), a simple 'poet' (37, 35; 52, 30), a copier of 'tales from the past' (68, 15), of using 'magic' (cf 43, 30). If God had appointed someone, then surely he would have appointed a powerful personality, a 'man who is prominent' (43, 31). Someone like that would have had more credibility than this Mohammed. Furthermore, Mohammed was accused of destroying the old tradition and of denigrating the fore-fathers (43, 21–23).

For over 10 years Mohammed suffered derision, defamation, con-spiracy and accusation. The stories of the patriarchs in the Qur'an therefore strongly reflect the virtue of faithful suffering and persever-ance for God's sake. However, they also reflect the final triumph of the career and message of the patriarchs. The texts of these early Mecca years are also influenced by the sharp dichotomy between those led into truth on the one hand, and those who err (*muslimūn* and *kāfirūn*), those who accept the message and those who turn away from it, the winners and the losers. The writings clearly condemn the hardening of the hearts of those who listen to the prophet and their resistance to the truth of his message, and threaten them with the coming final judgement and its punishments.

Emigration from Mecca (hijra)

In view of the hardening opposition during the late Mecca years, the Qur'an and his trusted prophet Mohammed moved towards *hijra* (emigration, not flight!), away from the restrictive confrontation with the rigid rejection of his own tribe, the Quraysh, and away from mere preaching, towards fighting by means of physical force. After 13 years of patient witness by word alone, and in the light of the rejection of Muhammad and his claim by the society of Mecca, who resisted him proudly and proved to be incorrigible, Mohammed opted for emigration. The failure of God's word and frustration of the 'manifest victory (al-fath al-mubīn)' of the 'religion of truth' were inconceivable and were not allowed to happen under any circumstances. In other words, failure had to be averted by any possible means.

To understand the emigration from Mecca (*hijra*) as failure, as though Mohammed had cast aside his calling and his responsibility, is a misunderstanding. Rather, looked at from the whole of the Qur'an's message, *hijra* is the obedient consequence of this calling. With the invitation to Yathrib/Medina and the promise to defend him and his prophetic claims, Mohammed and his followers received a unique opportunity to go united into self-imposed exile to create a solid foundation, an instrument with which the still neutral tribes and people in Yathrib could be converted to Islam by means of diplomatic skill and political pressure. It began to look possible that Mecca, which had refused to turn to Islam and its messenger, but which had not been able to prevent the messenger's emigration, would eventually be vulnerable to the returning exiles.

With his battles, the battle of Badr (624), Uhud (625) and the battle of the trench (627) Mohammed simply followed the basic logic of questioning the power of the tribe governing Mecca, the Quraysh, and attacking this tribe who protected pagan faith and its structures. From the beginning this radical questioning of the power of the pagan rulers of Mecca had been one of the aims and signs of Mohammed's mission. After the victory of Badr, which is described in the Qur'an as *yawm al-furqān* (the Day of Distinction, also Day of Decision, 8, 41), it became important to strengthen Medina's resources in steady, partly politically religious and partly military consolidation, to increase Mohammed's reputation, to conquer the surrounding tribes and finally, to return victoriously to Mecca.

For the non-Muslims of Medina the conflict resulted in suspicions or accusations of secretly agreeing with the opponents, or even of cooperating with them. Even neutrality became suspicious. The Jewish tribes of Medina were under particular suspicion, because the prophet's initial assumption that they would accept him turned out to have been erroneous. The forced banishment, the confiscation of property and the dispersion of the tribes are the saddest chapters of the *sīra* and the Qur'an. The most memorable victims were the Jewish tribes Banū Nadīr, the Qaynuqā` and the Qurayza, whereby the latter suffered the execution of all their male members and the sale of all their women and children into slavery, with Mohammed's specific approval.[3]

Yes, one can and should see beyond individual episodes, even if they are as tragic as those mentioned here, and include in the assessment the whole complex of tribal, ritual, cultural psychology and legal regulations, as well as the collective strategy of war situations. The harshness of the punishment could thus be legitimated and the accusation could be qualified. However, the more strongly these circumstances are used as explanations and even excuses, the more pressing the deep theological problem: How can the believer combine the Qur'an's endorsement and the use of political and military force by the prophet with the claim of Qur'an and *sīra* to final religious validity?

The armed *jihād* against Mecca led to victory and at the same time to *islām*, the act of subjugation of the conquered to the reign of Allah, as well as his prophet and his *umma*. The bloody battles of the first of the caliphs immediately after Mohammed's death showed the extent of fragility of tribe's *islām*, which was often no more than external subjugation to the power of the messenger, but lacking true faith. (cf sura 49, 4).

The ancient inscription on Mohammed's grave in Medina: ('Peace be upon thee, O Apostle. We witness that thou hast truly delivered the message, that thou hast striven in the way of God until God glorified His religion and perfected it.')[4] expresses poignantly the vital unity of the witness of the Word and the political and military efforts in the life and teaching of Mohammed and therefore in our understanding of the Qur'an.

The political and military dimension of Mohammed's life and teaching

When Muslims seek Christian acceptance of Mohammed they cannot avoid serious engagement with the historical information in the *sīra* and the corresponding texts in the Qur'an, and their normative meaning in the overall Islamic vision of faith. Islamic mystics and modern Muslim idealists use different methods for abstracting from the political and the military dimensions: that is, the *jihād*-dimension of the *sīra* and the corresponding texts in the Qur'an. But no picture of Mohammed can ultimately set aside or negate historic facts and their claim to be normative, and a Christian assessment of Mohammed must take account of this dimension in his life and his message. The fundamental problem Christians have with regard to Mohammed's own understanding of his mission is the use of violence because of holy indignation over the rejection of the authority of God and his prophet. From a biblical– prophetic and Christian point of view, the prophetic mission, in so far as it is implemented by using political and military force, loses those qualities of truth and justice it tried to justify.

The important contemporary thinker Fazlur Rahman (1919–1988) does not share this view:

> Mohammed never lost his hope for success, nor the truly terrible and brutal recognition that the requirement to be successful had been *his God given duty*. It is a component of the Qur'an's teaching that the mere bringing of the message, the experience of disappointment and the suffering of failure represent an immature spirituality.[5]

The question here is what, precisely, we are to understand by the terms 'immature' and 'spirituality'. In this context it is important to note that the Qur'an, and therefore Mohammed, simply turns the politically active patriarchs and judges of the Old Testament into true representatives of prophetic action: Moses, David, Abraham, the iconoclast. They are all of them heroes of success, examples for the prophet of Islam, while the

> Muslim's holy scriptures are utterly silent on the patient servants of the Word: Amos, Hosea, Isaiah, and especially Jeremiah, all of whom

turn away from power for the sake of the integrity of the Word, and who passionately believe that it is better to fail honorably than to obtain dishonorable success.[6]

This silence is not an accident; it corresponds with the norms and the spirit of the Qur'an. If the Qur'an and Mohammed's prophesies had included Jeremiah and all the suffering servants of biblical tradition, it would have resulted in an intolerable questioning of firm Muslim basic convictions, as they are expressed so clearly in Fazlur Rahman's statement. To put this another way: Mohammed does not stand in the tradition of the prophets who have become decisive for our picture of biblical prophets and the character of their message.

According to our conviction, the faithful 'mere' delivering of the message (*balāgh*), which Rahman so categorically condemns as an indication of immature spirituality, does not expose someone to the temptation to claim that which is God's alone (see sura 3, 79–80) in the same way as the implementation of the message by the determined use of force and violent means. The temptation to claim that which is God's alone threatens especially the messenger and the message, when they apply political and military force. Such political and military might requires and justifies self-interest as well as enmity, which in turn spoil and darken the message. In order to retain his freedom as witness of God's Word, Jeremiah had to ensure his own freedom of thought and to fight strongly against any possible political instrumentalization of his person and his message. Ultimately, he paid the price for this.

Also to be taken into account is that prophetic refusal to use force and violence is correlative to God's wish to receive a genuine answer to his invitation and his will from mankind. This answer must be based solely on love, not on the fear of punishment and the consequences people would have to fear from the prophet's hand if they rejected the call. The prophet's suffering in the service of the Word is no more and no less than his partnership with godly grace in its inherent abstinence from any force (*lā ikrāha fī'l-dīn*, sura 2, 256) in the face of violent rejection of God's will by mankind.

This explains why Muslim thinkers interpret the fact that Jesus' prophetic path does not include a political and military dimension as a 'privation' forced on him by the Romans, and not the perfect and final form of prophetic existence and prophetic fate.[7] Kenneth Cragg fittingly comments on this question by alluding to Paul's famous statement in 1 Cor. 1.24: 'according to the description of the Qur'an God's power and wisdom are not seen in the crucifixion of His servant Jesus, but in his rescue from the same.'[8]

Christian thinking, which has been shaped by the teachings of the Gospel, will always consider it to be a burden and a tragedy, that violence and the resulting force are so firmly and unquestioningly anchored in the normative sources, in the exemplary biography of the prophet of Islam. The pattern of Mohammed's *sīra,* from the *hijra* as conscious emigration to the final glorious conquering of Mecca, are in conflict with the way of Jesus the Messiah: via the humiliation of the cross to the resurrection, whose visible power and glory will break out and shine fully only in the coming world. From the living origins onwards there remains a disparity between Jesus and Mohammed.

Qur'an and Mohammed measured against the Gospels

We will not engage here in the traditional controversial critique of the central topic of this centuries old controversy, such as corruption (*tahrīf*) or the reliability of biblical writing, displacement (*naskh*) of Jesus' authority through Mohammed, the way to the resurrection via the cross, and finally the question of the definitiveness of the prophet and the message – although these topics will require continued discussion. Instead we begin with the central doctrine of the Qur'an and of Mohammed himself: the truth of God and humankind. Discussion of Christology and the doctrine of salvation has to take as its starting point the place where the deepest convictions of Islam and Christianity meet. There is a greater hope of being heard by our honestly enquiring Muslim discussion partners, if we place our questions regarding Mohammed's and therefore the Qur'an's message in a context that is their own. Maybe then Christian beliefs can be understood at the level that is so vital for understanding the deepest basic convictions of Islam from the point of view of the Christian faith.

The central concern of Islam is primarily to lead humankind on the right path before and to God. When we consider and describe the central concerns of the Gospel based on Islamic affirmations, we are not primarily defending Christianity. Rather, based on the relevant teachings of the Qur'an, we are concerned with the representation of God's sovereignty and 'justification' of humankind as described in the Gospels.

With this approach we are closer to Paul's own thinking and method: 'for we do not preach ourselves but Jesus Christ the Lord, and ourselves as your slaves for the sake of Jesus' (2 Cor. 4.5). From the perspective of the Christian faith we therefore ask: Is the depiction of God's sovereignty in the Qur'an sufficiently complete, deep and consistent? Can the Qur'an's understanding of the definitiveness of a message that does not go beyond the law truly convince us? Does the person, who according to the Qur'an is on the right path, completely and truly experience salvation?

Beginning and ending our conversation about Mohammed and the Qur'an with God, we cannot go wrong. It will help if we begin with the Qur'an's belief in Mohammed as the 'seal of the prophets' and the Qur'an as the 'seal of prophecy'. According to the Qur'an prophecy reaches its pinnacle in guidance, teaching, directive, warning and exhortation. Understood in this way the relevance of the creator is largely limited to the educational. The Qur'an sees prophets as the tutors of humankind. God's tuition illuminates, informs, guides, encourages and warns. It disciplines, prevents and binds. The whole world is a school. God's guidance through the prophet, who is God's 'representative' (*khalīfa*, sura 2, 30; 38, 26), instructs people to live a righteous life. In this consists the duty and the dignity of the person correctly guided.

Creation, revelation and lawgiving in the Qur'an

However laudable and magnificent the Qur'an's statements about God, creation and the law may be, compared with the revelation in Jesus Christ they are incomplete and fragmentary. Is guidance from God truly all that humankind requires? Is there not to be a 'more'? Does the teaching of the law through prohibition and commandment fulfill the deepest intentions of the law and the law maker? Do the biblical prophets and Jesus not help us to discover dimensions in God's sovereignty, which go far beyond the categories of 'education' and 'commandment'?

Matthew 11, 9 speaks of 'more than a prophet'. This 'more' determines the whole of the New Testament. It is the 'more' of the messianic actions towards salvation. It is the 'more' of God's loving engagement, beyond the educational and disciplinary measures of the law, that has always been rejected by humankind and will always be rejected. It is the 'more' of the coming of God himself in flesh and in person, in suffering and in salvation – far beyond the spoken word.

Guidance (*hudā*) and the Law (*sharīʿa*) do have their dignity and their benefit. However, the question is whether they provide a final and ultimately effective answer to mankind's continued half-heartedness, rebellion against the law, the questioning of the claims made by the law and the law maker, and, finally, pseudo-worship and a life altogether without God (*min dūni'llāh* 2, 107). Despite God's guidance, threats and punishments the core sins continue: hardness of heart, hypocrisy, pride, the admiration of oneself. What can guidance achieve in the face of the depths of evil in humankind, and of those people who ignore the guidance and make themselves immune against it? Is prophecy the only, unique and final means to heal these wounds of humanity? Only those who underestimate the seriousness of mankind's situation and the extent of God's authority will simply answer this with yes. The Gospels teach us to understand that the creed *Allāhu Akbar* (*see Deus semper major; God is always greater!*) has to be understood more broadly and deeply. Such a deep understanding of the true greatness of God should therefore be the main and most stimulating topic of theological conversation between Christians and Muslims. The issue is nothing less than the core belief about God in our respective faiths!

In sura 6, 91 it is said of the Jews of Medina: 'They have never valued God as He should be valued.' The Gospel of Christ says that pointing to God's transcendence alone is insufficient to value God. The emphasis on God's transcendence must be balanced and extended by another: the emphasis on God's involvement visible in God's uniting of His own self with humankind, beings of endless yearning and magnanimity, but also of weakness and addiction to the power of sin.

Through Mohammed, the Qur'an also speaks strongly of God's closeness to humankind: 'We are closer to him than his jugular vein' (50:16). The Qur'an thinks about this closeness in conjunction with distance and aloofness, which are matched by the submission and compliance of creation. The Gospels, however, speak of yet another dimension of God's transcendence: of a dimension that is realized in God's love, of the connection of God with humankind solely because of grace. As a consequence of vigorously rejecting any idol worship as well as any connection of people with idols, is it possible that Islam has suffered a tragic loss as regards God's association with humankind through grace? Maybe this loss resulted precisely from the prophet's urgent and uncompromising call to denounce God's association with idols. Christians will ask whether God's transcendence is most truly retained and valued when we defend it not only against pagan idols, but also against all human sin. According to Christian understanding, *Allāhu Akbar* ('God is the greatest') is a cry of joy about God's gift of salvation from sin, the ultimate healing of sin's deadly sting. The cry is more than a mere triumph over polytheism.

There can be no doubt that Muslims and Christians are united in their faith in the one God. The Christian faith, however, says: 'there is an immediate and unlimited concern of God for the wellbeing of humankind.' For God, creation also means risk, obligation, even God's free entering into a kind of liability.

Creation includes a plan from God: it is aimed at cooperation, at *islām,* at a submission of the created to God's call which is the creature's appropriate response. This intended free response of people in submission and devotion cannot be automatic, nor is it guaranteed. Puppets do not need prophets. That which God the creator has given through his guidance as His will for humankind must in turn also be wanted by humankind. But if that is how creation is enacted, does it then go hand in hand with a kind of 'immunity', with a kind of invulnerability and in this sense of 'exaltedness' of God vis-à-vis humanity caught up deeply in error and in sin, as the Qur'an does not tire to point out?

The same logic applies to God, the God of revelation and giver of the law, because guidance and law are at one with creation and express its goals. It can be said that there is, in principle, no divergence between Mohammed's and Jesus' teachings regarding God's involvement with human affairs. The debate centres only around its expression and extent. Do transcendence and God's greatness on the one hand and God's radical involvement with humankind on the other truly have to be seen as contrary and competing with each other? In other words, does God's way of looking after humankind have to be limited to the law, legal exhortation and judgement?

Christ's standard goes further, right up to the grace of self-giving in the incarnation and in suffering love. While the Qur'an does not entirely reject salvation as in consistent with God's sovereignty, for the Gospels life depends on God's free gift in Jesus Christ. Christians believe that our faith in the always greater God makes it impossible to reject this gift as too improbable. The Christian faith ascribes to God's greatness an ultimate freedom that has only one dimension – self-giving love. In the face of the Qur'an's claim that God was not allowed to and could not do more than send a prophet, the Christian belief proclaims God as the One who comes and gives himself in logos-love.

The image of God in the Qur'an and revealed by Mohammed leaves no room for a suffering God. Suffering is something put onto God externally, which would limit and disgrace him. God therefore has to be seen as free from suffering and incapable of pain. God's freedom from suffering understood in this way is something Christians can agree with. However, in the Christian proclamation of God as the Father of the Crucified One, a love is shown which is, completely sovereign and free and suffers purely for love. Seen in this way, in the light of the core meaning of creation and prophesy which has been shown to us by the revelation of Jesus, God's sovereignty is questioned much more deeply shown by a faith, that however pious, denies God the use of all his sovereignty against evil through the all-conquering majesty of his descending love, right up to Gethsemane and Golgotha. From the Christian point of view the concern about God's immunity from risk, relationship and sharing in suffering is, paradoxically, the 'infidel' proclamation of a misunderstood divine unity.

In conclusion we should say: Mohammed is an outstanding religious and political founder-figure, who has led many people to God, but who has not recognized the love of God and the greatness of his call to humankind, which has been shown in the life, suffering, crucifixion and resurrection of Jesus Christ.

Notes

1. See also: Emilio Galindo Aguilar, 'The Second International Muslim-Christian Congress of Cordoba (21–27 March, 1977)', in *Islamochristiana*, 3 (1977), pp. 207–228. As to the reactions to the lecture of Prof. Ruiz, see ibid, p. 214.
2. *Sīrat Rasūl Allāh by Ibn Ishāq* [ca. 704–767] (ed.) by Ibn Hishām [died. 833]. Trans. into English by A. Guillaume (Oxford: OUP, 1955).

3. Johan Bouman, *Der Koran und die Juden* (Darmstadt: Wissenschaftliche Buchgesellschaft, 1990), pp. 69–92, esp. pp. 85–86.
4. Quoted in K. Cragg, *Muhammad and the Christian: A Question of Response* (Maryknoll, NY: Orbis Books, 1984), p. 26.
5. Fazlur Rahman, *Islam* (Chicago and London: University of Chicago Press, 1979), p. 16, also p. 21.
6. Cragg, *Muhammad*, p. 43.
7. *Vgl. Ahmad Schawqi, Al-Schawqiyyāt* (Cairo1948), quoted in Cragg, *Muhammad*, p. 46.
8. Cragg, *Muhammad*, p. 46.

Index of Names